1 MONTH OF FREE READING

at

www.ForgottenBooks.com

By purchasing this book you are eligible for one month membership to ForgottenBooks.com, giving you unlimited access to our entire collection of over 1,000,000 titles via our web site and mobile apps.

To claim your free month visit:

www.forgottenbooks.com/free269155

* Offer is valid for 45 days from date of purchase. Terms and conditions apply.

ISBN 978-0-260-91725-6
PIBN 10269155

This book is a reproduction of an important historical work. Forgotten Books uses state-of-the-art technology to digitally reconstruct the work, preserving the original format whilst repairing imperfections present in the aged copy. In rare cases, an imperfection in the original, such as a blemish or missing page, may be replicated in our edition. We do, however, repair the vast majority of imperfections successfully; any imperfections that remain are intentionally left to preserve the state of such historical works.

Forgotten Books is a registered trademark of FB &c Ltd.
Copyright © 2018 FB &c Ltd.
FB &c Ltd, Dalton House, 60 Windsor Avenue, London, SW19 2RR.
Company number 08720141. Registered in England and Wales.

For support please visit www.forgottenbooks.com

HIGHWAYS AND BYWAYS
IN THE
LAKE DISTRICT

Troutbeck.

Highways and Byways
in the Lake District

BY
A. G. BRADLEY
ILLUSTRATIONS BY
JOSEPH PENNELL

Troutbeck.

Highways and Byways
in the Lake District

BY A. G. BRADLEY

WITH ILLUSTRATIONS BY
JOSEPH PENNELL

Highways and Byways in the Lake District

BY A. G. BRADLEY
WITH · ILLUSTRATIONS · BY
JOSEPH PENNELL

London
MACMILLAN AND CO., Limited
NEW YORK: THE MACMILLAN COMPANY
1901

All rights reserved.

RICHARD CLAY AND SONS, LIMITED,
LONDON AND BUNGAY.

CONTENTS

	PAGE
CHAPTER I	1
CHAPTER II	36
CHAPTER III	68
CHAPTER IV	92
CHAPTER V	121
CHAPTER VI	150
CHAPTER VII	180
CHAPTER VIII	217

RICHARD CLAY AND SONS, LIMITED,
LONDON AND BUNGAY.

CONTENTS

	PAGE
CHAPTER I	1
CHAPTER II	36
CHAPTER III	68
CHAPTER IV	92
CHAPTER V	121
CHAPTER VI	150
CHAPTER VII	180
CHAPTER VIII	217

viii   CONTENTS

		PAGE
CHAPTER IX	. . . .	248
CHAPTER X	. . . .	262
CHAPTER XI	. . . .	298
INDEX	. . . .	324

LIST OF ILLUSTRATIONS

	PAGE
TROUTBECK	*Frontispiece*
PENRITH CASTLE	1
BROUGHAM CASTLE	17
ASKHAM VILLAGE	31
EAMONT BRIDGE, NEAR PENRITH	33
ASKHAM	35
THE MONUMENT, ULVERSTONE	36
ULLSWATER, FROM NEAR GOWBARROW	38
HEAD OF ULLSWATER	40
BROTHERSWATER AND KIRKSTONE PASS	51
DACRE CASTLE	68
THE ROAD, KESWICK TO PENRITH	74
ON THE WAY TO THE LAKE, KESWICK	76
LANDING STAGE, KESWICK	83
KESWICK	87
CROSSTHWAITE CHURCH	92

LIST OF ILLUSTRATIONS

	PAGE
PORTINSCALE BRIDGE	95
THE VALE OF NEWLANDS	96
SKIDDAW FROM THE COCKERMOUTH ROAD	98
COCKERMOUTH CASTLE	100
SKIDDAW FROM THE FOOT OF BASSENTHWAITE	103
A SKETCH OF SOUTHEY FROM LIFE, BY A. T. PAGET, JULY, 1836. IN THE POSSESSION OF CHARLES E. PAGET, ESQ.	107
DERWENTWATER	110
VALE OF NEWLANDS	120
CRUMMOCK LAKE	121
THE BRIDGE AT GRANGE	125
HONISTER PASS	130
CRUMMOCK LAKE	133
LOOKING UP BUTTERMERE	134
BUTTERMERE FROM NEAR GATESGARTH	146
FURNESS ABBEY	149
APPROACH TO BUTTERMERE	150
CRUMMOCK IN STORMY WEATHER	155
ST. BEES	162
EGREMONT CASTLE	164
WHITEHAVEN	168
EGREMONT FROM A DISTANCE	171
CALDER ABBEY	173
NEAR CALDER BRIDGE	175
ON THE RIVER LEVEN	179

LIST OF ILLUSTRATIONS   xi

	PAGE
RAVENGLASS	180
MUNCASTER CASTLE	182
FROM THE TERRACE, MUNCASTER CASTLE	183
ESKDALE	185
NEAR BOOT	188
TROUTBECK	192
CONISTON FROM ACROSS THE LAKE	196
THE SCHOOL HOUSE, HAWKSHEAD	201
NEWBY BRIDGE	202
WINDERMERE	203
A STREET IN HAWKSHEAD	205
HAWKSHEAD, MISTY MORNING	208
WINDERMERE	214
THE MOUNTAINS AT CONISTON	216
WINDERMERE	217
THE MILL AT AMBLESIDE	220
RYDAL CHURCH	225
RYDAL	228
GRASMERE, LOOKING TOWARDS DUNMAIL RAISE	231
GRASMERE CHURCH	234
DOVE COTTAGE	235
THIRLMERE	242
HELVELLYN FROM THIRLMERE	244
ON THIRLMERE	247
HESKET NEWMARKET, NEAR CALDBECK	248

LIST OF ILLUSTRATIONS

	PAGE
MARKET PLACE, HESKET NEWMARKET	253
JOHN PEEL'S HOME	257
ROAD TO KESWICK	261
THE CASTLE AND EDEN BRIDGE, CARLISLE	262
NEAR HIGH HESKET	263
WIGTON	265
DALTON-IN-FURNESS CASTLE	266
THE MARKET, CARLISLE	275
DACRE CASTLE	281
GRETNA GREEN	292
ESKDALE	297
KENDAL	298
GREAT SALKELD	301
THE ROAD OVER SHAP FELL	302
SHAP ABBEY	304
HAWESWATER	306
NEAR BAMPTON	308
LOOKING WEST FROM SHAP ABBEY	309
LEVENS HALL	318
MILNTHORPE	320
FURNESS ABBEY	322
LEVEN BRIDGE	323

MAP OF AUTHOR'S ROUTE . . . . *End of Volume*

Penrith Castle.

HIGHWAYS AND BYWAYS
IN THE
LAKE DISTRICT

CHAPTER I

" No record tells of lance opposed to lance,
Horse charging horse, 'mid these retired domains
Tells that their turf drank purple from the veins
Of heroes fallen or struggling to advance."

THUS sings Wordsworth, and with small regret no doubt—but he puts my difficulties in a nutshell. For the English Lake Country, as a subject of literary treatment, differs in certain essential points from any other part of the British Islands, and on this account I feel most reluctantly constrained to preface my journey through it with a few explanatory words, and crave such small measure of indulgence from the reader as they may seem to justify. Now whatever comparisons may be instituted between the scenery of the Lake district and that of kindred regions in Wales, Scotland, or Ireland, it is quite certain that nowhere else in these islands is such a wealth and variety of natural beauty concentrated in so very small an area. At the same time, few districts are more naked in those human and historic interests about which the authors of this series find pleasure in gossiping.

I do not wish to be misunderstood. I shall no doubt be reminded of the abounding literary associations of the Lake Country on the one hand, and of its racy and independent peasantry upon the other. But in regard to the first it will be remembered that, with a single notable exception, they are not indigenous or of the soil, that they belong to a recent and brief period, and, moreover, that the subject has been treated by experts and enthusiasts, as a glance at the library shelves will testify, in the most exhaustive fashion, under various headings. Indeed, the enquiring stranger who had not realised the comparative limitations of Lakeland outside its physical beauties, might almost complain that the region had been wholly subordinated to the personality of the literary celebrities who in modern times sought a resting-place there.

Mountain and valley are not here, as in Wales, and in much of Scotland and Ireland, saturated with historic memories and eloquent with story for such as care to read it. And I speak, of course, only of that district which is usually visited and spoken of as "the English Lakes." Its story is merely such as can be made by a pastoral people, scarcely affected by the outer world, or by the usual feudal and social cleavages; neither makers of history, nor builders of castles and abbeys, nor passionate advocates of kings, princes, or chieftains; a people who within measurable times have neither been trampled upon, nor trampled upon others; who have merely desired to be let alone, and from their situation have offered small temptation to others to meddle with them. To the folklorist, or the ethnologist, or the specialist in kindred paths, the indigenous portion of the Lakeland people and their history have, of course, much to interest, but for the general reader I should be tempted, for the sake of brevity, to describe them as more adapted to be the background of a chapter than of a book. Moreover, a century of intercourse with a steadily increasing flood of visitors must inevitably affect so small a community however conservative. And, after all, the conservatism of the Northern Englishman is not that of the Celt, who in the back of his mind has always the impulse to heave a brick at the outsider, however much he may profit him, and in any case remains impassive to his influence. Indeed, if it were necessary to enlarge further on this topic, I might fairly quote the author of a deservedly popular guide-book, who in his enthusiasm for Lakeland scenery makes something like a merit of its freedom from such adventitious aids to interest as a stirring past may give, and almost lays the lack of them to its credit account.

I was already sufficiently familiar with the Lake Country to be fully alive to these and certain other difficulties, which, taken by itself, it would most assuredly present to any author of a volume upon the lines of this series. And as I sped northward by that admirable train which permits of a tea at Rugby, and a not unreasonably late supper at Penrith or Windermere, they were borne in upon me with a force inevitable to the situation.

It has been often and truly said that Lakeland is the playground of England. It is also in a high degree the holiday resort of busy people of culture and education. As habitual visitors, or often indeed as villa and property owners, there springs up a feeling of identification with the country, and part ownership, as it were, in its scenic glories; a pleasing and natural sentiment which has none the less scope from the virtual absence of old landed families and of a peasantry with the natural prejudices thereby engendered. Nearly all the enthusiasm of the Lakeland *habitué* is expended on the physical beauties of his environment. These are, of course, dwelt upon in great detail by many scores of intimate admirers, and are indeed the subject of no little rivalry between various sections. And I, a poor gossiping prose writer, have to ride through all these pet preserves, upon which such torrents of enthusiasm, such volumes of literature, such floods of verse have been expended.

Now in North Wales, the region physically most analogous to the Lake district, the conditions are wholly different. The Saxon, be he visitor or resident, cannot acquire that feeling of part proprietorship in the country or identification with it. It would be impossible in a country whose language he does not understand and of whose literature and past history he as a rule knows nothing, and whose people regard him, very possibly as a " nice shentleman," but most certainly as a foreigner to his dying day.

In the Lake Country there is nothing of this sort. To the simple dalesman, " the gentry," in which term he courteously includes all the well dressed and well behaved summer visitors or residents, have been almost the only social feature in the country since time, so far as he is concerned, began. He is hampered by no old allegiances, and, canny Cumbrian as he is, knows well on which side his bread is buttered. All these things were very much on my mind as I was whirled northwards through the green pastures of Lancashire just freshened by the genial touch of spring, and watched the sun sinking behind the level shores of Morecambe Bay. It was quite certain that neither my inclination nor my sense of proportion would allow me to attempt three hundred pages of unalleviated word-painting, which seemed from a distance the only treatment that the Lake district lent itself to. Even were I equal to achieving some measure of success in such a sustained effort, I felt sure that neither publisher nor reader would greatly thank me for it. I derived, however, some little consolation from the thought that we are, in the main, road travellers, that it was outside my province to grapple with that vague and vast field of hill-climbing, which, though it constitutes the chief attraction to the active visitor, might well give the boldest author pause. But if I had supposed that even the roads of Lakeland, using the term in its strict meaning and as defined by maps and guide-books, were my limit, I should have had grave misgivings. Happily, I was in no way bound to the chariot wheels of the Jehus whose daily rounds mark the conventional routes of travel. So long as I kept Skiddaw and Helvellyn in sight, there was no good reason why I should not occasionally stray into regions where the pulse of the old border life beat with a more strenuous throb than it did in the quiet backwater behind them. And I well knew that within sight of Skiddaw and Helvellyn there were regions as rich in story as Northumberland itself or the Welsh marches; and what more can be said! Cut and dried plans or a regularly progressing route seemed impossible in a country of such rugged and beautiful confusion and proved so, I determined therefore to let the fancy of the moment, in a great measure, be my guide, and to order both my steps and my pen as the spirit moved me.

Penrith, which I purpose to make our starting-point on this little journey, has for all time been on the great western highway between North and South, and a moment's glance from the lofty plateau above the town, on which the London and North Western Railway lands you, assisted by an only reasonable acquaintance with English topography, would be sufficient to explain the cause. For westward, the broken masses of the Lakeland mountains, beginning with the fainter outline of the Skiddaw group, and circling round in rugged and familiar detail to the lower moorlands over which our train has laboured on the way from Kendal and the south, unmistakeably proclaim the barrier they have always been. Looking eastward, the entire horizon, from the Scottish border to the south, as far as we may see, is filled by the billowy undulations of the Pennine range. Here in the wide vale between, down which the Eden rolls its broad and glistening streams towards the Solway, with the Petterell piping in feebler tones beside it, in its narrower trough, the obvious route from Scotland or from England, of friend or foe, of footman, horseman, stage-coach, or railway train, is written so large that any child may read it.

But to quite grasp the situation, it might perhaps be necessary to realise what broods behind these undulations to the eastward, which, though obviously barren of all human life, seem yet, by comparison with their savage neighbours on the West, so mild and gentle. Even Crossfell yonder, guarding the corner where the five northern counties almost meet, and actually within a trifling fraction of the heights of Skiddaw and Helvellyn, might for all the dignity and boldness it possesses be an outcrop of the Sussex downs! But a very different country to the Sussex downs lies behind these wild Northumbrian fells, for solitudes as rude and dreary as any English curlew ever screamed over lie about the sources of the Tyne and Tees and Wear. Everyone knows, too, that the Cheviots guard the greater part of the Northumbrian frontier towards Berwick, giving a choice therefore of only two routes to which nature had lent much real assistance. And Penrith, eighteen miles south of Carlisle, lies, as I have said, upon the western one.

Nowadays such a situation is an undeniable advantage. You have an admirable railway service; you build hotels, and receive with open arms a steady stream of visitors and a steady income. There was a time, however, above all in this part of the kingdom, when such accessibility was a prodigious inconvenience. You received, it is true, a spasmodic influx of visitors, but they were not of the kind to swell the local revenue; their sole object being to decrease it by violent methods. You did not build hotels to receive them, but castles to keep them out; and here by an irony of fate the railway station and the castle, the bustling present and the dead past, an ill assorted pair enough, stand side by side upon this lofty ridge looking down upon the town.

I think, had it been otherwise, I should have hesitated at this, the very outset of our journey, before my reader has even had time to get to his inn and deposit his luggage, to thus risk his goodwill, by buttonholing him beneath the ruins of a feudal castle. Perhaps feudal is, for once, the wrong word, seeing that these tall red freestone fragments, for they are little else, of Penrith Castle, enjoy the somewhat singular reputation of having been erected, not by a baron for selfish purposes, but by a community for their own defence. The castle is painfully modern from an archæological standpoint, not having been erected till the fifteenth century, when Penrith, sick and tired of being pillaged by the Scots, set to work, under the leadership of a Neville who was then in power, to rectify the evil by the erection of this once spacious fortress. Its history, too, is short, for in little over a hundred years it seems to have fallen into ruin. The fact is that Penrith, though a place of importance, had never been a chartered town nor the centre of barony like Appleby, Kendal or Carlisle; but for the most part a mere royal manor, till Richard the Second gave it to the Nevilles, who showed their gratitude by being among the first to welcome Henry of Bolingbroke to England and its throne. It was Henry Neville of Raby to whom the ill-fated Richard made a present of Penrith, or Perith as it was then often called, though the origin of the name is Celtic (Pen-rhydd, the red hill); and before that time it had the singular experience of being exchanged with the Duke of Brittany for Brest of all places in the world. But it was Ralph Neville who in the next century, with the co-operation of the citizens, built the castle, after a peculiarly harrowing and compulsory entertainment of their dear neighbours the Scots. Indeed, how open Penrith stood, should Carlisle flinch or fall before the loosened floodgates of northern invasion, I have already said, a child may see standing upon this very spot. But what chiefly entitles these ruins to our regard so far as personal history goes, is the fact of the famous hunchback Richard having been in charge here for some time, and according to tradition having lived as royally and extravagantly in Penrith as if he were already King, which at that time he was very far from being.

Now it is not my business to recommend hotels, and the Dockwray house, situated in a quiet square of the town, is a quiet and unpretentious hostelry of whose catering merits I know nothing, since I have only sought such passing entertainment there as would justify me in exploring its fascinating interior. If I were going again to Penrith, however, I should most certainly test its capacities, not merely for the sake of lying in a house where a King of England, even though a bad one, had once resided with much *éclat*, but because it contrives to look its part so thoroughly; from the enormous thickness of the walls, eight or nine feet in some places, to the oak panelling which graces almost every one of the small chambers. It is all very miniature, and even the old banqueting hall upstairs, of good dimensions in itself, is partitioned. Richard's own room is of course a matter of no little pride, and is thoroughly equal in appearance to what is required of it; and of walls that have listened to the troubled dreams of that monster of iniquity much is expected. The landlord tells me a good many Americans patronise him, which I can well believe, and the natives speak of a secret passage hence to the castle, which I may believe in or not as I choose, for we have descended near half a mile from the station through narrow and somewhat perpendicular streets, and are now among the irregular open spaces that are significant and pleasant features of a pleasant old-fashioned market town. I use the term significant advisedly for while still wondering how Penrith contrived to exist so long without any recognised means of defence, a local friend kindly demonstrated to me how every street leading into the town either was, or had been, of singularly narrow proportions, invariably, however, terminating in one of those open spaces where tradition says the cattle of the neighbouring country could be gathered in times of stress. You have only to lift your eyes too, and hanging some seven or eight hundred feet above the town is a wooded hill, whose beacon fires for centuries flared far and wide their warning of danger, death and woe. How often Penrith was raided and how often burned it would be ill saying. To the boroughs on the Welsh marches one might look for something of a parallel to these northern border towns. But there was almost nothing there but racial conflicts, which ended earlier, and, furthermore, the forces of law and order were comparatively near. But here in the lawless and ferocious north every community had to look after itself, and the motives for battle were not merely race hatred intermittently aroused, but that of plunder, which was ever present and irrepressible. Two centuries, indeed, after a man's stackyard was in normal times as safe in the vale of Clwyd or Glamorganshire as in Surrey, the farmers of the Eden and the Lowther and the Petterel valleys slept with their arms beside them, with the match handy and the beacon laid; while the whole forces of a market town were none too great when a thousand Armstrongs, mounted to a man and clad in steel, were on the war path, and all this, moreover, when the two kingdoms were not merely at peace but actually united under one crown.

And in the meantime one looks at the stalwart descendants of these borderers as they throng the Penrith streets on market days, and wonders how much of their character, expression, or physique is due to the strenuous times in which the breed was nourished. It is quite certain that a person who would feel no special cause for humility as regards his physical proportions in a southern country gathering would feel some thankfulness on market day in Penrith that might no longer ruled the day. A short time since I should certainly myself have been looking out for Celtic traits in Cumberland, and I fancy most people, particularly Welshmen, would here in this old land of the Northern Cymru—the very heart of Strathclyde—be possessed of some notion of this sort. Experts however are all agreed that there is very little left of the Kymri whom Cunedda ruled, but their place names, which are thick enough. If one traverses the history of this western border, however lightly, and reads of the harrowings and devastations that long before the mediæval period swept through a country which was chiefly wild mountain or thick forest, it is easy to see that the Briton of Roman times can have little claim of such kind as is based on his original ooccupation of the soil. That he contributes some small share we cannot doubt, but the prevailing factor after the long chaos, that has left its mark upon the race and soil, is with equal certainty the Scandinavian, filtering chiefly, it is said, through Northumberland. However that may be, the Cumbrian is a lusty soul and full even yet of a lively animal relish in his strength. It is always said that when serious fighting became no longer possible, to speak broadly, in the Stewart period, he betook himself, like the Welshman of an earlier epoch, under similar circumstances, to litigation, and thus worked off, with results sometimes as lamentable as those of war itself, his fighting zeal. The well known peculiarities of land tenure in these counties, whereby such a mass of yeomen were freeholders, or "statesmen," gave enormous scope for this amusement, which in more recent years, combined with whiskey, temptations to move away and the high selling price of land, has gone far to destroy, not the breed itself, but its position on the soil.

What I do think causes surprise to many people is the lucid English that the average country folk of Cumberland and Westmoreland address one in. To the man familiar with the common speech of the regions by which these isolated counties are surrounded, of Lancashire that is to say, and West Yorkshire, of Durham, Northumberland, the Lothians, and Dumfriesshire —the language of these others as now in ordinary use, sounds singularly pure. I have been often told that there are plenty even yet, of Cumbrians particularly, buried away in the hills, who can astonish you with the ruggedness of their speech. I don't venture to dispute it; but I have looked about for them, both among the hills and plains, without much success, and in the ordinary course of my mission and my inclination have forgathered with farmers by the score and in every conceivable situation, and often miles away from any tourist beat. The Cumbrian vernacular in print looks formidable enough; that it sounded so at no distant time I can quite believe, but to fully recognise its present lucidity you have only to stumble suddenly on a Durham pitman or a Lancashire millhand, a rustic from the North Tyne or the deep fallows of East Lothian. Indeed I met a young American at Carlisle who was filled with astonishment not unmingled with regret, at the comparative absence of those lingual obstacles he had fully reckoned on encountering.

He was not a Boston cosmopolitan, but an honest Western boy with the hayseeds not long combed out of his hair; a freshman in the Harvard Law School bubbling over with intelligent curiosity and packed with information. That he was a youth of some uncommon enterprise may be gathered from the fact that though he had never been either in England or on a bicycle before, he was making his first experiment of both concurrently. He had, in short, got right off the steamer in Liverpool and mounting then and there the "wheel" he had brought with him, essayed to push his painful way by road through Lancashire *en route* for Carlisle and the North of Scotland. It was here, as I have said, that his first serious mishap, caused by forcible impact with a fruiterer's truck, laid both him and his machine by for repairs, and gave me the pleasure of his passing acquaintance. He readily admitted to having encountered some diversion and some pleasing obstacles in the conversation of the wayside Lancastrian, but was vastly disappointed at the relapse into lucid English which greeted him in Westmoreland and Cumberland. He might just as well have been at home in Wisconsin he protested, so far as this feature of his tour was concerned. He had built up immense hopes from the English dialect novels, as well he may have, without being fully able to realise the geographical limitations which distinguish them.

"Yet there is one word" he said, "fairly gets away with me; one they've used right along from Liverpool to Carlisle here, and I'd like mightily to have your explanation of it. They fire it out about every five seconds, and seem to me to punctuate their conversation with it right along. I'd like to know how to spell it and what it means, any way." I told him that I believed the monosyllable that worried him was spelt a-y-e, that it meant everything or nothing, and, in short, that he was not far wrong in supposing that it was, upon the whole, a superfluous ornament to northern eloquence; and that it was sometimes used merely for dividing long periods of silence when there was nothing else to say. This by no means satisfied the youth's legal mind, but he made a note of it as the best I could do for him. I then proceeded to comfort him with the reflection, that unless the Doric of Southern and Eastern Scotland had undergone vast deterioration in the last twenty years, he would certainly find considerable entertainment of the kind he was looking for between the Solway and Aberdeen, whither he was bound by way of Edinburgh. I also assured him that as he got east he would encounter another little word, that would worry him quite as much as the North English ejaculation. That it had been made the subject of comic songs even by the Scots themselves, and was, moreover, unspellable, being feebly expressed by a couple of small m's and a hyphen. Having undergone a protracted examination as to the whole bench of British judges, past and present, in which I miserably failed, we parted—he in search of strange sights and strange tongues, I——well, it is of no consequence now, for we are in Penrith, and likely to be there, or thereabouts, for the rest of this chapter.

And I hope my reader will bear with me for not leaping on my bicycle at once and tearing off for the mountains and the setting sun at Keswick, or jumping on the coach for Pooley Bridge, and pushing straight for the head of Ullswater. My ways will not, I fear, be wholly those of the recognised interpreters of Lakeland, nor will my paths be always their paths. If such had been the possibility I should have flinched from such a contest. I have dared to hope, now that locomotion is so much more easy for so many people, that Cumberland and Westmoreland may be recognised by the traveller as having, like other English counties, some human and historic interests, and not wholly to depend on the natural beauty of their mountain regions and the literary celebrities who in recent times have been attracted by them. It will be very little I can do in this way, to be sure, having proper regard to the title of this book, but I purpose in any case to loiter in the neighbourhood of Penrith till this opening chapter has run its course.

Now while we were at Dockwray Hall we should have stepped across the square, or triangle rather, that it faces, the ancient Bullring in fact, and sought by means of a quaint passage in the walls the secluded hostelry of the "Two Lions." This, too, is more famous among antiquaries than tourists, for it represents with tolerable fidelity the town house of a notable member of the great Lowther family, by name Gerard, whose father was Sheriff of Cumberland in his day, and received Mary Queen of Scots when she crossed the Solway and threw herself on her royal cousin's clemency. The house dates in part from the fifteenth, but mostly from the end of the sixteenth century, and being a good deal cut about, will perhaps appeal more to the specialist than the amateur in such matters. But the old dining-room is still intact, with the unusual accompaniment of a daïs, and all the adjuncts of buttery hatch, and arrangement of retiring rooms that were the features of Collegiate architecture at that time. The plaster work of the ceiling is a fine example of the period, and bears among much other ornament the shields of the great families who then held in their hands the destinies of the two counties. The old inn is full of odds and ends dating from the Tudor period, while a bowling green smooth as a billiard table fills in the background, and is a great resort of those Penrith townsmen who follow the popular northern pastime.

There is nothing left of "the beautiful Gothic church" which Camden tells us stood in Penrith in his day but the tower. No man even knows what like it was, which is curious, seeing that the present edifice proclaims its comparative modernity in that unmistakable fashion common to most sacred buildings of the Georgian period. This one was built in 1721; and I am bound to say if the deplorable style of that epoch can ever find some justification in men's eyes it should do so in the spacious proportions and undeniable dignity of Penrith's square church. Perhaps the only detail of the interior that need detain us are two or three pieces of stained glass, rescued from the old church and set in the windows of this later one. One of these is a portrait, as is supposed, of Richard II., not favourable to that monarch's reputation for comeliness. The other is that of Cicely Neville, who, in a sense, is the most illustrious lady in the local annals of the district.

Now Richard II. not very long before his fall, had bestowed the honour of Penrith upon Henry Neville, who, as I have before remarked, showed the characteristic gratitude of a Norman baron by being among the foremost in welcoming his benefactor's enemy Bolingbroke to England and its throne. Neville, however, did yeoman's service for his new and much harried master in protecting Cumberland, which had now long been English shire ground against the Scots, for many years, though this in no way seems to have interfered with his domestic affairs, since he married twice and had two and twenty children. It is Cicely, the youngest of all these, that with pale face and golden hair now looks down on us from the window in Penrith church. She was a famous and haughty beauty, well-known in London, where she was commonly styled "proud Cis of Raby." Her chief claim to notoriety, however, lies in the distinction acquired by her marriage and her motherhood. For she became the wife of Richard Duke of York, the Yorkist heir-presumptive to the English throne, and mother of Edward IV. and Richard III. The first was captured at the battle of Wakefield and hurried instantly to the block, and his head, decorated with a paper crown, impaled on York gates. Their son, Lord Rutland, on this same occasion, begged on his knees for mercy from the Black Clifford, the fiercest member of the strenuous Westmoreland line. "As your father killed mine," cried the "northern wolfe," plunging his dagger into the boy's breast, "so will I kill you." Richard Duke of Clarence, too, who was slain by Edward IV., was Cicely's brother. She herself was grandmother to Henry the Seventh's Queen, while her nephew Warwick the kingmaker succeeded to this same manor of Penrith, where he kept prodigious state. He built indeed the upper part of this very church tower which still carries aloft at three of its four corners his well-known device of the ragged staff. So Proud Cis, it will be seen, paid for her distinction with a full measure of sorrow, the last fifteen years of her life being spent as a nun at Berkhampstead, whither so many royal personages of that day retired to brood over their sorrows and do penance for their sins.

It is probable, however, that for one person to whom the portrait of Cicely Neville inside Penrith Church possesses attractions, fifty will linger round the prehistoric puzzle which the churchyard boasts. As the Giant's Grave has wholly foiled the antiquary, the amateur may just as well fall back upon the local legend, which points to it as the resting place of one Owen Cæsarius, a giant, a soldier and a sportsman of the sixth century—a century that must have been a strange enough one to live in, if all the saints and sinners and monstrosities it is credited with really walked the earth. The grave is fifteen feet long, with rudely ornamented stone pillars ten feet high at the head and foot. Large semicircular stones also showing traces of ornament, connect them, by some supposed to represent the backs of the huge boars which our departed giant was accustomed to encounter in the adjacent forest of Inglewood. These remains are spoken of in the oldest writings extant, and must really have been prized by the Penrithians even in the darkest hours of sensibility to such things. For when the present church was built in the time of George the First, and the churchwardens, true to the instincts of their period and their class, commenced to break up and make away with the stones as rubbish, the population rose as one man, and the rivets with which they repaired the mischief already perpetrated may yet be seen.

There are still left in Penrith not a few quaint corners and old bits of architecture, but speaking generally it has been refashioned to the needs of a modern country town of some ten thousand souls, and entertaining for a portion of the year a good deal of passing traffic. Nor is there anything particular to be noted as we drop down from the market-place into the wide street leading out on to the old Southern road, and turning sharply to the left at the outskirts of the town head for Appleby. It is but a short round that I am bound on, not a two hours' walk if there were nothing to stop us by the way. And by any quicker means of progress there would be scarcely time to note how rich and fair the rolling foregrounds showed beneath the dawning summer, and how fast the cloud shadows race along the green billows of the Pennine range before the great red ruins of Brougham Castle, standing grim and lonely amid the summer fields, fill the eye Beneath its walls the now united waters of the Eamont and the Lowther leap and flash in curious contrast to the quiet scene around. No modern buildings mar the dignity of the slow crumbling pile by their contact. There is no incongruous union here of the living and the dead; no later mansion tacked on to the old walls making vain efforts to reconcile the outside comforts and necessities of the twentieth century with the ghost of feudalism; no flower beds, no tennis courts, no farm buildings even are here. A grove of stately trees, lime, elm and ash, murmurous just now with rooks and cushats, lift their boughs above the roofless walls, and a herd of milk cows champ the thick carpet of grass that spreads between the ruddy bastions

THE VIPONTS

and the silver stream. Roman roads converging from the south, and leading to Carlisle and Hadrian's wall, made this the Roman fortress of Brovacura, a noted spot even in days when Cumbria was thick with such, and widely different from the semi-wilderness it afterwards became. But we must limit our reflections to the life of the hoary pile before us, which in the twelfth and thirteenth centuries belonged to the Veteriponts or Viponts, who for three generations were the feudal magnates of this whole region, and whose memory

Brougham Castle.

yet survives in the annulets that may be seen in the quarterings of so many northern houses. But three brief and significant words carved above the gate, "Thys made Roger," tells the story of its prime, and carries my thoughts away for a moment to the marches of South Wales, where all that is left of Clifford Castle, the birth-place of fair Rosamund, looks down through bowers of leaves upon the glancing rapids of the upper Wye. For the Viponts ran a briefer course than most great houses of that day, ending in Henry the Third's time in two little girls, who were consequently at the King's disposal. The elder one was sent as ward to Roger Clifford of Clifford, and in due course reappeared in the north as his wife, endowing that comparatively needy noble with the vast estates of her ancestors, her sister dying childless. Well may her husband have written "Thys made Roger" on the gate of the castle he so magnificently rebuilt. For three centuries the history of the Cliffords is practically that of England, and no race on the north-west marches was so continuously great. Fierce, vigorous, and of enormous wealth they fell foul more than once, as was inevitable, of their sovereigns, and as often suffered the attainder and confiscation which in those times was so readily, and in their case so invariably, revoked. Black Clifford, the fiercest of them all, we have already met in the murderer of the Neville lad upon the field of Wakefield. That the Yorkists as soon as they had the chance took his life and stripped his family of everything goes without saying, and the late Chancellor Ferguson quotes the finding of the jury on his body which seems to have a grim finality.

"The jurors find that he was attainted of high treason by virtue of an Act of Parliament in 1 Edward IV.: that he died on Palm Sunday *and held nothing in any county.*"

This may well have looked like an end of the Cliffords, and indeed his widow was so alarmed for the safety of her two sons, then children, that she sent them in hot haste abroad, where one died, the other being brought home again, to become the hero of perhaps the most romantic incident of its kind in border story. For his mother, who had in the meantime married Sir Lancelot Threlkeld, a famous country gentleman of that day, whose house we shall shortly pass, went still in such fear for the life of any child of the terrible black Cliffords that she sent him privily to a shepherd's house upon the slopes of Blencathera, as is generally said, to be brought up as his own son in ignorance of his name and race. And here till he was thirty years of age or more he led the life of a rude Cumbrian peasant. But the sequel shows how strong must have been the instincts of his race, for with the advent of Henry VII. his identity being disclosed and certified to, he was restored to his estates, and proved a model of virtue and wisdom.

The fighting instincts of the Cliffords, however, would appear to have been effectually stamped out by his Arcadian life, which seems to have made an astronomer of him, for in the study of this science he spent the rest of a long life. He married twice, in the first instance from the neighbouring family of Lowther; and his famous descendant, Anne Countess of Pembroke, wrote of him a century later: "He was a plain man and lived for the most part a country life, and came seldom to Court or London; but when he was called thither to sit as a Peer of the realm, he behaved himself wisely, and like a good English gentleman." "The Shepherd Lord" was just the man to catch the fancy of Wordsworth, whose verses in his honour will be familiar to all the poet's admirers.

Long before the time of the Black Clifford and his Arcadian son, Balliol King of Scotland had come on a visit to Brougham, when a memorable staghunt took place under the auspices of the Clifford of that day, who in his passion for hunting failed to meet his end, like all Cliffords before him, and most of those after him, on the battle-field. The stag on this occasion was roused on Whinfell over yonder, and led the chase the entire length of Cumberland to the Scottish border, and then back again to Whinfell, where the noble animal after leaping a wall fell dead upon the far side of it. But the point of the story is that a gallant hound named Hercules, who was close on the quarry's heels, struck the same wall a moment after, in his efforts to clear it, and fell back also dead within a few yards of the deer.

The latter's horns were nailed to an adjacent oak tree, and becoming imbedded in the trunk preserved the memory of this great run till the time of Charles I. The oak itself lived for two centuries after the horns had disappeared, and was known as the Hartshorn tree. Indeed, Wordsworth says he well remembers it himself in his youth, tottering to decay beside the Appleby and Penrith road. An old couplet, too, has come down with the story—

" Hercules killed Hart a greese,
And Hart a greese killed Hercules."

Brougham Castle is indeed a noble pile, and the more notable from the fact of its presence in a region somewhat poor in the more imposing monuments of feudal days, a poverty in great part owing to the fact that in these two counties every man's house was very literally his castle. The peril was too constant and too near for any other arrangement, and, moreover, the feudal custom was never applied in its full sense to the greater part of Cumberland and Westmoreland. With Brougham went Appleby, Skipton and Pendragon. But the former only is in our beat, and memories crowd so thickly on us in the blessed silence that seems to reign here, it is perhaps just as well. For we must not leave without a word of that celebrated lady already briefly mentioned, Anne Countess of Pembroke, in whom the long line of Clifford eventually determined. I should like to have said something, too, of that audacious Clifford who made a royal messenger swallow the large waxen seal which fastened the King's writ, and must certainly not pass over a much later one, who sailed the Spanish Main with Drake in the biggest vessel (900 tons) that a subject had ever built, and with a force of 800 men in his constant pay. Like the rest of them, he tried a business partnership with the Virgin Queen, but found her both too timid and too greedy, till his passion for buccaneering on a great scale, joined to a love of horse-racing when on shore, and an immense popularity at Court, where he was the Queen's "Champion," well nigh ruined him. Finally, says Mr. Watson, to whom I am much indebted in all that concerns Brougham Castle, he ranged himself among the Immortals by commanding a Queen's ship in the fight with the Spanish Armada.

But all this is not the Countess Anne, and it is a good thing our journey is short and the summer day is long. The extraordinary succession of deaths, which left this last representative of the Cliffords, after two unhappy marriages, a widow in sole possession of their vast estates, does not concern us. The point is that at the demise of her second husband, the Earl of Pembroke, this sprightly and nimble-minded old lady, for she was then over sixty, returned to the north and sat down at Brougham, her birth-place, with the fixed determination of restoring the glory of the Clifford name and fortunes. This was the more creditable as there was no Clifford to succeed, nor even had she herself a son. If family pride can be accounted a virtue, surely the Countess Anne was both virtuous and single-minded in her efforts to mark the exit of her race from the stage on which it had played a leading part so long, with such honour and distinction as was in her power. And her power was very great, seeing that she laid out £40,000 in building, and repairing her castles alone. Cromwell was then supreme, and as the greatest dismantler of all time it so enraged him to hear of this noble lady's building activity, he sent word to her that he would knock her castles about her ears as fast as she built them up. But the Countess replied with spirit that as fast as he pulled them down she would of a surety rebuild them. She had the liturgy of the Church of England, too, read publicly every day in her chapel, and dared the authorities, who raged and threatened great things, to do their worst. And she travelled about her estates looking closely into the leases and agreements of her numerous tenantry, which had fallen into much confusion. If she was just and generous, she was also a woman of business, and refused to be imposed on to the value of a single farthing, and set so many lawsuits afoot that the local attorneys held her for long in blessed memory. She spent £200 in sueing one Mr. Murgatroyd, a retired clothier of Huddersfield, for the payment of a single "boon hen," and ultimately won her case. She thereupon asked her vanquished opponent to dinner; and when the sole cover of the first course was removed, the identical bird which had sealed her victory was displayed upon the dish, and amicably divided between the lady and her tenant. She disapproved of the manners of Charles II. and his court as much as she had done of those of Cromwell and his friends. When Sir Joseph Williamson, the King's secretary, rashly assumed that he could impose a member on the borough of Appleby, and wrote to that effect, the aged Countess replied, "I have been bullied by a usurper, and neglected by a court, but I will not be dictated to by a subject. Your man sha'n't stand." She set clerks to hunt up and record the doings of her ancestors, and has left voluminous manuscripts in her own hand descriptive of her sentiments and her life, which, to judge from the extracts made by those who have seen them, one might well wish were published.

In these, she describes with much minuteness and delightful self-complacency, the early beauties of her face and figure, and the abiding qualities of her mind and heart, attributing the singular combination to the astral influences under which she was born. She found herself, moreover, High Sheriff of Westmoreland by inheritance, for the office in this county had been hereditary since the days of the Viponts. That a lady would occupy the situation, however, had never entered into the calculations of either Kings, Cliffords, or people, and it did not now till the venerable Countess sent off the nearest male relative who claimed the honour with a flea in his ear, and herself assumed the duties and responsibilities of the office, taking her place upon the bench between the judges of assize. She was particular, too, to have it stated on her coffin, which lies mouldering below St. Lawrence Church in Appleby, that she was "High Sheriffess by inheritance of ye County of Westmoreland."

With this uncommon lady, the great and strenuous race of Clifford, after thirteen generations, vanished from the north, and Brougham Castle echoed no more to the sound of theirs, or probably of any human voices. It was left to a daughter of our Countess to carry away its wide domain to the Kentish family of Tufton, and the severance was made complete by the dismantling of her castles, and the sale of such material from them as could be marketed.

But I have lingered here longer than I intended. We must leave the Eamont river and the broad Appleby road, to follow each their pleasant course into the Eden valley, and turn our backs upon the smooth Pennine hills, and set our faces towards those other and more rugged heights that seem to call our tardy steps towards the West.

A couple of miles of uneventful byway, and we are out upon the great North road, along which, before the days of railroads, the stream of travel ran 'twixt Carlisle and the south. It is dead enough now to all but local traffic, for people do not cross Shapfell to Kendal when they can go by train, unless, indeed as we shall do later in our journey, for a summer day's jaunt. There was life enough here, however, at the close of the year 1745; for close to Clifton, the point at which we strike it, and just three miles from Penrith, there took place the very last battle which was ever fought on English soil. It was on a gloomy evening, in late November, when the Duke of Cumberland caught Prince Charles's rearguard and forced them to stand in the enclosures about the village here, and fight an indecisive action in the dark. The Pretender's people were then, of course, in full retreat from Derby and hastening on to Carlisle, which was being held for them by friends. No difficulties had been encountered till Westmoreland stretched its inhospitable hills across their path, and they began the ascent from Kendal into a country that even in the after days of coaches and Macadam was dreaded by the traveller more than any single stage in England. That adventurous Franco-Scotsman, the Chevalier Johnstone, who had a command with the Prince, and was as ready with his pen as his sword, has left us a vivid account of the struggle over Shapfell with guns and waggons, threatened by three parallel forces and pushed at the sabre's point by one of them. The Chevalier indeed, unlike the Countess Anne, could have been born under no lucky star, and was fated to chronicle the triumphs of his foes; for he was not only at Culloden but was at Montcalm's side fourteen years later on the Plains of Abraham, for which, seeing his literary tastes, I have myself had cause to be, in quite another place, extremely thankful.

It was just before sunset on the 17th of November, when the rebel rearguard reached Clifton, the main body being already between that village and Penrith. A hundred and twenty of their horse had the day before, a Sunday, made vain endeavours from their base at Kendal to cut their way into Scotland down the Eden valley. But the Penrith people, and the country folk had turned out in force and hunted these Jacobite hussars back upon their army to their no small discomfiture, and the elation of the others.

As to this twilight and moonlight affair at Clifton, there are several accounts of it from both points of view, but I do not think it would be worth the while of any one, unless he were a local antiquary whose ancestors took part in it, to try and describe such an involved and hurly-burly business in detail. About 2,000 Highlanders seem to have been in action, while another thousand, the Brigade of Athole, held the Lowther bridge towards Penrith. The rest were either in the latter place or marching on to Carlisle. A muddy narrow lane, bordered by high walls and hedges, then ran where is now this ample highway, while fenced enclosures and wet ditches abounded on both sides. Those hardy annuals of that period, Bland's, Kerr's and Cobham's dragoons, who we sometimes see running away like demented hares, and at others fighting like heroes, formed the chief attack, and on this occasion played the nobler part. There were also with them the Yorkshire foxhunters, full of amateur zeal. The men they met were those of Cluny, Appin, and Glengarry, and the Edinburgh regiment. Night fell before they had well warmed to their work. There was then much wild shooting, and a great deal of very pretty hand to hand cutting and thrusting, with sword and claymore, in narrow lanes, and amid small enclosures. An early moon struggled fitfully through rolling clouds, and gave fresh stimulus to a fight that threatened to collapse at times, from sheer inability on either side to see where to shoot or when to strike. For in these intervals of moonlight, says a combatant, the white belts of the dragoons, who were of course dismounted, showed out conspicuously, whereas the plaid enveloped clansmen were by no means so easy to see. The rebel cavalry, the Loyalists declare, fled at once, and their own commander, Murray, says, " our horsemen on seeing the enemy *went to Penrith*," which confirms in terse fashion their enemies' report, and shows some consideration for their feelings on Murray's part!

Mr. Thomas Savage, a Quaker, who occupied a house in the very thick of the fun and stuck to it, has left a graphic account of what he saw and did. When the Highlanders had had enough of it and followed, though leisurely, their cavalry to Penrith, and Thomas Savage was congratulating himself on coming so well out of the scrape, there came a thundering knock at the door which made him jump. It proved to be the Duke himself, who, liking the look of the honest Quaker's house, had decided to spend the night there, "and pleasant agreeable company he was, a man of parts, very friendly and no pride in him." What caused Thomas Savage still more gratification was that none of his cattle had been hit, though they had been between the two fires through the whole business. And while the Duke's people camped upon the field, and his Royal Highness snored peacefully between the Quaker's sheets, the poor Highlanders were tramping through Penrith and along the road to Carlisle in the mud and darkness.

The local hero of the fight was Colonel Honeywood, squire

of Howgill. Mr. Ferguson relates how a Highlander after the fight was heard to say, "We did vara weel till the lang man in muckle boots came o'er the dyke," alluding to the gallant Colonel, who was eventually " got down " and wounded three times. Considering, however, that he had received twenty-three sabre wounds at Dettingen and a couple of bullets which he still carried about in him, it is not surprising that he made light of the Clifton matter, and lived for forty years afterwards, being much of that time M.P. for Appleby. He was Colonel of the Twentieth Regiment in 1755, when James Wolfe, who for some reason resents his appointment in his private letters, was as Lieut.-Colonel making that corps the best in the British Army, and creating for himself those opportunities of which he made such noble use. As to the number of the killed and wounded in the Clifton fight accounts are hopelessly conflicting. But before leaving we will step inside the ancient little church, and, with the vicar's leave and help, turn back the pages of the register, and note the following entry, not because it throws any light on the above matter, which is of really no importance, seeing that every man who fought here was dust ages ago, but because these entries are somewhat unusual in the humdrum tale of a parish record in peaceful England.

Here they are :

"19th of December 1745 Ten Dragoons to wit, Six of Blands, three of Cobhams and one of Mark Kerrs regiment buried, who was killed ye evening before by ye rebels in ye skirmish between ye Duke of Cumberland's army and them at ye end of Clifton moor."

Then comes a later entry, a wounded man evidently : " Robert Atkins a private Dragoon of General Blands regiment buried ye 8th day of January 1746."

We are within a mile or two of Lowther Castle—immense, magnificent and modern—but are much nearer than that to the Park edge, for we can hear the river, noisy with the tribute of distant and stormy fells fretting in its rocky bed, and see what looks like miles of woodland rolling away towards the hollows of the hills. But Lowther is too big a subject to grapple with at this late period in the day; though, having gossiped so much about the Viponts and the Cliffords, it would seem only fitting to say something of the potent race that, so far as changed times admit of, have succeeded to their honours.

But we have had enough of great folk perhaps to-day. Our backs too are turned on Lowther and our faces set towards Penrith, and scarce a hundred yards along the road and so close that there is no overlooking it, as characteristic a remnant of old border life as could be found in Westmoreland. I have remarked before, that in this north country every man's home in former days was very literally his castle, and here in yonder little Peel tower was the castle of the Wyberghs, who built it in the 15th century and own it still.

Fallen indeed is this particular Peel tower from such distinction as it once enjoyed, for it has been rejected even of the farming folk who for generations lived here, which, taking note of the prodigious rents across its scarred face, I am not surprised at; but it has the rare merit of standing quite alone, just as it came into the world, so to speak, and affording an admirable object lesson in the evolution of the border family and the border country house. For the Peel tower was the rock on which both were founded, the chrysalis from which they almost invariably sprang. To go about Cumberland and Westmoreland without a knowledge of the Peel tower germ, would be wandering in the wilderness indeed, so far as such interests are concerned. In the larger houses they have been so built in, duplicated or otherwise disguised, one feels inclined on coming in sight of an ancient mansion or farm-house to think of the familiar puzzle of the dog in the tree and exclaim, "Find the Peel tower."

Indeed, from the battlements of this tottering Clifton tower one may see, not a mile away, the stately walls of Brougham Hall, as conspicuous an illustration of the highly elaborated Peel as could be found in the two counties, to say nothing of the finest avenues in the country, and of the famous Lord Chancellor of that ilk whose family bought it early in the eighteenth century and live there yet. But this cracked old relic in the Clifton stack-yard is in its way more interesting. Like the old log blockhouse or frontier cabin that you may sometimes see preserved with reverence amid the brick homesteads of Virginia or Kentucky as a relic of a rude and bloody past, so the old Peel tower of the north, which has a much more dignified position, reminds the Cumbrian of a much remoter past and of the fierce fashion in which his breed was nurtured. There is nothing resembling it in the south. Think of these scores of country squires scattered from Kendal to the Solway, all boxed up on the first story of their tiny castles, and compare the situation with the spacious, gabled, lattice-windowed mansions of their south country equivalents of the Tudor period and the placid life that if they wished was theirs. Clifton is a fair specimen of the Peel tower, though rather a small one, for the dimensions of course greatly varied. Oblong, like most of them in shape, it may be thirty feet by twenty or rather more, and of three stories, with a spiral staircase leading through them on to a battlemented roof, in one corner of which is a small watch-tower. The space usually admitted of two or three living rooms on the first story and as many sleeping apartments on the upper one. The ground floor was more frequently reserved for storage purposes, and was often without a door, being entered like a cellar from the rooms above. The squire's front door being thus on the first story was only available by a ladder; and as this could be hauled up at a moment's notice, the security of the owner and his family against ordinary intrusion was singularly complete. Swung, so to speak, in mid air and snugly ensconced behind walls of stone five or six feet thick, he could snap his fingers at the whole kingdom of Scotland, and, what is more, shoot arrows or lead at his visitors to his heart's content.

But this mere saving of his skin was of course only the method of procedure when odds were hopeless. The Scottish wars were intermittent, but the moss trooper was perennial, and might turn up at any time and in any strength, from a dozen to a thousand. Booty of course, and cattle mainly, was his immediate object; human life, his own or other people's, was only an inevitable factor in the trade. So beside every Peel tower was an enclosure, or a "barmkin," into which at the first warning of danger, heralded by fugitives or beacon-fires, the cattle were driven, and around this outer rampart of the little fortress the fiercest battles raged. Nor must it be inferred for a moment that these conflicts took place only or even mainly on the English side. The Scottish borderer took, perhaps, more positive pleasure in this ill doing; but, on the other hand, the country north of the Solway lay even more generally open to attack than Cumberland, and led upon the whole as anxious and precarious an existence. But Carlisle will be a better point at which to talk of these and kindred matters. I will only here remark that the Peel tower did begin to expand itself before these evil days were over. Southern influences slowly but gradually crept into the north as the Tudor period advanced. The squire, and his ladies too no doubt, began to realise that their quarters were not only cramped but no longer suited to their station. Then began that rage for building in the two counties, which, stimulated we may be sure by social competition, sacrificed something of the old security for added comfort and improved appearance. Long, low two-storied Tudor wings crept out from one side or other of the old Peel, sometimes terminating in a second tower—sometimes forming two sides of a square, or even expanding gradually to the dignity of a complete four-sided court-yard, with chapel, gateway and outbuildings. But, unlike their larger southern prototypes, they could not throw off the guise of war nor forget for a moment the enemy at their gates. Though panelled walls and decorated ceilings and rich oak carving began to distinguish the interiors, the light of battle to this day still gleams through the low mullioned windows, and defence if not defiance is written all over the massive stone walls, while the flanking Peel towers, battlemented, loopholed and slotted, give a distinction to the whole picture which the small scale of the building in no way detracts from. On the contrary, it adds, I think, some charm and character to it, and suggests a type of man and a style of life that had no analogy elsewhere in England. On this very account however it is in what are now farm-houses that the best examples are usually to be found, for the others have, with some notable exceptions, been much obscured by the increasing requirements of modern social life. The near neighbourhood of Penrith abounds in admirable specimens. Yanwath is close by us and practically within sight, and one of the very first of the Peel tower manor house combinations, being mostly late fifteenth century work according to the late Dr. Taylor, of Penrith, the greatest of authorities on this particular subject. The Threlkelds lived here from the time of Edward the First to that of Henry the Eighth, and it is still much as they left it. One of them, it will be remembered, married the widow of the Black Clifford who secreted her son the " Shepherd Lord " in his youth. It was their boast that they had three noble houses—one at Crosby Ravensworth, with a park full of deer; another here at "Yanwath nigh Penrith, for profit and warmth to reside at in winter;" a third at Threlkeld, "well stocked with tenants to go with them to the wars."

Cliburn too, close by on the other side, has a Peel, and a smaller tower near it, covering a well. Sockbridge, still nearer, the home for centuries of Lancasters and Tankards, seems an unnoticeable farm-house till you get close up to it. Askham lies behind us close to Lowther Castle, and is now a rectory.

Over the gateway of the court-yard, beneath a helmet and a boar's head, the quaint inscription may be read:

> Thomas Sandford Esquire
> For this paid meat and hire
> The year of our Saviour
> XV hundred and seventy four.

And he got his money's worth, for it is a most beautiful and not greatly altered house, set well upon a wooded knoll, with the Lowther breaking finely at its base.

Askham Village.

Thomas Sandford doesn't suggest as a name in our confused English social jumble very much distinction, but it was one to conjure with for many generations in the north, and, what is more, carried with it to battle one of the largest bodies of armed and mounted retainers in the two counties. Nor again would the homely patronymic of Dawes convey to the average ear much social lustre. But at Barton Kirke, over yonder beyond the Pooley road, you will find not only a quaint and ancient church with the most remarkable chancel arch I ever saw, but an old manor house as well, where in the court-yard armorial bearings, showing a fess between three Jackdaws, tell the old familiar tale of a forgotten race. But there is always one spot in a country parish where these vanished men and women are still permitted to prattle to us of one another from the walls in such pathetic unconsciousness of the oblivion that is sometimes to come over the very sound of their names. I am free to confess that these mute voices, who in stone or marble tell us the eternal story of life and death after the varying fashions of their period, are apt at times to hold me longer than the buildings which enclose them. Here in Barton church for instance is the lament of Lancelot Dawes, lord of the manor in 1676, for his young wife of two and twenty, a Fletcher of Great Strickland, over yonder behind the Lowther woods:

> Under this stone reader Interr'd doth lye
> beauty and vertues true epitomy
> Att her appearance the noone sun
> blush'd and shrunken c'ause quite outdone
> In her concentor'd did all Graces dwell
> god pluck't my Rose y^t he might take a smell
> I'le say noe more but weeping wish I may
> Soone wth thy Deare chast ashes come to lay.

Just the man, the unfeeling reader will remark, to marry again within the year and live to be ninety. Doubtless; but the mural records of Barton church preserve a decent silence if this indeed were so. They do, however, tell us by inference that in a hundred years the bearers of the "three Dawes" escutcheon had vanished from the old manor house, and one Nicholson had died possessed of it, a fact commemorated by the united efforts of his ten grandchildren, whose satisfaction that their grandsire lived to see them all married and settled is quaintly expressed upon the tablet. But this is wandering far from the Penrith road, and to very little purpose I fear some may say. So, leaving for the present, at any rate, all further mention of the many other Peel towers of this district, let us hurry on across the bridge of

Lowther, where the Highlanders of Athole stood on that dark night and listened to the clamour of battle on Clifton Moor, and on yet to the more ancient bridge across the Eamont, which lands us once again in Cumberland and within a mile of Penrith town.

There is quite a village here at Eamont Bridge, and one by no means devoid of interesting features, if one might note them. But I have gossiped quite enough for one day of things dead and

Eamont Bridge, near Penrith.

gone; and we will shake the dust of tombstones and ruins off our minds in a little honest mirth at the gorgeous work of art with which the "Welcome Inn" at the bridge end greets the visitor to Cumberland. It rivets one's attention instantly from its conspicuous position, and seems for the moment to exclude all other features of the landscape, and is to me at any rate, as often as I pass this way, an unfailing source of entertainment. For we have here the full-length portrait of a mammoth Highlander in the height of war paint, whom a diminutive gentleman in a tall hat is shaking by the hand and bidding in very large type " Welcome to Cumberland." Now the Cumbrian, together with his neighbour east of the Pennine range, is accustomed to regard himself as the lengthiest among Britons, while the physical virtues of the Highlander we all know do not lie chiefly in his inches. By the same inverted process the Gaelic visitor is entering the canny county by a strangely circuitous route—unless indeed, which seems hardly likely, the illustration contains a really unkind reference to Clifton Moor, for this is assuredly the only time that kilted Highlanders ever entered Penrith by Eamont bridge. And to suggest that the Penrithians on this occasion met their visitors with the hand of friendship and tricked out in their Sunday suits is jesting on a serious subject with a vengeance and trampling on the feelings of both parties. For it may perhaps be remembered how the locals turned out with guns and pitchforks and made things very unpleasant indeed for any parties of Prince Charles's people, who straggled from the main body and drove numbers of them, it is said, into the Eamont, which was then in flood. Still it is a great picture, and for the man who doesn't appreciate it, I wouldn't give much as a vagabond.

Like the coach travellers of olden times, we enter Penrith at the lower end, and the distant Castle shows out finely on the hill behind, to the complete effacement of the railway station and public houses, which on close acquaintance jostle it in such incongruous fashion. And above all, if the western sky be glowing with the approach of sunset or fiery with its lingering lights, the ragged line of broken walls standing out against it makes a most effective picture.

I shall be told, I know, of the places I have passed unnoticed, even in this short round—of Eden Hall, and Carleton, of Brougham church, and the Countess pillar and what not. But it is my privilege to go where fancy leads me and linger where I like; and, having thus weakly made rejoinder to a possible but unreasonable complaint, I shall make no more. If it is of any use to assert that I am not writing a guide book, as every author in this series has done with pathetic reiteration, I hereby do so.

It was on September 30th, 1769, that the poet Gray was tramping into Penrith for the first time along this very road. He tells us how he came by Brougham Castle and "Mr. Brougham's new house" and over Lowther and Eamont bridges, and so to Penrith, where he "dined with Mrs. Bucken on trout and partridges." May we fare as well!

Askham.

The Monument, Ulverstone.

CHAPTER II

TALKING of guide books it will, I fancy, be news to many that Wordsworth condescended to write one. I suspect, however, that tourists who are accustomed to place themselves with such well-merited confidence in the hands of Mr. Baddeley or his rivals would think Wordsworth's guide a very poor affair. Indeed there is not perhaps a great deal to be said for it from any point of view—though it must have an abiding interest from the mere personality of its author. It was sixty years before this again that the first guide book to the Lake Country was written. The author was one West, who had been a teacher on the Continent, but ultimately became a resident in Ulverstone, and acquired a knowledge of the district, which he put to a practical use by conducting "genteel parties making the tour." It will be seen therefore how early the Lakes began to attract tourists. Taste in landscape had then barely emerged from what may be called the "Richmond Hill" stage, when crags and mountains and solitudes and the nobler forms of nature created only repulsion, and received epithets accordingly. "Lakers," as we know, were a recognised social development in Jane Austen's time; and indeed West's Guide in 1774 is sufficient evidence of the tendency even thus early, while of Gray's tour and journal some years previously I have already spoken. So far as I know, the famous author of the "Elegy" is the first outside voice that comes to us from the Lake Country. He walked to Ullswater from Penrith, climbed Dunmallet Hill, and thence looked up the lake, lying motionless beneath a grey October sky. He followed the road we are about to travel as far as Watermillock; gazed at the mountains "rude and awful with their broken tops"; and then, warned by lowering clouds and the waning light of an autumn day, turned homeward. A guide book written twenty years before Wordsworth sang his first lay has obvious claims on our curiosity. West, however, is at no loss for poetical quotations, and draws heavily on Richard Cumberland, who in sounding periods gives Ullswater the palm not only of all neighbouring, but of all British and Irish Lakes. None of them, he sings,

"Shall shake thy sovereign undisturbed right,
Great scene of wonder and sublime delight."

West's table of altitudes is a remarkable testimony to the vagueness of the period in such matters. Snowdon he has with tolerable accuracy, Helvellyn and Skiddaw are only two hundred feet or so amiss, but the Yorkshire hills of Whernside and Ingleborough, he doubles in height, placing them far above Snowdon and nearly a thousand feet above the Lake mountains!

We are now traversing the four miles of road between Penrith and Pooley bridge at the foot of Ullswater, and I ventured on the foregoing disquisition, since so far we have been covering old ground. Now, however, we are across the Eamont again into Westmoreland, and turning to the right abruptly leave our route of yesterday. The sun is bright, and the sky is clear, for it does not always rain in the Lake country. On the contrary, these mountain fringes of the island with their watery reputations are, in my experience, apt to be as dry as Kent or Sussex in the spring and early summer. Some seasons I have known them to be drier, and this was one of them. Need I indicate my method of progression! There are coaches travelling this easy undulating stage, even now with much regularity—but I have not yet come to that, while the most ardent pedestrian in these days does not waste his powers, as of old, upon dusty highways, but uses the choicest gift that the gods in recent years have conferred upon mankind, to place himself with

Ullswater, from near Gowbarrow.

expedition where his legs may be utilized to the best purpose, and the greatest enjoyment of his eyes and brain. There are still belated beings here and there, who affect to sniff at the cycle, but they really are not worth powder and shot, for within easy memory, there was still a prejudice against railroads, and the one will go the way of the other. There is the young person of either sex whose supreme ambition is to be thought horsey and to whom a few cheap sneers at the cycle seem calculated to foster the delusion. Then, there are the old people, God bless them. Human nature is on their side and they have, upon the whole, been extraordinarily tolerant. Lastly, we have those who would like to ride and for various reasons cannot. To many of the latter the situation of a cyclist in motion appears one of perennial tension and anxiety. They do not realize the secret of habit and balance, nor that at an easy pace of seven or eight miles an hour along a country road, the most ordinary rider experiences no sense of effort whatsoever, and can look about him with almost as much ease as a pedestrian, and very often see over fences that hide the country from the latter's view. Nor need I dwell on the supreme advantage that pertains to the cyclist when a few miles of dull or very familiar road have to be travelled and a journey that on foot is wholly tedious and wearisome is surmounted with brevity and exhilaration. I think I hear some carping souls exclaim, Fancy a bicycle in the Lake country! as if one were proposing to take it up Skiddaw or Scafell, or over Black Sail pass. The fact is, a cycle, to those who use one, is never a superfluity. If you elect to walk upon the mountains for a week or fortnight, as any one with strength sufficient would surely do, the iron horse, secure in the Inn coach-house, requires neither food nor thought and is at hand for those less ambitious expeditions by road, that play a greater or a lesser share in almost every programme of Lakeland-travel.

Look at the coaches again, which go lumbering past us, always in a hurry, and bound for some train or steamer, when one would fain loiter, or at other times leaving one to kick one's heels for half a day, where an hour would well suffice.

If we were a passenger, we could not cry halt just here, for instance, and leaving the road for a few minutes cross this ox pasture on the right to where the screen of trees yonder marks a spot worth seeing. I would not stop for a mere cromlech or an ordinary so-called camp, for their name is legion in these parts and unless you approach these prehistoric matters as a separate subject and with becoming seriousness, it seems to me there is nothing to be done except allude to their situation. But what is known as the Druid Circle at Mayborough challenges one's attention in no ordinary way. It is a massive rampart of loose stones, though for the most part overgrown with turf, and enclosing a circle of about one hundred yards in diameter. In the centre is a huge stone twelve or fourteen feet in height, the survivor I believe of several which once upon a time stood round it. It is a fortuitous circumstance perhaps that makes the spot more suggestive to the ordinary eye than other remains of a similar kind. For on the ridge of the high encircling bank a

Head of Ullswater.

growth of timber, oak, ash, and sycamore, has sprung up, which gives to the level grassy arena thus enclosed, a singularly realistic look—while experts I believe encourage the notion that would spring at once to the mind of the ordinary observer, namely, that this was a place of high ceremonial in Druid times. Indeed, it would be difficult to conceive a spot more suitable for a great gathering to-day. The Welsh possess some British camps more interesting than this, but the Welsh bardic societies would give much for a gathering-place at once so accessible and so strikingly appropriate as the Mayborough circle. But the

Dane and the Saxon are stronger far in Westmoreland than the Celt and a wrestling contest would, I fear, draw much larger crowds to Mayborough than any amount of musical or intellectual exercises suggestive of the spirit of the place and of the past.

A smaller circle lies across the way; but we must on to Ullswater at best pace along a pleasant undulating road. The Eamont valley lies upon our right. Beyond it spread the woods of Dalemain where Hassels have lived since the days of the Tudors, and not far behind in a secluded valley stands the beautiful Peel tower manor-house where Huddlestones have been their .neighbours for at least as long. In the morning light against the western sky lie piled the pale grey and shadowless masses of Blencathra and its satellites. Close above us rises the wooded height of Dunmallet which Gray climbed for his first view of Ullswater and in less than no time we glide through a cluster of snug-looking inns and a cheery commotion of horses, ostlers, and coaches in various stages of their day's work and so out on to the old stone bridge of Pooley under which the Eamont rushes from the shining lake beyond. There is no choice of sides for those on wheels of any kind who like ourselves would penetrate to Patterdale at the head of Ullswater nearly nine miles away, for the road by the eastern bank only extends to Howtoun, less than half the distance. It would be no bad plan indeed to take the little steamer which is even now puffing at the pier end as if in a hurry to be off with the score or so of travellers that the Penrith coaches have set down. But the lake side road is not one to be missed, whereas I will assume that the traveller who reaches Patterdale will have the good sense to linger there, and thus doing will take boat at some time and contemplate with a mind at peace from the jingling of wandering minstrels and the flavour of orange-peel the noble proportions of the finest of English lakes.

We have a smooth road before us, a luxury, let it be said

at once, not too common in the Lake country. For a region whose life-blood is locomotion, it is surprising how diseased are some of its arteries. The roads of North Wales as a whole are better graded and better kept. But there is no cause for complaint here, even if one were in the mood for it on such a day and in such a place. It is good to be anywhere away from bricks and mortar, when a bright May is merging into a brighter June, but above all it is good to be among British hills and mountains. There is no season like it and there are surely few regions elsewhere so perfect and so entirely fair. Why, it may be said, thus tantalize the reader by discoursing of June woods that blow along the feet of mountains and glimmer in the rippling surface of May-fly haunted lakes, or of June streams which shine amid leaf and blossom as they will assuredly never shine again. For it is few people now-a-days that the demands of business or pleasure ever permit to see the best of England at its best. But there are compensations in the reverse and the traveller who has to woo nature in her late maturity or in actual decay may well find them voiced in Keats's famous lines:

"Where are the songs of spring? Ah! where are they?
Think not of them, thou hast thy music too."

Ullswater possesses a peculiar charm in the way it gradually unfolds its glories to those who pursue its winding course upwards from Pooley Bridge. It is rarely more than half a mile wide and is divided into three distinct reaches, each one of which exceeds the last in beauty, till the blend of wild overhanging mountain and rich homelike foreground which marks its head fills the visitor with a delight that is perhaps the keener from the skilful way in which this great masterpiece of nature has drawn him into her presence. For the first few miles our road lifts us up at times to some height above the lake and gives us glimpses of the distant mountains clustering thick about its head, with Catchedicam's pointed peak, posing for all the world like the monarch of a group which the broad summit of Helvellyn in actual fact easily dominates. We pass the high-perched inn at Brathenrigg, drop down past Watermillock towards the lake edge and thence, once more thrust inland by the intervening woods and parklands of Hallsteads spread beautifully along the margin of the water, go rising and falling in gentle fashion along a quiet and leafy road, till a final descent to the lake shore leaves us there for the remaining five miles of our journey.

The banks of Ullswater are practically unspoiled. The villas that in some other lakes have seized upon conspicuous points and contributed nothing to the landscape but their own inharmonious presence scarcely trouble this one. Such habitations as are here have the dignity of broad acres and of sufficient age to have surrounded themselves with woodlands that now spread far and wide in rich maturity. Across the lake is the leafy bay and snug hamlet of Howtown, where road traffic upon the further shore terminates, and the mountain wilderness, over which the only wild red deer left in the north have still a range of some forty square miles, begins to rise with something of savage grandeur from the water's edge. With a bend to the right the second reach now opens up to view. A single sail, barely tightened by the light and fitful breath of the south-west wind, makes a charming picture, drifting idly along, the sole object it would seem on the wide expanse of blue water. If you look closely, however, you may make out a boat or two here and there lying motionless against the greenery of the further shore. Each of these will contain a trout fisherman, sore at heart and whistling for a wind, for Ullswater is the best of all the larger lakes for trout, for the simple reason that it enjoys a blessed and rare immunity from that water wolf, the pike.

But here is Gowbarrow park; no tract of ox-fed pastures, no stiff rows of elm and limes, but a real chase is this in all its pristine wildness and a seat moreover of ancient time. Indeed the chieftain Ulpho who is supposed to have given his name to the lake once lived here, and, where his keep stood, a Duke of Norfolk early in the past century erected a small castellated shooting lodge which time and ivy have contributed to mellow into much harmony with the romance of its situation. The present Lyulph's tower stands just above the road and lake, while the deer park descending from steep and craggy fells behind, leaps over ravines noisy with falling streams, spreads over rocky slopes, the home of birch and thorn, to drop near the lake shore into soft glades of grass and fern shaded by immemorial oaks. Within its limits too, and just above us, is Aira Force, where the stream of that name takes a clear leap of 80 feet into a rocky chasm.

> " List, ye who pass by Lyulph's Tower
> At eve, how softly then,
> Doth Aira Force, that torrent hoarse,
> Speak from the woody glen."

This spot is the scene of a famous legend which it would require some hardihood to ignore.

Now, in the predecessor of the present tower—how long ago history does not say—there dwelt a lady of the house of Greystoke to whom this estate, then as now, belonged. Her beauty was famous throughout the land and she was betrothed to a gallant knight. The lady's name was Emma and the knight's Sir Eglamore. Though affianced to so fair a damsel this young cavalier was not a man to sacrifice Mars to Venus and so he set out after the custom of his kind to roam the country in search of adventure, or in the words of one teller of the tale, "to make children fatherless and their mothers widows." He met with such success that his name was noised far and wide and the fame of his deeds even filtered through the wilderness behind which Ullswater lay. A betrothed maiden must have had many heart-pangs while her lover was scouring the country as the professed champion of ladies in distress. Sir Eglamore was so industrious in this pursuit and so long absent, that grave doubts of his fidelity preyed on the mind of the gentle Emma, and she contracted the dangerous habit of walking in her sleep, the object of these midnight rambles being always a spot upon the banks of the Aira where she had first plighted her troth to this adventurous knight errant.

In the meantime, the latter still faithful and now full of honour and crowned with laurels, was wending his way home again, to lay them at his mistress' feet. It was so late at night when he arrived within sight of the tower, runs the story, that unwilling to disturb its inmates, he decided to rest by the stream till morning dawned and the world awoke. It was natural enough too that he should be drawn to the spot most closely connected with his present mood; and it so happened that on this very night the fair somnambulist made one of those weird excursions to which anxiety had unconsciously accustomed her. The knight was aroused from his musings by a figure clad in white which he took for a phantom, but with a hardihood not too common in that superstitious age he undertook to put the matter to the test of touch. His grasp however awaked the fair sleep-walker so suddenly and with such a start that she fell headlong into the foaming torrent before her lover could realize the situation. When the terrible truth flashed upon him he lost not a moment but plunged into the stream, only however, to bring the maiden's bruised and dripping form to shore in time to receive a single glance of recognition before the gentle spirit fled. The knight it is said turned hermit on the spot, and a better locality for this particular calling could hardly have offered itself than the place which witnessed his bereavement.

From the mountain parkland of Gowbarrow, still clinging to the lake shore, we pass almost at once into the woodlands of Glencoin. Here upon every side of us are tall forest trees, oak and beech, ash and sycamore, elm and pine, spreading their fresh leaves over banks of fern, over outcrops of grey lichen-covered rocks, over glades of short and dewy turf. Upon every side is the hand of some long-departed planter, whom all generations who visit Ullswater shall rise up and call blessed. Rabbits dash across the unfenced road, cock pheasants call from the depths of the wood, and the squirrel scuttles on the bough, while just below us the clear waters of the lake sleep quietly in rocky coves and reflects the colour and the motion of the green leaves that quiver above its surface.

For the second time to-day we are passing from Cumberland into Westmoreland, and it was just here where the rocks press closely on the lake that a troop of Scottish moss-troopers was once repulsed with much *éclat* by one Mounsey at the head of his brother statesmen. Now the Mounseys were the largest landowners in this remote community of statesmen, and for this exploit the hero in question was dubbed the King of Patterdale as we shall see. What is more, however, the title became hereditary, and Patterdale had its royal dynasty till the last sovereign some fifty years ago parted with his property and consequently with his crown. Of this, however, more anon, for we have turned the last corner of the lake and the upper and shortest reach breaks finely into view. The eastern shore has now assumed the full measure of its wildness in the fifteen hundred or two thousand feet of rugged front that rises up from Silver Bay and culminates in the rocky crown of Place Fell. All round the lake end which is now before us the mountains crowd in grand and dominating fashion. Many regard this as nature's greatest masterpiece in all Lakeland, a rare distinction indeed if it be admitted. It is not my business to catalogue the wild array of mountain tops that on south and west and east shut out the world and fill the sky. It will be enough to know that yonder ridgy hog-back overtopping everything on the right, with the shadow of a precipice on its hither side, is Helvellyn, and that it starts the long procession. Low in the foreground the mouth of Patterdale spreads a rim of gleaming meadow, and a fringe of dainty woodland along the shining margin of the lake. Thence lies the only outlet to the south, to Ambleside and Windermere and Kendal, and you might well wonder where any road could break its way over such a barrier as seems to shut out the further world. And indeed, when four miles up the dale you understand how the coachroad contrives its exit, and mark its strange contortions as it zigzags up the Kirkstone pass, the desire to stay in Patterdale which takes hold of every one who enters it will probably grow still stronger. Many are the cyclists who, dropping down here in too reckless fashion from Kirkstone, remain against their will, and a local doctor tells me he regards the lunatics who in the teeth of warning and past mishaps come to perennial grief on this precipitous descent, as quite a regular asset in his income.

But how describe the wealth of colouring and of detail, of hill and meadow, of rock and wood, that is so marvellously grouped around the head of Ullswater, between the mountain background and the glittering lake. Let us rather look at it and enjoy ourselves instead of boring the reader with a page or two of futile word painting.

The abundant life that in village, hall, and farmhouse clusters by the lake head and straggles up the dale beyond, seems so contrived as to be free from all offence and to form part of a harmonious whole. The delightful seclusion from the outer world that distinguishes Patterdale above all other Lake districts of equal population, contributes something doubtless to its charm. And I use the word seclusion strictly in its geographical sense, for it would be idle to deny that the world, in a touring and a tripping sense, is partial to the head of Ullswater. But after all how transitory and how trifling is this ebb and flow of human ants when measured by the scale of the surrounding hills and vales, and yet more when the gregarious and unadventurous habits of most of them are taken into account. The man would lack enterprise indeed, who sought solitude and could not find it here even in August, and at this early season he may have more of it, perhaps, than is precisely suited to everybody's taste. There are two hotels near the waterside, both of which in their respective ways are unsurpassed in Lakeland. The larger of these is the Ullswater, a celebrated house, at the foot of whose gardens the steamer discharges and receives its passengers. In the Lake district, where the hotels are almost invariably good and their landlords, unlike so many in the far north, invariably obliging and never extortionate. A hotel with a reputation needs no word from any one. But I am not myself over partial to being a number in the best regulated establishment, and always, when possible, seek out some house of entertainment conducted upon personal lines, if on a less palatial scale, and where some sort of local atmosphere is floating about. I like too, to be in touch with mine host, whose discourse is apt to be more purposeful and to the point when one's interests are worthily engaged in local matters, than that of the most genial guest from Liverpool or London in immaculate dress clothes. And in countries like this your landlord of the better sort is apt to be a sportsman, a farmer, and a stockbreeder, as well as a man with infinite opportunities of observing his fellow creatures from outside. His local interests are of necessity far reaching, and he not only knows the country round for many miles, but everybody in it. He deals in sheep or cattle with the larger farmers, and takes eggs or poultry from the humble dalesman. Many months of comparative leisure fall to his lot, and he hunts with the mountain hounds, and is familiar with every fell and crag, as well as with the trouting capacities of each lake and stream. The very eccentricities and differing tastes of successive waves of guests make him a many-sided man, and bring him all sorts of odd adventures, not of his own seeking, by flood and field, and such as would hardly befall the average mortal. As likely as not, too, he is the parson's right-hand man, for when the fair-weather gentry have all fled, and the snow lies deep round their deserted lodges, and the little stone church, so crowded at other times, is now cheerless, mine host will be there to a certainty, with the offertory bag in the corner of his pew, and supported by his domestic circle. Very often he will be the saving of the situation, from a congregational point of view, for a month of Sundays at a time. Such indeed, with more or less completeness, are many landlords of my acquaintance, and they seem to me a vastly more interesting type than the bottle-nosed individual, of rotund person and torpid habits, that has been the subject of so much prose and verse.

But I must not be suspected of applying these general observations in quite literal fashion to the management of the private hotel at Glenridding. I was but picturing a type with which many of us, I am sure, are familiar. I shall merely remark, for the benefit of any one who, like myself, prefers to be a name to a number, when taking his ease at his inn, that he will find here a regard for his comfort and welfare such as would be an admirable object lesson for many landlords who are accounted well up to their business and certainly account themselves to be so.

It is a milky stream, alas, that comes prattling past the door at Glenridding and tells a tale—happily the only one hereabouts —of lead-mining desecration in the once beauteous dale that wanders up towards the mighty shoulder of Helvellyn. One route to the top of the famous mountain leads this way, or you may pursue the high road for half a mile and turn up Grisedale, whose unsullied charms are accounted the fairest of all the glens that cleave the steep sides of the Helvellyn and Fairfield range. You will make acquaintance here with the ancient little church of Patterdale (Patrickdale), one of the rare dedications to St. Patrick, and supposed to be a survival of the fifth-century Christianity of the Strathclyde Britons. It is probable, however, that the beautiful woods and grounds of Patterdale Hall, with the Grisedale beck glittering through them with merry music, will hold your fancy more, for a fairer foreground to the chequered hills that in their summer dress rise green behind, and the dark crags that far above them again loom silent and solemn, it would be ill to find. If the poets who

E

have sung of this Lakeland deserve such immortality surely those also who have been conspicuous in preserving and adorning it should have their meed of recognition. The Marshalls came into the Lake country, bringing wealth and taste with them, nearly ninety years ago, and their name is written large all over it in such a fashion as does it honour. What extent of land their descendants may own on the various lakes I know not; but not only here on Ullswater but on Coniston and Buttermere and Derwentwater you will find them the pervading influence. The saplings that these earlier Marshalls planted have long sprung up into noble woods of oak and ash, beech and sycamore, that roar finely in wild weather above the breaking waves, and in quiet sunny weather make a fringe of twinkling foliage between lake and mountain that is wholly charming.

Now I cannot think that the disguising of any British mountain side with a covering of larch or pine wood is of any advantage whatever other than a commercial one. It is consoling to find that so eminent a judge of nature as Wordsworth held this view very strongly, denouncing in no measured terms the wholesale planting of these stiff exotics, though the larch, it is true, has the merit of being the first tree to feel the touch of spring. Sprinkled here and there among forests of deciduous trees, the Scotch fir gives an admirable touch of colour. In isolated groups, upon crags or lonely hill tops, they have a character of their own, and a weird charm that is undeniable. In dull and level countries forests of pine are serviceable to the landscape, especially in winter, are good to walk in, while their music on a windy day is of a high order. But both in America and on the Continent you may freely gauge the measure of their monotony when covering the surface of a hilly or a mountain country. It would be a strange taste indeed that would prefer them to the varied detail and matchless colouring that glows upon an English mountain side, and above all upon a Cumbrian one. Indeed, that very scantiness of heather which every one remarks upon, and some people without much discrimination deplore, is almost an advantage. The sportsman of course has associations connected with the mountain plant which make a just estimate of its decorative value difficult, and many sportsmen only see it for the few weeks of its bloom and beauty. Perhaps of the mass of tourists the same may be said. But for many months in the year it is surely the ugliest growth, regarded from a distance, that a mountain produces? We call it russet, and

Brotherswater and Kirkstone Pass.

speak of it in endearing fashion, unconscious that other influences are working in the mind, or else that we are talking something like nonsense. It seems ungracious and unnatural to depreciate heather; but as the Lakeland mountains are often criticised for their scanty growth of it, it is only reasonable to ask the reader to consider himself, in spring, summer, or winter, standing opposite a mountain clothed with heather upon the one hand, and on the other showing a varied surface of rock and fern, of many coloured bog grasses, of bright sheep-nibbled turf, and to honestly say if he would wish to exchange the bright and changing hues of the one for the sombre monotony of the other. I think he would not.

Now Patterdale as a district, or "kingdom" which it formerly was in the Mounsey period, runs some four miles up from the head of Ullswater, wedged in between the mountains, till the little lake of Brotherswater fills the narrowing vale and marks the commencement of the steep climb over Kirkstone. A straggling village, in no way unsightly, which is creditable under the circumstances, follows the highway for half a mile or so, and a snug old-fashioned-looking hotel suggests in its exterior the post-chaise period of Lake travel, though, for aught I know, it may be fitted inside with electric light and every "modern convenience." Meadows now laid up for hay, for the most part cover the levels, and twisting through their midst the silvery streams of the Goldrill shine in the open sunlight, or twinkle through screens of willow and alder. Farmhouses, in white or grey, nestle beneath either mountain foot; and though most of these, I fancy, lay themselves out for rustic entertainment of summer visitors, there is little or no sign of the private villa, which even in the Ambleside and Grasmere district, to say nothing of Windermere, is somewhat over pushful.

One can well imagine that Patterdale was a sufficiently secluded spot in the year 1745, and that many of the people in the low country around Penrith, at the first rumours of the Pretender's army having crossed the Solway, sent their valuables up there for security with much confidence, is not surprising. It is curious, too, to read Wordsworth's encomiums on the wonderful perfection which the art of news transmitting had achieved in his time, as compared with a period then comparatively recent. These particular remarks were occasioned by his receiving the news of Trafalgar and Nelson's death on November 10th while breakfasting in Patterdale, and this, it may be noted, was exactly three weeks after the battle! During the past year, it is hardly necessary to say, one heard in Patterdale at breakfast of some things at least that had happened the day before in South Africa.

It was in this same year, too, of Trafalgar, 1805, that an unfortunate youth, whose name, Gough, has by a fortuitous circumstance been immortalized, left Patterdale to cross the Helvellyn range to Wythburn and Thirlmere, no very desperate performance of a truth under ordinary conditions. It was to his dog however, a small yellow-haired terrier bitch, that his memory owes such measure of notoriety as surrounds it. Scores of people have lost their lives amid these lakes and mountains since Gough's time, and passed into oblivion, while he and his dog have been sung of by two great poets, Scott and Wordsworth, and to this day are the occasional subject of articles and paragraphs. The young man seems to have been of a cheerful disposition and popular with the natives, and much addicted to fishing and mountaineering, always being accompanied by his four-footed companion. He belonged to a respectable middle-class family in a northern town, and seems to have been amusing himself for a few months prior to entering on some definite career. Snow had fallen lightly on the morning in question (April 18th), but Gough was familiar with the route, and as he proposed to be away for a day or two, little notice was taken of his absence, till it was discovered that he had not been heard of on the other side. In brief it was three months before his body was found, and then only through the barking of what was left of his faithful terrier, who had watched all these weary weeks by her dead master's side. The body was found by some shepherds, near the banks of Red Tarn, a wild spot, under Swirrel edge, and the flesh had been eaten from the bones by birds of prey. Whether the young man fell from above, or whether he was overcome by illness or exhaustion, remained a mystery; but it is of small consequence nowadays, though the gist of the story which relates to the amazing fidelity of the little dog well deserves immortality. It made, indeed, quite a stir at the time throughout England; and people unfamiliar with the mountains not unnaturally gave credence to a ghoulish story, that the terrier could only have maintained life for so long by feeding on her dead master's flesh. But as a matter of fact, the number of sheep that die every year on the fells of maggot and other causes, and are left to rot where they fall, banishes any horror or mystery from this part of the story, though it in no way detracts from the wonder of it. The dog recovered, and was taken away by Gough's friends after they had buried him in Penrith. Let us hope she was cherished as she deserved.

But let us away with such melancholy tales, and eat our dinner with a good appetite, though the beck by whose fountain springs the poor man died and the faithful dog watched sings cheerily under the window. The lake lies smiling before us; and what better finish to a day on the road than a night on the water at such a season as this? So let us take boat and rod, and our landlord too, who is both a sportsman and a waterman, and see what Ullswater looks like beneath the sunset, the twilight, the darkness and the moon, for we shall have the last if we are patient.

If any breeze was moving before, it is dead enough now, for the upper bay is like a mirror, on whose surface rocks and mountains, trees and islands with all their wealth of colouring live again. As we glide out on to the lake, the sun is just drooping behind the northern shoulder of Helvellyn, and the mystery of the afterglow is drawing its purple mantle over a world of detail on the hither side of it, that but a moment ago shone with such conspicuous clearness.

And in no long time the shadows on the lake edge grow blurred, the water changes from glass to polished steel, and the latter slowly fades into the leaden hues of twilight. The last gleam has vanished from the mountains around Kirkstone and the head of Patterdale, and died away upon the summit of Placefell. But in the meantime we have not been drifting idly, even in the presence of a transformation scene so exquisite as this, but have passed the steamer landing, and looked in at the rocky caves and wooded, cliffs that culminate in the much painted crag of Styborough. We are the only boat, save one, on the whole visible portion of the lake, which strikes one as a strange thing at this most jocund season of nature's year. Even the single boat in question is but carrying two natives across the bay, armed with gigantic rods, to where the Goldrill beck finds its outlets. The native of this Lake country has no faith in anything much less than sixteen feet in the way of a rod, with a strong preference for something even longer, whether to catch salmon or three-ounce trout. These sportsmen are going " bustard " fishing, and the bustard is a peculiar and time-honoured institution in the Lake country. The trout of the two counties are well educated—not a doubt of that, but at the same time they have been, by some means or other trained up to an hereditary appetite for the bustard, an article that I am quite sure the most unsophisticated fish of other latitudes would scorn either by day or night. The bustard is well named; it is the size of a moderate salmon fly, and resembles nothing that crawls upon the land or sails over the face of the waters. It has a rough yellow body and white wings, as monstrous and clumsy a caricature of an insect as was ever offered to a trout. But the trout of Cumberland and Westmoreland, I am assured, have a wonderful liking for it between sunset and midnight, and vastly prefer it to the cunning and delicate contrivances most of us are accustomed, even at that hour, to think almost indispensable.

There is still plenty of light, though a grey tinge rests upon the world. We are beside a shelving gravelly beach, and my companion proclaims that if we are to catch trout this night, it should surely be here, and indeed for this long time the fish have been breaking the water with some show of activity, though in what mood who can say? I will not bore the reader with the details of our industry. They are not remarkable, but the interest at any rate is sufficiently sustained to enfold us in the wings of night before we seem to have got well to work. Still, even four or five handsome little fish, weighing a pound and a half between them, which is Ullswater size, make a tempting breakfast at any rate. A light breeze is springing up, and there is a touch of chill in the air: the moon will soon rise, and when my guide suggests putting out a trolling line, and taking a further journey under the steeper eastern shores of the lake, I am nothing loth, though trolling for trout as a sport is to my mind of the poorest. But there is a certain weirdness about the situation, and sensations that recall night journeys in frailer craft than this stout boat, and through scenes wilder though assuredly no grander than these, are in no way interrupted by the light responsibilities of holding a trolling line. The breeze blowing down Patterdale through the gap at Kirkstone is beginning to moan in the trees, that cling precariously to the rocky foot of Birkfell, and to make music under our keel. The night shadow of this same Birkfell too, with its thousand feet or so of precipitous and naked boulders, lies somewhat awesomely across our path, and we can well understand at this eerie moment why the mountain foxes are so partial not only to rearing their cubs in its fastnesses, but to turning their faces thither when hard pressed by the exigencies of the chase.

But stay! Here is a fish. He has not much chance if the triple hook is in his jaws, nor is there any great measure of excitement in bringing him up to the boat, though he weighs some three quarters of a pound. Ullswater trout are of the bright and silvery kind, differing much from those of Derwentwater, which run larger, and are thick, short and richly marked. Ullswater, too, is one of the lakes where that eminently local fish, the char, is found; but this species of the salmonidæ has little sporting value, as it lies in deep water and can only be caught by methods that hardly commend themselves to the angler who is not fishing for his living. The char run mostly three or four to the pound, and may be roughly described as trout richly tinted with red and orange hues. On the rare occasions when he takes the fly and leaps from the water, the angler who might perchance have caught American brook trout in their native haunts, would be instantly put in mind of the fontinalis, who are held, I believe, by some to be of the char species. Such at least was my experience. But prowling around somewhere, in the depths of Ullswater, with three or four hundred feet of water above them, are the great grey trout of fabulous size that are never omitted from ancient accounts of St. Ulpho's lake, and are still, I believe, reckoned among its inhabitants. In old days, however, they figured as a regular item in its table of contents; but I have observed that the most sanguine tackle makers of the district do not hold out hopes to their southern customers of drawing such a prize, which I may take conclusively to mean that it is no longer to be drawn. At any rate my companion, who is a most ardent Patterdaler, has not suggested that our minnow, spinning merrily through the dark water forty yards behind, is likely to have a visit from one of these monsters of the deep. Indeed it has ceased apparently to have attraction even for the small fry atop, and it seems we are opposite Gowbarrow near half way down the lake. The long-looked-for moon has now risen in full orbed splendour, and shows even to my inexperienced eye the suggestive embattled outline of Lyulph's tower, and the shadowy parklands with their scattered trees stretching upward to the fells beyond. We can hear quite plainly too, the steady roar of Aira force, though the wind is soughing almost ominously in the woods upon the bank, where an owl is dolefully hooting, and the ripples beating on our keel with something of the force of waves. Clouds too are chasing across the moon, and surely the wraith of the fair Emma might well choose such a night as this to steal across yonder stretch of light and shadow, to where Aira force is sounding the same notes that it sounded six hundred years ago. It must be near midnight, and full time we turned. The lights that were twinkling here and there along the shore are now all quenched, and the fish have long ceased to feed before the rising wind and waves.

> Each bird or beast
> That haunts the tangles of the brake,
> Or dwells beside the silver lake,
> In placid slumber, lies released
> From trouble by the touch of night.

We ought to be quoting Wordsworth here, not Virgil. But in truth, there will be no further opportunity for such philanderings, for there is a four mile row against a head wind and rising sea in prospect; and Ullswater when it chooses can put up a storm in which no ordinary boats that ply upon the lake can live. Indeed, the wind rushes down betimes with such sudden fury from the mountain passes that the over confident visitor is apt to find himself storm bound at Gowbarrow or worse still at Howtoun with nothing for it but to get back by land as best he may, " and we," says mine host, " have to get the boats back as best we may."

It is an hour past midnight, when, not without relief and our task accomplished, we push our boat's nose out of the rough water into the lea of the landing place. The shadowy forms of the mountain tops loom in sombre silence above us, for the clouds, though moving swiftly, are moving high, and there seems no real ill humour in the night. The thought occurs to me, as we walk across the meadows to where a single light gleaming from the sleeping village marks our bourne, that we of this generation in England are inclined to overlook the outdoor attractions of the night in curiously wholesale fashion. Many of us, no doubt, at some period of our lives and in some quarter of the world, have been obliged to travel often and far beneath the moon and stars; and speaking for myself such journeys seem to have left anything but barren memories. The modern dinner hour accounts in part no doubt for this neglect of night's sombre charms. Wordsworth, De

Quincey, and the rest of them—not as enthusiastic naturelovers, but as a matter of course,—when paying visits and so forth, used to walk great distances at night, both in winter and summer. Wordsworth, for instance, leaves his friend's house at Patterdale on the occasion already alluded to at ten o'clock on a November night, to walk the twelve miles home to Rydal, over Kirkstone Pass, as a most ordinary proceeding.

While the tourist will find upon the western or Helvellyn side of Patterdale the finest blend of dale scenery and notable mountain tops and routes that land a good walker by luncheon time, if he so wishes it, at Grasmere, Thirlmere or other desirable centres, upon the other or eastern side a country no less worthy of exploration stretches away from the very shores of Ullswater. In fact when you have crossed the valley meadows at the head of the lake, and climbed on to the top of the lower rampart of Place Fell, there spreads before you a practically illimitable stretch of sheep and deer forest, unbroken by house or village or fence or wall. A fine vista of rolling moorland and bold outstanding hills is here, with the long ridge of the High Street (vulgarism of Ystryd) bounding the eastern view. Hartsop and Rest Dodd, Gray Crag and Kidsty Pike, and many other hills of rugged character, and twenty-five hundred feet or thereabouts of altitude, break the surface of a prospect that is more suggestive of continuous solitude than almost any part of the Lake Country. Boredale, Martindale and Bannerdale, lonely glens enough but for the joyous becks that water them, drop down through the moorland wilderness towards the green levels of Howtoun. The High Street ridge, like a mighty wall, with its red, stormwashed sides, hems in, as I have said, our vision. It takes one's fancy too from the uncompromising directness with which for miles it cleaves the sky line. It is prominent from every peak of note in Cumberland or Westmoreland, and well deserves such distinction, if only for the great Roman road that may yet be traced along its summit. Hidden behind it, like a miniature of its greater sister here. beneath us, Haweswater winds its beauteous course amid woods and rocks, and, with Mardale at its head, may be said to divide the Lake district proper from the moors of Shap.

Over all this country, the ancient red deer roam in their wild state, as on Exmoor. But the range is much smaller, nor are they systematically hunted, which no doubt accounts for their being more frequently in evidence to wandering anglers or pedestrians. I have myself had no such luck, but I have been told by men who often fish the lonely lakes of Hayeswater and Angletarn, that it is no uncommon thing to see a herd of these noble animals drinking on the shore. They must be familiar enough however with the note of hound and horn, for the Ullswater fox-hounds, kennelled in Patterdale, regularly hunt these solitudes. It is lonely enough as it is lovely in June, and I have wandered here all day without seeing a sign of human life but an occasional farmer looking up his sheep. For these last, at this season of the year, are sorely beset by the maggot, that curse of the fell countries, which drives the wretched animals into all sorts of holes and corners, where they perish to a certainty if not hunted up and doctored. The life of the fell farmer is very far from all that fancy is apt to paint it. When wool was two shillings a pound, and Herdwick wethers fifty per cent. above their present figure, it was another matter; but nowadays, with the first at sevenpence, and the last at twenty shillings, to speak approximately, it must somewhat take the heart out of the further struggle with floods and foxes, summer maggots, and winter snow storms. The sheep industry, I need hardly say, is far and away the chief business of the mountain districts. Quarrying and mining occupy but a fraction of the people, and, happily for the landscape at any rate, there are no Festiniogs and Bethesdas here. The country too has probably the finest breed of mountain sheep to be found in these islands, and it has been cherished for centuries with care and pride. From Skiddaw to Black Combe, from Ennerdale to Shap, the Herdwick sheep is the pivot on which all local life not wholly absorbed in the tourist business turns. Yet I met a midland county sheep breeder the other day who had never heard of them, so little does one half of the world know how the other half lives, even when occupied in the same trade! The Herdwick runs a trifle heavier than the Welsh or Exmoor, though of course lighter than the Cheviot, or black-faced Highlander, which, seeing that, like the former, he makes his living without help to speak of, is to the credit of his stock, admitting at the same time that the mutton is as good, which is, I think, the case. The merest amateur in such matters, too, will see at once that the Herdwick carries a heavier fleece than the Welsh. Above all, the grey colour of the wool will be immediately noticeable, though the stranger would at first probably take it for granted that it was merely the result of dipping, and make no comment. Nothing, strange to say, is more like the grey colouring of the fleeces grown on these pure sweet fells than that you sometimes see on sheep pastured amid the smoke of a great city, and it is remarkable that the wool of Herdwicks bred in Wales turns to pure white again. The lambs are mostly piebald, black and white, with a humour of appearance all their own, though their fleeces tone down afterwards to the right shade. Farmers tell me, however, that the tendency to black wool is always very strong with Herdwicks, and has to be contended with in breeding. They are apt, moreover, to run to horns in the ewes, which is incorrect. The Lakeland farmer is for the most part of the smaller yeoman variety. With the inevitable exceptions he is a plain working farmer, employing little labour outside his own family, and personally tending his own stock. Most of them were at one time freeholders, using the term broadly; a few of them still are. The Westmoreland and Cumberland statesmen (*estatesmen*) were once the leading feature in the social economy of the country, varying in their holdings from thirty to a thousand acres.

They were not ordinary yeomen, these Bells, Brownriggs and Bowes, Hodgsons, Nicholsons, Bowmans, and the rest of them, like those of whom so few survive in the South, and whose small estates have lain for all time wedged in between those of greater folks, to whom they paid unquestioned social deference. The Cumbrian or Westmoreland dale was often a small republic, among whom the larger freeholders were only "primi inter pares," making no pretension to social exclusiveness. There had naturally been small temptation in old days for knights and armigers to acquire property and take up residence in such outlandish regions. So while in the more lowland districts squire and statesman flourished side by side, occasionally overstepping the social line that divided them, the latter had the mountain country almost entirely to himself. All this is intelligible enough to any one going over the country with an outline of its history in his mind. But what does come as a bolt from the blue to the most patient of inquiring strangers is a paper written some years ago from a most distinguished local antiquary, entitled, "The Heraldry of Cumbrian Statesmen." Turn a statesman into an armiger, and he loses all interest at once! If his escutcheon meant anything, he was simply a country gentleman in a region and at a period when education, luxury and refinement were not necessary adjuncts to consideration. But we gather from our author that the devices such statesmen aspired to wear, "mostly on the back of their tombstones," were irregular. In which case it strikes one only as suggesting an interesting excursion for the student of heraldry. These escutcheons had not the cachet of the Heralds' College; but any official, says Chancellor Ferguson, who had ventured to call in question the right of these warlike yeomen to exercise their heraldic fancies, would have run a grave risk of being made a spatchcock of, or, in other words, of his head being stuck in a rabbit hole, and his legs staked to the ground. But that of course is another story altogether!

Democracies, we well know, are prone to drift into absolutism, and I have already alluded to the notable example which was furnished by the rise of the Mounsey dynasty to power here in Patterdale. In the obituary column of the "Gentleman's Magazine," for October, 1793, I find the following entry: "On the 21st, at Patterdale Hall, in the parish of Barton, co. Westmoreland, in the 92nd year of his age, John Mounsey, Esq., commonly called King of Patterdale, the owners of which place from time immemorial have been honoured with this appellation." Then follows a page or two describing the habits and manner of life of this singular monarch.

"The palace" (on the site of the modern Patterdale Hall), so says the writer, "makes but an indifferent appearance; neglect for half a century hath made it almost a ruin." His Majesty himself seems to have been a sad miser, and altogether a most undesirable person. With an income of £800 a year, his ambition was to keep his expenses down to £30; and in this he was more than successful. He rejoiced in his physical strength, which was prodigious, and used it to row his own slate and timber down the lake to market. He toiled from morning till night at the hardest manual labour, and exhausted his ingenuity in saving the expenditure of a penny. When it was necessary for this penurious monarch to spend a night outside his dominions, he slept in barns and under haystacks, to avoid the cost of an inn. On one occasion, when riding with a neighbour on the banks of Ullswater, he suddenly jumped from his horse, stripped off his clothes, and plunged into the lake, emerging triumphantly with an old stocking. The sight of a stocking that did not float suggested infinite possibilities to an eye so eager for gain that the impulse was irresistible. His own, says his biographer, were invariably heeled with leather when first purchased, and he always wore the wooden clogs of the country, shod with iron. To save the expense of buying or wearing a respectable suit on occasions when one was an unavoidable necessity, he used to commandeer those of tenants or neighbours, leaving his own rags in the house, to be assumed again when the function was over. His tenants had to supply him with so many meals a year in addition to rent, a plan in which he unconsciously imitated the system of the earlier English kings, whom we all know moved their court about, levying heavy contributions of food stuffs on the localities thus honoured. He was so fearful of being robbed that he used to hide his money in stone walls and holes in the ground, and this well-known propensity of his Majesty's seems to have had a somewhat demoralising effect on some of his subjects, who spent in vain hunts for this treasure trove much time that might have been better employed. Shortly before his death this penurious autocrat derived much satisfaction, we are told, from haggling with various persons about the fee to be paid for the making of his will. The Patterdale schoolmaster bid lowest and got the job, tenpence being the contract price. But the codicils and alterations were so numerous that the dominie struck for half-a-crown, and thereby lost all.

It is satisfactory to learn that his eldest son, who succeeded to the throne, was in all respects the opposite of his father, and possessed every virtue. He was, I think, the last of a long line, making those sales of his property which marked the beginning of the new era in Patterdale.

But before turning our backs on Ullswater and Patterdale I must say another word about the trout fishing, as this is upon the whole the best district in the Lake Country for the casual angler. This, be it remembered, is not saying very much. Still there are compensations for even indifferent sport in such a country, and there is great variety of ground, and good baskets are frequently made. A day on a mountain tarn too has a fascination peculiarly its own, and such as the pedestrian who merely passes along the shore and is gone knows nothing of.

Angletarn is about three miles from Patterdale, set high

among the hills to the eastward, and as wild a spot as ever the lover of mountain solitudes could desire. Its waters are of a clear amber tint, being fed by peaty streams, but full of trout from a quarter to three quarters of a pound, somewhat dark in colour, and a trifle "soft," as is only to be expected, but rising freely to the fly and showing excellent sport. There is a boat, the key of which may be had, but the lake can be readily fished from the shore, and better still by wading. It is by no means easy to find, and however carefully the stranger takes his bearings before mounting out of Patterdale, he will most probably end by climbing to the summit of "The Pikes," which overlooks the surrounding moorlands, before solving the problem of its situation.

I have spoken too of Brotherswater, that charming little lake, which, skirted with woods and bright meadows and overhung with heaped-up fells, fills the narrow head of Patterdale. Near its banks, and by the side of the coach road which ascends the Kirkstone pass, is a homely little inn, kept by a most worthy couple, where I feel quite convinced the hardy angler would find such full measure of simple comfort as he could reasonably desire. The landlord rents the lake, which is crammed with free rising trout: but I am bound to add that these have become so small as to give much cause for surprise that something is not done to remedy the evil. There are two boats on the water, which, small as it is, is sometimes lashed into a perfect fury by the storms which tear down between Red Screes and Caudale moor, or the more westerly gorge of Dovedale. I have very vivid and recent recollections of struggling nearly the whole of a June day with lashings of rain and wind on this little lake; and though the labour of sculling back against the drifts was intensified by the dimensions of a boat which were ample enough for the needs of a man of war, I felt amply consoled for what seemed like such superfluous toil when rolling back again with the gale.

Indeed, it is almost worth a ducking, even if a basket of

fish were not thrown in, to witness the wild rage with which the south-westerly storms, with their endless battalions of whirling clouds, pour through these mountain passes; lifting at times to show the soaking rocks and the white rills leaping down the turf-clad steeps; then in a moment swallowing everything, mountains, woods, meadows, and leaving nothing visible around the rocking boat but a little world of black waves, hissing and spouting, and throwing up clouds of white spray to join the mad race of driving rain.

An ancient manor house of the ruder kind, with tall chimneys and overhung with trees, stands amid the meadows at the head of Brotherswater—a surprisingly sequestered spot for a Tudor house of even such modest dimensions as this one. I do not remember the history of Hartsop Hall, now for many generations the home of statesmen or farmers; but an ancient right of way runs straight through the house, and I am told that once a year, with great punctuality, a venerable dalesman, possessed of an abnormally developed concern for vested rights and usages, makes a special expedition to uphold the maintenance of this one. At the lower end of Brotherswater, a deep valley opens from the east, and from it emerges a good sized beck and a rough road. The first is Hayeswater gill, and rises in the lake of that name some two miles distant, and about a thousand feet above us. This latter, something more than a tarn, is one of the best trouting waters of the district. At the mouth of the valley, where the sportsman would leave his trap or cycle before beginning the ascent on foot, is the little hamlet of Low Hartsop, a collection of ancient buildings nestling beneath a canopy of oaks and sycamore leaves, that has scarcely its like in the whole Lake Country as a picture of times gone by. There is nothing here of what one means by a picturesque village in the ordinary sense of the word; a mere cluster only of farm-houses and cottages, straggling along in more or less propinquity to a leafy lane. But the look of mellow age and rude simplicity in these old stone homesteads, so snugly nestling at the mountain's foot, would arrest the steps of the most impatient angler; and one's fancy is still further touched by the ruins of other buildings, which, if not more ancient, have at any rate sooner outrun their span of life. The moss has gathered thick upon their broken roofs; ferns and wild grasses riot in rank profusion in their gaping doorways and sightless windows, and they would almost appear to be seeking that oblivion from nature's kindly covering which the thickness of their walls has denied them by the ordinary process of decay.

It is a pleasant walk up the dale beyond till it narrows to a deep glen, down which between high slopes waist-deep in bracken, the beck which guides us tumbles its silvery streams. I found much consolation one bright summer day, when an absence of breeze made Hayeswater unfishable, and the beck was clear and full, in quite a good basket of small sweet trout, picked out with fly from its boisterous streams and pools. At one point indeed it makes a clear leap of quite forty feet over a precipitous rock, the white water shooting in exquisite fashion through trailing boughs of birch and mountain ash. Above this is a stretch of open moorland, and then Hayeswater spreads away long and narrow, walled in upon three sides by steep mountain sides. Here too is a fine solitude, though of a different kind from that of Angle tarn, with its dark waters, its boggy banks, its craggy promontories and storm-beaten look. Hayeswater is bright and silvery. So are its fish, and it runs like a trough deep into the mountains; Gray Crag, Kidsty, and the end of the High Street range, dropping to its shores with abruptness in all places, and at some with striking precipitousness. Here, with many apologies for so long a digression to those readers who follow not the gentle art, we will leave the angler and all that concerns him, only wishing him a good breeze, without which his mission would be a fruitless one indeed, and reminding him that this otherwise excellent trouting lake is at some disadvantage in this respect from its sheltered situation.

Dacre Castle.

CHAPTER III.

I HOPE to get to Keswick within the limits of this chapter, an achievement which would be simple enough if we went by the shortest route, namely, the one which leaves the lake at Gowbarrow and cuts across to Troutbeck station on the Keswick and Penrith road. But I will ask the reader to transfer himself once more to the foot of Ullswater, and by the steamer this time if he will; for a mile or so short of Pooley bridge at Waterfoot a road bends away to the left, which will serve our ultimate purpose well enough, and, though somewhat rougher than the other, is perhaps more interesting.

For leaving the Eamont on the right and passing through Soulby, another two miles brings us to a stream, a castle and a village; on a small scale, to be sure, all of them, but the cradle of a mighty, though long vanished race. Dacre Castle stands in the middle of a pasture field, lifted above the woody banks of the stream which shares its famous name, and sings plaintive airs upon the rocks to its departed grandeur. Half castle, half embattled manor-house, small for the first, uncompromisingly stern for the last, it is well worth a visit. A plain rectangular fortress under a single roof, and flanked at each angle by a tower, it still looks, save for some later windows, very much what it was in the 13th century, when the Dacres built it. They were then but tributary chieftains to the great neighbouring barony of Greystoke. Later on they became the greatest power in Cumberland, as the Cliffords were in Westmoreland. It was largely indeed at the expense of the Cliffords that the Dacres rose, and by means chiefly of two daring elopements, if this indeed were not too gentle a term.

For in the time of Edward the Second, the heiress of the great barony of Gilsland lying beyond Carlisle against the Scottish march, was in the safe keeping, at Warwick Castle, of Beauchamp, its famous earl. She was destined for a Clifford. But Ranulph de Dacre had the address and hardihood to carry her off even from such illustrious guardianship, and thus secured her vast estates. Seven or eight successive Dacres were wardens of the western marches, living chiefly at Naworth and Kirkoswald. Their red banner, with its silver escallops, their war cry, "*A Dacre a Dacre, a read bull a read bull!*" was the bane of generations of Scottish invaders. At Flodden Field Thomas Dacre, "Dacre of the North," with his strenuous following, was a prominent factor in the victory. This same Thomas, too, was as successful in love as in war, for he carried off the second great heiress from the hands of the Cliffords in the dead of night, even from their own stronghold of Brougham Castle, and took with her the barony of Greystoke, and vast estates besides. It was not till Elizabeth's reign that the succession failed, the only boy, a little lad, being killed by a fall from his vaulting horse. There were then three girls, but there was also a collateral male Dacre, a plausible claimant. But the Duke of Norfolk had obtained the guardianship of the ladies; and as he had three sons, this settled the question, the collateral Dacre being able to make no head, in spite of much endeavour, against such a combination of destiny and power and marriage bells. And that is how the Howards became great landowners in Cumberland.

To-day, a labourer's family inhabit some of the rooms of the castle and show all of them; and they are worth seeing, both those above ground and those below. One room is called the "King's Chamber," after a doubtful tradition that the Kings of Scotland and Cumbria there swore allegiance to Athelstane, of England.

After passing by Dacre Church, with the great stone bears, brought centuries ago from the castle, squatting weirdly about in the long grass of the grave yard; and traversing Dacre village, a gem of old world cottage architecture, and following for a mile or so an indifferent road, we come out on the main highway between Keswick and Penrith. Happily too it is running just here along a lofty ridge, and gives us the last fair look we shall have of the rich country stretching northward towards Carlisle, with Greystoke Park full in the foreground, spreading its six thousand acres of timber and pasture over hill and dale.

It is a stately enough pile that the Howards of Greystoke now inhabit, and looks finely out at us from embowering woods, but, like Lowther, it is comparatively new, having been twice burnt, once in the civil war, and again some thirty years ago. Away into the distance beyond towards Carlisle and the north stretches the country covered in ancient days by the forest of Inglewood. Even in Wordsworth's youth, a hundred years ago, the last of its original trees had vanished, "o'er its last thorn the nightly moon has shone." Around the far reaching limits of Greystoke Park many of the Peel tower manor-houses that held of that barony in the middle ages with their Tudor additions are still standing. Hutton John of the Huddlestones, nestling in the glen behind us, and still their country seat, has been mentioned in a former chapter. So has Catterlen, a farmhouse now, but still carrying over the door of its latest Tudor wing the Vaux arms, and the notification, "*At this tyme is Rowlande Vaux Lorde of thys Place and builded this Hall y^r of God* 1577. Of Blencowe too I have spoken, also a farmhouse, now half ruinous and wholly striking. The Blencowe of that period so distinguished himself at Poitiers that he was allowed to bear the Greystoke arms, and Blencowes were here till the beginning of the century, when the Howards absorbed them, as the Lowthers absorbed so many like them. They were connections of Lady Jane Grey, and over the door is carved the enigmatic sentence, "*Vivere mori, vivere vitæ,*" which some think an allusion to that unhappy lady. Away yonder, at the northern edge of the park, lies Johnby, whose large seventeenth century barns alone would give it some interest, even if this charming little manor house with its outside tower and newell staircase was not full of Elizabethan work. Musgrave arms are graven here, as well as many curious inscriptions; there is a wonderful kitchen and some fine old chambers. A Welsh family, oddly enough, owned the manor from the civil war onwards. Greenthwaite, now inside Greystoke Park, is considered too a gem of its kind. It was built by the last of the Haltons in 1650, whose Lady, Dorothy Halton, was a sad poacher, or something worse, for she used to tempt the deer from the Duke of Norfolk's park over her boundary with green oats, and then shoot them with a cross bow. Nor was she impelled to these unneighbourly acts from sporting motives, but only by the sordid aim of feeding her domestics at his Grace's cost, till they themselves cried out at being treated to "black mutton four days in the week." She was also addicted to snaring the small game in Greystoke Park, and practising all kinds of poaching wiles. Dame Dorothy was at length summoned to the assizes at Cockermouth, to answer for her unneighbourly depredations. One of the Fletchers was counsel for the prosecution on this occasion, a family who had recently achieved landed position through success in the wool trade, and were rather touchy on the subject. "Here comes Madame Halton with her traps and her gins!" called out the incautious barrister as this Diana from Greenthwaite entered the court; "*And there,*" retorted the lady, "*sits Counsellor Fletcher with his packs and his pins!*" a ready-witted rejoinder, that, in Ireland at any rate, would have ensured her a legal as well as a controversial triumph. Of how she fared history says nothing.

But we are rapidly leaving this bit of green low ground, so rich in soil, in foliage, and in memories, behind us, as we pass through the little hamlet of Penruddock, another reminder in its name of dim Celtic times, and see Blencathara, yet another one, looming large before us. We are still, however, in this most notable parish of Greystoke, which numbered within its bounds for centuries a ducal family and at least half a dozen manor-houses of repute. It is not many country churches of comparative aloofness from the world that from the Tudor to nearly the Victorian period can boast of ringing to church on Sundays such a substantial gathering of land-owning armigers as this one of Greystoke, which can be plainly seen standing apart from the village which clusters round the park gates.

No traveller indeed who cares for such things should miss Greystoke Church. Its low warlike-looking tower of red freestone needs no reminder of the sort of service it has sometimes been called upon to render. The body of the church, which is of late fourteenth century creation and of noble proportions, contains three aisles, and covers the site of a former fabric with, as is supposed, tolerable accuracy. It had a collegiate character, and its founder, a knight in chain armour, lies at full length in alabaster within the building, while the old sedilia occupy their proper position in the spacious chancel, which, by the way, is a modern replica of an older one. There is also a fine old screen, and windows emblazoned with the arms of Howard, Blencowe, Huddlestone, Vaux, Musgrave and others, who have been, or still are, lords of manors in this distinguished parish. Most of the great Strathclyde missioners too passed up and down this country. St. Patrick we have already met with; St. Ninian was here, and, according to Bede, performed miracles at Dacre; Kentigern, who went to Wales and founded St. Asaph, was almost certainly a frequent visitor. The next parish of Mungrisedale itself commemorates his other name of St. Mungo, while the famous church of Crosthwaite at Keswick is also a Kentigern dedication.

But enough of Celtic saints. We have reached the watershed, and at the same time the half-way house on the eighteen miles run from Penrith to Keswick. You might well think that the only road entering the Lake Country from the east would be a much travelled one. But in many journeys over it, and for the most part in the finest of weather, I have rarely met any one but farmers. It is a tolerable road too, though it has to cross at Troutbeck some high ridge land. But what chiefly keeps it so quiet I have no doubt is the railroad that follows almost the same route. For in the Lake Country a road that does not actually climb a pass or border on a lake is usually written down by the authorities as dull. Those however who are not pressed for time will do well to take this one, for here, on the dividing ridge at Troutbeck, and for some miles on either side, you are lifted well up above the world, and it is a fair world too that lies between the Eden valley and Saddleback or Blencathara—between the Pennine and Helvellyn ranges. This Troutbeck, by the way, must not be confused with that other one near Windermere. There is in truth little here but an inn and a few cottages, set high in a windy country of reclaimed moorland. There is a rifle range, to be sure—an object just now of welcome significance, and apparently well patronised. The smooth bulk of Mill fell too, which is such an outstanding feature here, should be large enough to stop the wildest bullet that ever sped from a recruit's Lee Metford.

Over the green and russet uplands of Matterdale Common yonder, where plovers and curlews are screaming above their fresh hatched young, the white high road winds to Gowbarrow on Ullswater, but five miles distant. So the tourist usually trains to Troutbeck, and is carried thence by the friendly char-à-banc, or some more exclusive vehicle, to Patterdale.

We have a long downward run into the valley of the Glenderamaken, which, right in front of us, opens a gateway between the northern limit of the Helvellyn range and the Skiddaw and Blencathara group. Before beginning the descent, we may enjoy a really fine outlook over Matterdale and Threlkeld Commons, and the wild moors that from thence swell gradually upwards to Clough Head and the Great Dodd and the other shoulders of the Helvellyn range. On the right, the foot hills of Saddleback are beginning to shut us in, though not before we have caught just a glimpse of the Caldbeck moors, and John Peel's country far away to the north. A

The Road, Keswick, to Penrith.

lonely house—indeed it is a lonely road—stands by the wayside, some halfway down the slope. Approaching it from the east, it is not in the least likely that any cyclist would be going slow enough to notice a small inscription on the wall. A frivolous rider would almost certainly be in the full enjoyment of a two mile run with his feet up, while the more sober wheelman, under the stimulus of a good road and a gentle downward slope, would be enjoying the delightful prospect that had just opened ahead of him. It is, to be sure, quite possible that either of these might take the solitary building at Moor End for a house of refreshment—as indeed it once was—and in looking for the long vanished sign by chance encounter the plate on its whitewashed wall bearing the following inscription—

> This building's age
> These letters show
> Though many gaze
> Yet few may know
> MDCCIX.

The architect evidently did not rate the intelligence of the neighbourhood in 1709 very highly.

This was once a busy hostelry enough, though now so lonely and forlorn, and was known in the coaching days as the *Sun Inn*. It was kept from 1790 to 1850 by a well known couple named Hutchinson. The old lady, who went on crutches for the last part of her life, was a popular gossip, and no regular travellers when the coach stopped there failed to visit the chimney corner in the kitchen and have a crack with her. Mr. Wilson, of Keswick, has preserved a somewhat characteristic reply given by old Isaac Hutchinson to Bass's agents when they first travelled the country, placing large orders everywhere, in consequence of the increasing demand from tourists.

"I git aw my yal," said the old Tory, "fra Alfred Eemison o' t' Burns, an' it's allus varra good; bit I divvent want to be unneighbourly—what, ye mun send me a hofe quarter" (4½ gallons).

At the foot of the long hill we cross the babbling current of the Glendermaken on its way from Mungrisedale, and, running parallel with its course, go rising and falling with the road over the rough toes of Blencathara, and beneath its mighty shadow to the ancient village of Threlkeld. Down in the meadows on the left, the tall stone chimneys of Threlkeld Hall rise above the trees, a venerable farmhouse, once a seat of the potent knight of that name, who, it may be remembered, married the widow of the Black Clifford, and the mother of the " Shepherd Lord." The manor was even in those days, according to the owner's own showing, full of fighting yeomen.

A still greater Conservative than even Sir John Threlkeld, I have heard somewhere, lived at Threlkeld Hall not very long ago : for when the landlord, to the immense satisfaction of the tenant's family, proposed to refloor the ancient kitchen, the old gentleman in possession, whom age had consigned to his arm

On the way to the Lake, Keswick.

chair, offered the stoutest resistance, urging the time-honoured plea, that as it had done well enough for him and his ancestors, it should be more than good enough for degenerate moderns and their descendants. As this stout preserver of ancient monuments refused to move, he and his chair were lifted bodily about during the progress of the work, under a steady fire of protest.

The valley is still fairly populous; grey or whitewashed homesteads, blinking between the fresh June leaves of the sycamore, which is the great "shade tree" of the Cumbrian farmhouse, are everywhere in evidence as we descend it. They do not shelter fighting, but fox-hunting yeomen nowadays, as is sufficiently indicated by a monument in Threlkeld churchyard, which we must by no means pass by. Here indeed is a memorial I will venture with much confidence to assert is unique of its kind; for near the gate of the graveyard, which opens on the village street, is a homely cenotaph of local stone, and on it are inscribed the names of over forty fox-hunters, natives of Threlkeld parish, who have died within the last twenty or thirty years.

"*A few friends*" (we read) "*have contributed to raise this stone in loving memory of the undernamed, who in their generation were noted veterans of the chase, all of whom lie in this churchyard.*"

Then comes the long list of typical border names—Cockbains, Hudsons, Brownriggs, Bells, Atkinsons, and so forth, giving the date of the birth and death of each departed sportsman. Around the cenotaph, and below the names, we may read, though not without some difficulty,

> The forest music is to hear the hounds
> Rend the thin air, and with a lusty cry
> Awake the drowsy echoes and confound
> Their perfect language in a mingled cry.

A space is left for the names of those still living who may be thought worthy of this measure of local immortality, when the day comes that they are called to more shadowy hunting grounds. The most famous perhaps of all Cumbrian sportsmen, though over four score years of age, is still hale and, what is more, residing within a few hundred yards of this very spot —no less a person than Mr. Crozier, the present master of the Blencathara hounds, who seeing that he has hunted them for sixty years may fairly be accounted the Nestor of his profession in all England.

Threlkeld churchyard is certainly an ideal spot for the last resting-place of fell fox-hunters. Blencathara, with its steep sides riven into dark gorges and its huge supporting buttresses, towers over it on the north, while to the south, not a mile away, leap up the northern outworks of the Helvellyn range. St. Kentigern himself is said to have preached where the church now stands, which last, in the way of remarkable ugliness, wholly mitigated by antiquity, is well worth a look inside. From what point of view it thus repays inspection is another matter, certainly not from either the Early English or the Perpendicular. For it is a barn pure and simple: not indeed very far from an actual square, and carrying a bell turret; but then the fact of its being such an ancient barn just makes all the difference. The whole floor of the west end is sloped like the pit of a theatre; and the pews would cause infinite anguish of mind to experts in church furniture, for they suggest the two first Georges in uncompromising fashion. The general appearance is that of a conventicle; but a conventicle of the Civil War period at least, it is so quaint. Restoration is of course in the air—or rebuilding as it would practically mean, which is a costly business, and Threlkeld would seem to have neither resident magnates, nor many summer visitors. It may seem unkind, but I trust Threlkeld Church may be spared to us. Restored churches are as common as blackberries, but I do not think there can be more than one Threlkeld. There is a rugged simplicity too about it, which is in keeping with a graveyard so plentifully strewn with the remains of simple hardy fox-hunters.

Very different indeed are these Lakeland sportsmen from the smart gentlemen who take hunting boxes in the shires. They know as little of cross-country riding as perhaps some of these latter do of hounds and foxes. Social statisticians of a cynical turn sometimes amuse themselves by guessing at the proportion of Englishmen who hunt from other reasons than love of it. Nobody ever gets up at six in the morning and goes a-hunting with the Blencathara hounds—who by the way are kennelled here, or any of the Lake packs, for other reasons than to see hounds hunt. It is needless too, to remark that the horse plays no part whatever in the business. Every one, including the master and whip, goes afoot, a proceeding which one glance at the country would make immediately explicable, though a horse might be used by some to get to the meet, just as a cycle or a trap might be by others. Indeed, I met Beaumont, the veteran huntsman of the Ullswater mountain hounds, one summer day in Patterdale, exercising his own pack, as well as a low country one that he had in charge, on a bicycle, and I confess to being struck by something of incongruity in the spectacle. Now, Beaumont, with one exception perhaps, has killed more foxes and walked more thousands of miles than any Lake country sportsman. It is said of him, with pardonable hyperbole, by his friends, that he could go blindfold from Kidsty to Scafell on a misty winter's night, but all the same he is sadly unmindful of his dignity. If he were only the popular huntsman of the Blankshire Blazers, he would know what was expected of him, and the right attitude to assume towards the unspeakable bike. But here was this simple Cumbrian sportsman quite enthusiastic with his mount. He could exercise his hounds to greater advantage on it for both himself and them, he declared; and it saved him many a weary mile of road tramping in the hunting season.

These mountain hunt clubs are democratic associations. Subscriptions range from £10 to a shilling, and the smallest subscriber is as welcome as the largest. The Dale farmers, who turn out in great strength, are their chief mainstay; but many of the local tradesmen are zealous and experienced sportsmen, farmers' sons some of them, and bred to hunting in their youth. There are four packs of hounds at least in the Lake country kept entirely for fell hunting, to say nothing of two or three more who divide beween them the adjoining low country, and occasionally run into the mountains. Ten couple is about the number of hounds usually kept in work, some of which will be on the flags through the summer, and some at walk with various members of the hunt. These mountain hounds, it goes without saying, have been carefully bred for their special work for generations, and can make fast going over precipitous and rocky ground that would bring an ordinary foxhound to a standstill. The killing of foxes too has here a double significance—that of real necessity as well as sport; for even four packs find it by no means easy to keep the stock in the Lake country within reasonable limits, and the toll of lambs levied is a high one. One large sheep farmer of my acquaintance averages his annual loss at thirty! Hunting is, on this account, often carried on till very late in the season, and I have heard the woody cliffs of Borrowdale echo to the crash of hounds in full cry as late as the end of May.

The mountain foxes breed as a rule in screes and rocky wastes in lofty and remote situations. Sunrise is the primitive but profitable hour for commencing operations, unless of course there has been much frost on the mountains. There are no coverts to draw, and Reynard must be hunted on the drag in the early morning as he returns with supper undigested from his nightly rambles. The main pleasure of the business consists of course in seeing hounds work and run; and the experienced fell hunter, with average luck, and his own knowledge of the sport and the country, can by judicious manœuvring see a great deal of this. These foxes do not as a rule, unless very hard pressed, leave their particular country. Those for instance on the Fairfield and Helvellyn range will not usually cross the Threlkeld valley to Skiddaw and Blencathara; while the Skiddaw fox, with the wide range of his own forest and the Caldbeck fells, would have to be in sore straits before he faced the Greta and the vale of Keswick, and trailed his draggled brush into the wilds of Whinlatter or Wythop. But as it is, he often runs away, and the hounds with him, from the most vigorous and most knowing of the field, leaving them nothing for it but to go home and speculate on the probable issue of the chase. The dogs frequently sleep out on their own account after long runs, putting up at any friendly farmhouse that happens to be handy. Foxes too being plentiful the small pack often divides, and two or three couple of hounds frequently kill their fox after a long run. I am assured, by well-known members of both the Blencathara and Ullswater hunts, that there is scarcely an old hound in their respective packs that has not at some time or other hunted and killed a fox single-handed. In the bye days at the close of the season, provoked by the bitter cry of sheep-farmers, the small pack is sometimes split up into two, or even into three small drafts, so that more than one district can be dealt with on the same day.

There are always plenty of terriers out too, both regulars and volunteers, and they play an especially prominent part in these mountains: for some of the holts among the rocks are of prodigious depth. Sometimes the terriers fail altogether to regain the upper air, and are not unfrequently lost for days in these subterranean labyrinths, turning up at home after they have been given up for lost and duly mourned. I have seen one tyke, still in full work, who once spent eleven days in the bowels of Raven crag, over yonder towards Thirlmere. In this precipitous country it is quite a frequent thing for a fox, and indeed for hounds and terriers too, to get "binked"[1] in the heat of the chase—to find themselves, that is to say, on a ledge of rock from which they can neither go back nor forward. If Master Reynard lands himself in this predicament, stones are used from above as an inducement to him to take the risks, while a dog can as a rule be rescued by a crag climber and a rope. It is a fine wild sport this, and has immense fascination for those who are fond of hound work. A few strangers do come north for it in the winter, and it is only surprising that there are not more. There is certainly no part of Great Britain where the farmers, and for obvious reasons, are so generally addicted to foxhunting. The

[1] "Bink" is an old border term for shelf.

horse question, of necessity limits the number in a lowland country, while following on foot under such conditions has none of the advantages for seeing the sport offered by the great bare and mostly grass-covered mountains of Cumberland and Westmoreland. Besides the two packs already mentioned, there are or were others at Coniston and Wastdale Head respectively, which hunt on the same lines.

Threlkeld is four miles from Keswick. We have not gone one when the Greta, noisy with such streams as the Manchester Corporation can spare from Thirlmere, sparkles beneath the road, and away into that series of wooded glens that make its descent to Keswick so notably romantic. Rising the hill beyond, the vale of St. John opens out on the left, and squeezing between Naddle fell and Wanthwaite crags vanishes from sight in the direction of Thirlmere. Saddleback, on our right, gives place to Skiddaw. Lattrig, crowned and robed with woods, confronts us; while the Borrowdale fells, rolling round the head of the dark hollow where Thirlmere lies, join the Helvellyn group at Dunmail raise upon the verge of sight. Another low hill and we are atop of the last ridge, Bassenthwaite gleams ahead and beneath us, in the lap of woods and hills. The whole range of mountains that divide that lake and Derwentwater from the west bursts into view, all gloriously illumined by the slow descending sun, and showing so obviously the path by which the waters of all this country below us travel to the open country and the sea. It is wonderful indeed what bold shapes these miniature Alps assume as the shadows of approaching evening begin to creep among them. The outstanding Pikes of Grisedale and Grasmoor, of Robinson and Causey, are none of them three thousand feet, nor in the glare of morning or mid-day do they look it; yet touch them with storm or shadow, a golden sunset or a black thunderstorm, and their altitude in figures becomes a thing of nought.

The descent into Keswick is more gradual, and nothing like the fearsome business it is by the more travelled route over yonder to the left, which comes from Thirlmere and Ambleside, and pitches you down to the lake level in a way to be remembered. We may here run down gradually, and with sufficient confidence, to spare a glance over the left shoulder to the house on Chestnut Hill where Shelley, at nineteen or thereabouts, lived for some months with his girl bride, and as a mere stranger aroused the indignation of the good natured Southey by the rent that an over-greedy landlord was exacting of his youthful inexperience. We come upon level terms

Landing Stage, Keswick.

with the rocky loud roaring Greta at the same instant the pleasant suburbs of the town are entered : and, after following its course for half a mile or so, are landed fairly in Keswick streets.

Now the situation of Keswick may in truth, and fairly, I think, be claimed as the most beautiful enjoyed by any town in England. When guide books enunciate in dogmatic fashion that this pass or that valley " has no equal in Great Britain," thus intruding individual taste or perhaps even local prejudice in the garb of information, one is apt to wax impatient. But Keswick could be proved by mere geography to occupy a site that no other town of several thousand souls in England can offer any parallel to. At any rate if there be such a town I cannot imagine what or where it is. For immediately behind Keswick the noble mass of Skiddaw fills the whole sky upon the north; and Skiddaw, though sneered at by cragsmen, is in outline and dignified independence of position one of the finest as it is almost the highest of northern mountains. Upon the other side, and almost from its doorsteps, the only lake that in beauty is generally thought to rival the head of Ullswater spreads away to the southward, and gleams among its marvellous setting of wood and crag and mountain. To the west the vale of the Derwent spreads a rich green carpet of pasture, wood and meadowland, through which that turbulent river, just released from the upper lake, rolls beneath high and grassy banks to merge itself again in the quiet depths of Bassenthwaite. Keswick itself is a cheery little place of some three or four thousand souls, that in the days before railroads must have enjoyed a great measure of seclusion from the outer world. It has no social and historic memories such as cling to Penrith. Save for its dim associations with the Derwentwater family, it was but a gathering place for statesmen, and a sprinkling of small gentry—a little mountain capital, where wool was woven and sheep bought and sold. The only remains of the ill-fated house of Radcliffe are the stones of the Town-hall, standing in the centre of the wide high street, which are said to have come from the old mansion on Lord's island, together with a bell that certainly once hung there.

Lead pencils are the industry that Keswick chiefly plumes itself on. A hundred or two souls thus make their living amid an aroma of cedar that floats not unpleasantly about the banks of the Greta, whose roaring stream turns their factory wheels. Many hundred tourists however deem it incumbent on them to go and see these same pencils made, and stimulate the industry, no doubt, by buying many contrivances in cedar they do not want, and would not dream of purchasing at home. I was myself several weeks in Keswick, and successfully resisted the still small voice which every wet afternoon—though these, I am bound to say, were not many—tortured me with whispers of the pencil factory, till the very last day, when I weakly yielded. My forebodings were more than justified, and I am supplied with pencils and penholders for the rest of my life; to say nothing of some wholly useless cedar boxes, and a monstrosity called a pencil walking stick. All these things too I purchased with a deliberation that in the open air afterwards seemed incredible; and the more so as I am bound to say, no sort of pressure is put upon the intelligent visitor. His craving to support a local industry, beyond the main one he is already supporting, is, I fancy, as spontaneous as it is evanescent.

Having purchased the esteem of the pencil makers I was also entitled to their confidences, which led me to suppose, among other things, that they do not hold our American cousins in any great regard, declaring that, while their interest in the machinery is greater than that of others, and the questions they ask more numerous, a desire to possess themselves of samples of the work is conspicuously lacking. But Americans surely have some excuse if any is needed. Those in Lakeland will for the most part be either at the beginning or the end of a European tour. If the former, they will not be anxious to carry Keswick wares to Paris, Rome, and Vienna; if the latter, their trunks will be full to bursting. As a matter of fact, however, Americans seem curiously unpopular with all the catering fraternity of the Lake country, except the proprietors of the hotels they actually stop at, which to be sure is an eminently saving clause.

The vendors of photographs or curiosities declare that American tourists give them no end of trouble, and buy nothing. The tip-expecting class complain that their most obvious and most equitable claims are often disregarded—a note which, I believe, is being sounded, and not wholly without justice, even in London, and a sharp reaction surely from the lavishness in this respect that was the burden of the British tourist's complaint in former days. The fact is, I take it, an immense number of Americans of a class that did not formerly travel now cross the Atlantic. Strict economy is often necessary to the accomplishment of the projected tour, and the disposition to distinguish between superfluous or extortionate fees and those which are as equitable and as morally obligatory as if posted on a tariff, seems to be lacking. This probably arises more often than not from a very natural inability to adjust their ideas to circumstances which are genuinely different from any they are used to at home.

One minor cause of complaint is not without its humorous side, and proceeds from the wayside hostelries where coaches stop for changing horses, or for quenching the thirst of man and beast. Now one of the features of American life is of course that unnatural craving for cold water, iced if possible, which, stimulated by habit, amounts almost to a vice; for it does sound somewhat abnormal to hear a coach load of young women on a chilly morning speculating as to the earliest chance of gratifying an appetite so morbid and unseasonable. But the rosy-faced matron of the *Black Bull* or the *Dun Cow* has yet more practical objections to so untoward a practice. Carrying out gratuitous glasses of the hostile element not only to young women but to able-bodied men goes sorely against the grain. She would scarcely indeed be human if she did not resent a tax upon her good nature that added something of insult to the injury. Englishmen would not dare thus much, even supposing they followed the pernicious habit of drinking cold water between meals, and iced water at all times. I think the publican who has enterprise enough to store ice and retail iced water to American tourists at a penny a glass has a bright future before him. People who often begin their breakfast with this cheerless draught in January will not stick at a penny on a dusty road in July or August,

Keswick.

and there is really no reason why any bad habit should be indulged in gratis. I have made a present of what I believe to be a really valuable suggestion to every wayside innkeeper in the Lake Country of my acquaintance. I doubt, however, but that the question of ice has even yet too unattainable a sound about it for the rural Englishman.

Various small local industries are pressed upon the attention of the visitor as he saunters about the pleasant streets and lanes of Keswick. But it really is so very obvious that its absorbing industry is entertaining tourists, driving them about, rowing them on the lake, bedding them, feeding them and supplying them generally with all the necessaries and such superfluities as they want, that the overwhelming predominance of so cheerful a trade makes one inclined perhaps to be a bit cynical about the "local industry," and lukewarm in one's curiosity as to whether this one employs fifty hands or that one three men and a boy. Places are apt to occur to one where five or ten times the entire population of Keswick are hanging for their daily bread upon some precarious production or the slight turn of a market. Skiddaw and Derwentwater are much better than a gold mine to Keswick, which is also a great distributing centre for notable places around. From May till October char-à-bancs and coaches perambulate the outskirts of the town each morning in a steady stream, and the eagle eyes of the competing Jehus search every cranny of your domicile. You may be shaving at an upper window, or having breakfast at a lower one, or discussing household matters in the basement, but they will never fail to find you out and compel your attention to the fact that they are about to start for Buttermere or Ambleside.

Keswick, as I have said, is a cheery place, and should be a prosperous one. It is void, or nearly so, of architectural offence, but has nothing of particular interest within the town limits. The public gardens are delightful, stretching along the banks of the Greta. And it may be well perhaps to remind the reader that this is not the Greta of Rokeby and of Scott. Its banks, like those of the other, are "gay," and its woods of a truth are "fresh and fair." But Brignall is fifty miles off, while this Greta, "Southey's Greta," as some of the handbooks call it, not Scott's, rises in Thirlmere, as I have already intimated. With all the claims that Southey has to our admiration, it seems a trifle incongruous to link him in such fashion with a turbulent mountain stream, even though it did flow near his house; for if ever there was an indoor man and a bookworm it was Southey. His friends used sometimes to wonder that he enjoyed such good health with so little exercise.

Greta Hall, where part of the time as Poet Laureate and for the greater part of it as the most industrious prose writer of his day, Southey lived for forty years, lies on the western outskirts of the town. It is an ugly but capacious house, redeemed in some sort by the big trees around it and the glorious mountain view that it commands. To many people Greta Hall will be the most interesting spot in Keswick. For Southey came here in 1803, and rarely left it till his death in 1843, maintaining by his pen a comfortable home, not only for his own family but for that of his erratic genius of a brother-in-law, S. T. Coleridge, and his wife's widowed sister, Mrs. Lovel. Cured of his youthful phantasies, when he came to Keswick, Southey presents us with the none too common picture of a famous poet and author whose private life was neither disreputable, eccentric, nor peevish. All one hears of him as a man compels our admiration. Till his well-earned fame brought him, together with many other honours, a pension from the Crown, Southey's indefatigable pen was the only means of livelihood, not only for his own family, but for those other relatives to whom in the kindness of his heart he gave a permanent home. His industry, as all the world knows, was quite phenomenal. His books and poems were supplemented with a continual flow of essays and reviews, his long connection with the "Quarterly" being one of the leading features in his literary career. He succeeded in maintaining the establishment at Greta Hall with its numerous inmates in sufficient comfort and simple refinement, and steadily refused all increase of fortune which would have necessitated leaving Keswick. Southey was in short a blameless and a well bred gentleman. He had neither the undesirable habits of some of his contemporaries nor the boorishness and fecklessness of others. His hair was black, his face pale, his features clear cut and refined, as is well shown by his marble effigy in Crosthwaite Church across the meadows yonder. He was neat in dress and particular about his person; polished and courteous in manner, practical in his affairs—an astonishing combination surely for a man of his peculiar genius —Southey's great passion was books, and he collected at Greta Hall a most valuable library, to which he was devotedly attached, handling the precious volumes with dainty and loving care. He used to say that letting Wordsworth, who seems to have had few books and those ill arranged and ill preserved, into his library was like "turning a bear into a tulip garden." Though one of the hardest working men of his day he bore the inroads upon his time made by visitors introduced to his hospitality with a serene good nature that is rare enough. In matters of honour he seems to have been almost hyper-sensitive, and De Quincey declares that a more exemplary man than Southey in all probability never lived. The same distinguished author makes an interesting comparison as regards the smaller matters of life between his two friends, Southey and Wordsworth, who, the reader may perhaps be reminded, were for most of their lives on by no means intimate terms.

The former, says De Quincey, is "certainly a more *amiable* man than Wordsworth. He is less capable, for instance, of usurping an undue share of the conversation; he is more uniformly disposed to be charitable in his transient colloquial judgments upon doubtful actions of his neighbours; more gentle and winning in his condescensions to inferior knowledge or powers of mind; more willing to suppose it possible that he himself may have fallen into an error; more tolerant of avowed indifference towards his own writings; and finally, if the reader will pardon so violent an anticlimax, much more ready to volunteer his assistance in carrying a lady's reticule or parasol."

The chief hotel at Keswick is a very grand establishment, standing on high ground outside the town and hard by the station, with a fine outlook. The others are of the old-fashioned description, and, I have no doubt, comfortable, but are mostly in the centre of the town—a situation which does not commend itself to me when touring in a fine country at midsummer. On the side, however, nearest the lake there are terraces of excellent houses facing the mountains and the open country, and commanding beautiful views, where most comfortable quarters can be had at extremely reasonable rates. My experience of this particular class of entertaiment in the Lake Country leads me to think well of the local landlady. There is little perhaps of that conspicuous and demonstrative interest in your comfort which makes so many Welshwomen past mistresses in their art. You would not expect it in a country where the Celtic strain is slight, but there is a high average of integrity and sufficiently good manners. Many people will prefer the privacy of apartments to the crowded rooms of an hotel, and cherish a fancy for regulating their own hours and their own menu. In the case of a family too the cost of living, with, upon the whole, an equal amount of comfort, is just about half that of the most reasonable inn. For such people Keswick seems to me to offer the best headquarters on many accounts in the Lake Country. With the help of the railway, in addition to coach or cycle, more, I think, can be accomplished without shifting quarters than from any other centre. Lastly, as at Penrith, there is a most admirable reading room and library, an advantage which the traveller may in the anticipation perhaps make light of, but will probably find reason at some time or other to be thankful for.

Crossthwaite Church.

CHAPTER IV.

LET us away then over Greta bridge at the western end of the town, past Southey's now somewhat forlorn-looking house again, and so along the smooth surface of the Cockermouth road, till in less than no time St. Kentigern's ancient church at Crossthwaite confronts us and calls for something more than a passing allusion. For this is in fact the old parish church of Keswick, though lying a long half mile away amid the quiet fields and woods. One of the largest and most important in the whole Lake Country, it has its roots in the early British Christianity of the Strathclyde period, before Angles, Danes and Norwegians filled this region with their " wicks and thwaites," and " thorpes " and " bys," their paganism and their strenuous blood. Whatever building or buildings marked the sacred spot through these dark centuries, the massive tower of this one, looking almost as old as Skiddaw itself, which frowns behind, makes an impressive picture set thus in the very bosom of so sweet a vale. The body of the fabric is of Perpendicular style and generous proportions, and beneath its roof, among other things, is the marble effigy of Southey before referred to, and a monument to John Radcliffe Earl of Derwentwater, reminding one of the time before the 'fifteen, when that unfortunate family lost their mountain kingdom in no ignoble if mistaken fashion.

The wide-spreading churchyard too, whose heaving turf and battalions of grey tombstones suggest such a store of local memories, is not surpassed for charm of situation by many churchyards even in England; and here also are the poet and the painter, the traveller and the brief sojourner, whom grim death has caught perhaps unawares and sent to lie under the shadow of Skiddaw among the burghers and statesmen whose names so unmistakably proclaim them natives of the soil in which their bones are mouldering.

Even in the time of Elizabeth, Crossthwaite still possessed quite a valuable collection of plate and vestments, due in part no doubt to the fact that no great landowners would have ventured here, where the statesmen's interest was so strong, to rob the church of its valuables, as was done elsewhere. Bishop Barnes, of Carlisle, however, in 1571 ordered both plate and vestments to be sold, and part of the proceeds applied to purchasing the simpler accessories required for the Protestant ritual. The Reformation fell with peculiar hardship on these two north-western counties, the people lost everything, and gained almost literally nothing. The " Rising of the North," with the restoration of the ancient faith as a leading object, instigated by Leonard Dacre, and known as "Dacre's raid," had just been suppressed, as, thirty years before, "*Aske's rebellion*," or the "*Pilgrimage of Grace*," in which the two counties joined with Yorkshire, had similarly failed. The gentry, who had been such great gainers by confiscated Church lands, could hardly be expected to risk their heads for mere sentiment, but among the people generally the same hatred of the new order of things smouldered as in Wales. Clergymen and churchwardens were enjoined to special strictness, and to make presentments against all offenders in their parishes. Here are some specimens from the Court of High Commission at Carlisle.

"William Smyth, curate of Edenhall, presented to wear his hose lowse at the knees.

John Dockher, for playing on his pipes when the curate was at evening prayer.

Anna Harrison, widow, suspected of witchcraft.

Maria Hutton, a widow lady, for wearing beads.

John Taylor, for suspect of sorcerie for that he had knyt in cows taile staves, salt and herbes.

Thos. Hodgson, for ringing a bell at the last flood to provoke people to prayer.

Agnes Watson, for keeping a dead man's scalpe.

Hugh Askewe, for burying a quick nowt and a dog and a quick cock."

Others, again, refuse to learn their Catechism, curse their father and mother, their ministers and their wives, scold their husbands, practise usury, "are medicioners for the waffe of an ill winde and for the fayryes," while one audacious individual is reported to have cast his glove down in Irthington Church, and offered to fight any one that would pick it up. Such were the peccadilloes, real and imaginary, of a Cumbrian parish in the days of Raleigh and Spencer.

The Derwent murmurs gently now between flowery meadows and waving hay-fields, and hedgerows laden with the snowy blossoms of the May. They are thin enough now, these amber streams, that swish between the arches of the bridge which lifts us over into Portinscale; but there are seasons in the Vale of Keswick when the channel of the Derwent is quite inadequate for the demands that two big lakes—for Thirlmere and the Greta come this way, and a score of lusty tributaries—make upon its space. Portinscale is one of those names that suggest the expulsion of the Celt, and the lodgment of the Norseman, with a force sufficient to pierce the most indifferent ear. Otherwise this prosperous suburb, if it may so be called, of Keswick is chiefly notable for its big hotel with gardens stretching lakewards, where visitors of leisurely habits, and a good deal of luggage and gastronomic proclivities, seem at all times to foregather in great abundance, and small blame to them.

In five minutes we are crossing the mouth of the Vale of

Portinscale Bridge.

Newlands, and the well-known beck which drains it is rippling beneath the road in low and murmuring fashion. We may bestow a reminiscent thought perhaps as we cross it on the wild spot that gives it birth, where the traveller, after surmounting the crest of Buttermere Hause, sees a silvery thread trailing from the summit of a grey precipice; and let no man lingering in these parts neglect the ascent of this ever charming Vale, as we are forced to do. It is narrow enough even here at its mouth; and at the farther side the village of Braithwaite nestles beneath the fells, as old-fashioned and self-absorbed looking a place as if its people spoke another language and worshipped other gods from those of the tourists who have raised its dust for the last hundred years. Here, among other places, is still held a manorial court, where the curious rights of the old border tenure are jealously watched over as matters not of sentiment but of some practical importance. A first-class coach-road bears us smoothly onward through the hamlet of Thornthwaite,

The Vale of Newlands.

and away down past the old Swan Inn beloved of anglers to the margin of Bassenthwaite. The Vale of Keswick, with the meandering Derwent glistening through green marshes into the lake head, spreads upon our right to the foot of Skiddaw, while upon the left Barf mountain and Thornthwaite fell shut out the higher and wilder hills behind.

And now, for four miles, the lake's full length, we slip along with scarcely a rise or fall, through almost unbroken woodland, and, but a stone's throw distant, the water glimmers and twinkles

through a screen of freshly opened leaves. But once in a while
the woods open and expose to view the whole shining surface
of the lake, with the groves and parklands that adorn its further
shores, and the majestic pile of Skiddaw, with its storm-washed
and buttressed sides, and its bold crest towering above all
Nor is it borne in upon one with much insistence that a railway
runs along the wooded bank between road and lake, so hidden
for the most part is its track. At long intervals there is a rattle
and a brief commotion, a cloud of smoke, a stampede of wood-
pigeons, a scuttle of rabbits, and the horrid thing is gone, and
there is peace for the next hour or two. But now in June,
saving always Whitsun week, there is very little traffic of
any kind even here. This shore road is quiet, and the leaves
rustle and the water laps softly on the rocks below, while a
born in the fells above, splashes now and again
on to the road side, and burrows its
The thorn and hazel
are hoarsely noisy in
:t up on this latest of
various shades strag-
ts,

warm beam

han there used to be
and fewer   the usual order of
things, which I am told is due   ine washings having
affected the spawning beds of the former to the obvious advantage of the others. This long western shore of Bassenthwaite is
moreover unbroken, or nearly so, by human habitation. Above
us, though mostly unseen, are the fells, around us the woods.
As the road turns round the lake end, at Peel Wyke a British
camp will be found by the curious in such things upon a hill top
near the water, while hard by it stands that snuggest looking
of small hostelries, the Pheasant Inn.

This is the last hotel in the Lake Country. As we turn the corner and run along parallel with the wide end of the lake we are on the very limit of tourist enterprise. Just beyond the railway and small station a broad highway swings to the left, and a milestone somewhere about proclaims that Cockermouth is six miles distant. I have a notion that very few tourists ever go a furlong beyond the foot of Bassenthwaite. A properly constituted Keswick hack driver would, I think, almost refuse to set his horse's head towards a region so unorthodox and insignificant. I have more than once, in answer

Skiddaw from the Cockermouth Road.

to inquiries as to route or distance, been earnestly besought by venerable inhabitants of the lake shore not to waste time and energy on a region so utterly devoid of "anything to see." If one does go to Cockermouth the only conceivable reason from the laker's point of view would be to see the house where Wordsworth was born; and I have here to admit that I went to Cockermouth, and spent two hours in the Castle, and never once remembered this other "point of interest." I confess I do not much care for inspecting houses that are merely connected with a poet in his pinafore period; and

Wordsworth left Cockermouth very young, his father, who was agent to the first or "the bad" Lord Lonsdale, dying prematurely. In these blessed days of bicycles, however, when it is much less than an hour's run over an admirable road, I would advise the reader by no means to omit the pilgrimage. There are two ways of making it, the one just mentioned, and another by a rougher and hillier road down the valley of the Derwent, which river, after breaking out of Bassenthwaite, pours a noble volume of water through a winding vale that in other regions would enjoy much distinction for scenic beauty. To go by the first road and return by the second is the obvious thing to do. The former carries you in gentle undulations through pleasant grass farms, where the meadows are well forward, and the clover fields already ruddy with blossom. Shorthorns are fattening on the pastures; and big Border Leicesters, sweltering in their heavy fleeces, look a strange contrast to the nimble little Herdwicks so lately left behind. Solid Cumbrian homesteads, with their grey roofs and whitewashed walls and black window borders, stand grouped about amid protecting groves of sycamores, while small streams gurgle shyly amid the lush grass and the fells which gave them birth, rise near at hand, and roll away southwards, behind Embleton, smooth, vast, green and solitary.

There is not much to be said of Cockermouth. It has seen better days, and been a place of some importance, and is not without quaint characteristics. The broad and turbulent streams of the Derwent beat against its back doors for a long distance, recalling for a moment Llangollen and the Dee. The Cocker, still noisy with the music of the fells, clatters through its centre, bearing quickly onward the clear waters that were so lately sleeping in Buttermere and Crummock. Its main street is wide, and for some distance bordered with young trees, giving a further look of repose to an evidently drowsy place. But Cockermouth Castle is not only proudly placed above the town and the Derwent, but well worth seeing. The towers and outer walls of grey limestone are still fairly perfect. Portions of the building have been kept up for habitation by the Wyndham family, the proprietors, and were for a long time and till comparatively recently the chief abode of some of them, to the joy and advantage of Cockermouth. Over the great gateway is the blue lion of the Percies, who when Earls of Westmoreland counted this among their strongholds. Hither, too, was brought Mary Queen of Scots when she crossed the Solway to throw herself

Cockermouth Castle.

with such sadly misplaced confidence on Elizabeth's mercy. She landed at Workington, some eight miles hence, now a busy centre of coalpits and ironworks, whose smoke and chimneys are only too visible against the western sky, and was entertained by the Curwens of Workington Hall, who are still its owners and accounted the oldest family in Cumberland.

No one indeed would wish to go beyond Cockermouth. Over the Derwent which sweeps in noble curves through parklands at our feet, and beyond the nearer woods and hills into which it disappears on its seaward journey, the summer sky is charged with horrid clouds that come neither from the mountains nor the sea. So having looked down the most gruesome of dungeons, seen the underground chapel and listened to the inevitable civil war siege, let us away back to the shores of Bassenthwaite by the longer and rougher road which follows the Derwent valley. And on the way I shall stop for a moment at Isell, not only because it is a fine specimen of an embattled Peel tower manor-house and beautifully placed on wooded slopes above the Derwent, but also for another reason altogether that plays no part whatever in local guide lore and seems to be not generally known. Isell now belongs to Sir Wilfrid Lawson: a hundred and fifty years ago it belonged to another Sir Wilfrid Lawson, and it was from this remote grey manor-house, old enough even then, that the lady came who laid such hold upon the affections of the famous General Wolfe as to cast quite a shadow over several years of his too short life.

The story is not without pathos, though it ends like an American novel in both hero and heroine going their own way without any apparently sufficient reason and each dying unmarried. The Miss Lawson of Isell of that day was maid of honour to the Princess Charlotte, and the hero of Quebec was a gallant major, a most precocious youth of twenty-one, and a veteran of six years' service in the French wars. They met in London, and Wolfe formed an attachment to the lady of so ardent a nature as to prove destructive to his peace of mind for an unconscionably long period. It is difficult to tell from his letters to what extent the attachment was mutual. His mother was so determined that he should marry an heiress, pressing upon him more than one from aldermanic quarters, and was so hostile to the Lawson project, that it seems likely she actually came between them. At any rate she said things about the maid of honour's health which were harmless and perhaps true, and she said other things neither harmless and certainly not true, which caused the only approach to a quarrel which

Wolfe, who was a devoted son, ever had with his mother. The disconsolate lover went on garrison duty for some years in Scotland, and never again set eyes upon the beloved object. His disappointment cut him to the quick, and he frequently alludes to it in his correspondence. Years afterwards the mere sight of her picture hanging on a wall took away his appetite for dinner, so he tells us, though this is not perhaps a romantic way of expressing so delicate a situation. He regarded his heart, in this respect, as dead, which in the case of a man of his deep feelings was probably no affectation. At any rate, for the remaining ten years of his life, though a lover of society, there is no hint of his losing it, nor yet of matrimony till his engagement with Miss Lowther, just before he sailed for Quebec. But this was a much less ardent affair, so far as one may judge from scanty evidence.

Miss Lawson died early and unmarried. Miss Lowther, by a curious coincidence, for Wolfe had no connection whatever with these two counties—was a neighbour of the General's early love, being a sister of that same Lord Lonsdale for whom Wordsworth's father acted, and whose financial eccentricities, to put it mildly, threw the Wordsworth children in so unjust a fashion upon the charity of their relatives. This lady became Duchess of Bolton and lived to a green old age. From the little one hears of her it seems probable that whatever good things might have been reserved for Wolfe, had he survived his glorious victory, matrimonial felicity of a high order was not one of them. The manor-house too, whence came Miss Lowther, though dropped this long time to a farm-house, is still standing. Meaburn Hall is far enough out of the beaten track, lying as it does between Appleby and Shap. But for the sake of the old oak staircases, the wainscoted rooms and the Lowther associations that still cling to it, some few local antiquaries and an occasional traveller yet find their way there. I myself, not alone perhaps on that account, but partly on Wolfe's, have made the pilgrimage from Penrith with much satisfaction, for the house is a most beautiful specimen of the Peel tower manor.

But we must linger no more at Isell, not even on the old bridge by the Vicarage, beneath which the Derwent rushes so finely, spreading out below into such a breadth of shining rapid as it washes the foot of the lawn and goes roaring off into the woods beyond. Salmon run up here freely, travelling through both Bassenthwaite and Derwentwater, affording a

Skiddaw from the foot of Bassenthwaite.

little sport to the rod hereabouts, and a good deal of unseasonable fish meat later on to the farmers and quarrymen at the head of Borrowdale. But faster even than a salmon, and much faster than we should travel in the flesh over the rough and hilly road, we must ourselves get back in fancy to the shores of Bassenthwaite.

Now the Castle Inn marks the homeward turning point in the drive round Bassenthwaite, and lies in the opposite corner of the lake end from the Pheasant, though much further removed from the shore. To reach there we have a mile or two of level going, more or less overshadowed by the woods and plantations of Armathwaite Hall, between whose foliage we may here and there get charming peeps up the whole length of the lake, with the mass of Skiddaw on the left and the mountains of the Armboth and Helvellyn ranges beyond Keswick filling in the background. At this same Castle Inn, a small but notable house of call, our road turns sharp to the right and up the lake again for Keswick. Here also two other roads diverge, but going, so far as the Lake tourist is concerned, into the wilderness, one to Carlisle, the other to Caldbeck; we shall have reason to follow them both later on.

Skiddaw assumes a most imposing shape as we approach its northern slopes, the points of its supporting spurs springing heavenwards with surprising boldness, and making a beautiful picture, framed in the arching tree tops which fringe our road. On this side, too, there is quite a wide strip of country between road and lake. We are lifted well up for the most part, and get fine views of the fells which culminate towards Buttermere in Robinson (of dreadful name!) and Grassmoor, in Causey and High Pike, while homesteads and country houses lie all about us, stretching away towards the heathery wilderness that lies at the back of Skiddaw.

The shadow of the great peat mountain, however, is soon upon us, though it is a pleasant enough country this Hundred of Underskiddaw, this strip of foothill by the lake shore facing the south-west; an old abiding place of virile stocks, whose members, for lack no doubt of scope and elbow room, went out often into the world, to the East and West, to the North and to the South, making fortunes for themselves, and leaving names not unknown to fame. The Brownriggs of Ormathwaite and Millbeck, now extinct, seem in the seventeenth and eighteenth centuries to have been most conspicuous among these people, and to have occupied or owned most of the farms in Underskiddaw. A learned doctor of this clan had enough distinction in the world of science to attract Benjamin Franklin as a guest to Ormathwaite Hall, when the two savants successfully experimented with oil on the troubled waters of the lake. The face of Underskiddaw has altered much since the days when its own natives were the only dwellers on the soil. Fine woodlands have grown, old houses have been furbished up, muddy and rutty lanes have given place to the admirable highway on which we are now travelling. Villas, though mellowed hereabouts, it is true, by the woodland growth of quite a reasonable period, have sprung up, and stand by the roadside or lie tucked away under the mountain foot, awaiting their August occupants, while Skiddaw dominates all, with sides as precipitous as those of a mountain can well be which is almost devoid of cliff and crag.

Millbeck, some three miles short of Keswick, and just off the high road, is a spot no one should pass. A mountain stream here issues from a gorge in the breast of Skiddaw amid a wealth of old timber and orchards, and an ancient hamlet, white and grey and mossy, sleeps beneath their shade. Chief among its buildings is Millbeck Hall, a diminutive Elizabethan manor-house of the statesman class, lived in by many Brownriggs, but built and owned by one Nicholas Williamson, who, if he had no armorial bearings, was determined to follow, so far as he could, the quaint conceits of his superiors, and in this case particularly those of the Blencowes of Blencowe. For here we may read over the door the same inscription that looked down on us from above the portal of the statelier manor-house near Penrith :—

> 1592. QVORSVM, N. W.
> VIVERE-MORI—MORI-VIVERE
> NICHOLAS WILLIAMSON.

These aforesaid Brownriggs too founded a family in Ireland, who achieved the distinction of a baronetcy, and, for aught I know, may be flourishing in Wicklow still. The beck plunges joyously now before the door, splashing as it passes the mossy roots of sycamores and oaks, while the noisy clamour of three or four score Herdwick wethers down from the fell, with the yapping of their canine warders fills in the measure of the rustic chorus. There are some cottages too in Millbeck whose appearance almost justifies the fabulous tales told of their antiquity, and they have been the joy of generations of artists. A much less romantic object is that of the long disused woollen mill higher up the stream, though even this is not without some special interest as having been the occasion of a remarkable diatribe by Lord Macaulay, of which the unfortunate Southey was the victim.

The then Poet Laureate, in his "Colloquies on Society," had drawn a vivid contrast between these ancient dwellings and a row of cottages erected here for the workers at the mill. "The old cottages," he writes, "are such as the poet and the painter equally delight in beholding, substantially built of the native stone without mortar, and their long low roofs covered with slate; if they had been raised by the magic of some indigenous Amphion's music the materials could not have adjusted themselves more beautifully in accord with the surrounding scene. The ornamented chimneys, round or square, less adorned than those which, like little turrets, crest the houses of the Portuguese peasantry, and yet not less happily suited to their place, the hedge of clipt box beneath the windows, the rose bushes beside the door, the little patch of flower ground with its tall hollyhocks in front; the garden beside, the bee-hives, and the orchard with its bank of daffodils and snowdrops, the earliest and profusest in these parts, indicate in the owners some portion of ease and leisure, some regard to neatness and comfort, some sense of natural and innocent and healthful enjoyment. The new cottages of the manufacturer are upon the manufacturing pattern, naked and in a row. How is it that everything which is connected with

A Sketch of Southey from Life, by A. T. Paget, July, 1836. In the possession of Charles E. Paget, Esq.

manufactures presents such features of unqualified deformity? From the largest of Mammon's temples down to the poorest hovel in which his helotry are stalled, these edifices have all one character. Time will not mellow them; nature will neither clothe nor conceal them; and they will remain always as offensive to the eye as the mind." Thus moralised Southey seventy years ago among the leafy bowers of Millbeck and Applethwaite in the adjoining glen. "Here is wisdom!" thundered Macaulay, when he read it. "Here are the principles upon which nations are to be governed! Rose bushes and poor rates, rather than steam engines and independence. Mortality and cottages with weather stains, rather than health and long life with edifices which time cannot mellow. Mr. Southey has found out a way, he tells us, in which the effects of manufactures and agriculture may be compared. And what is this way? To stand on a hill, to look at a cottage and a factory, and see which is the prettier, &c." . . . .

While upon the subject of Southey, and as we are traversing the easy three miles between Millbeck and Keswick, I will turn over the pages of an old manuscript diary which happens to lie before me, because it is that of my own grandfather. The diarist was then archdeacon in a northern diocese, and in June, 1831, seems to have been on a visit to the Curwens of Workington, lately mentioned, and to have taken the opportunity of calling, not apparently for the first time, on Southey at Greta Hall. Three or four closely written pages preserve a part, at any rate, of the conversation that took place in Southey's library on this occasion, partly on politics but chiefly on theology, and of no great moment here; but it may be worth noting that the poet struck his visitor as " very much of a *white man, i.e.*, white coat and trousers, white hair, and a white face, a semicircular profile, very Roman nose, an expression of remarkable shrewdness, shaggy eyebrows, with a quick and severe eye." "Whenever the conversation became animated," says the archdeacon, " he rose and paced the room (which was filled with books, as were also two other rooms) in various directions, so that he was sometimes behind me while I was speaking to him." Among other anecdotes that passed on this occasion, Southey mentioned a delusion of Robert Hall's, the famous preacher, who was subject to them, to the effect that the angel Gabriel had fitted him with a crown a size too small! The two girls are noted in the journal as kind, courteous, and pretty; Mrs. Southey as stout and contented looking.

I am quite sure that the citizens of no town in all England, to say nothing of the passing sojourner, have such a promenade for the enjoyment of their post-prandial tobacco as have the good folks of Keswick in that leafy walk which borders the Derwentwater boat landings and ends at Friars Crag; whether the sun is still drooping in fiery splendour to the rim of the overhanging hills, or has sunk behind them, leaving its trail of glory and tender afterglow upon land and water, this lower end of Keswick's enchanting lake is not easily surpassed. Like Ullswater, so Derwentwater in its somewhat differing style holds a place of its own among English lakes. There is not, to be sure, quite the wildness or solitude of Ullswater— certainly not on a fine summer evening off Friars Crag, when humanity plays an active part in the bright and everchanging scene. For boats are then gliding between the wooded islands and promontories, and bright patches of colour flit over waters, here black beneath some upstanding crag, there quivering in the sun's trail like molten gold. Song and laughter blend not inharmoniously with a scene so instinct with light and form and colour; and, behind all, the silent mountains, piled up one above the other, yet close at hand, complete a picture that is not given to many English townsmen for contemplation of a summer evening within a gunshot of their doors.

A hundred and thirty years ago, before the era of the tourist, and when Keswick was but a small place, the poet Gray stood upon this very spot, and has told us how he watched "the solemn colouring of the night draw on, the last gleam of sunshine fading away upon the hill tops, the deep serene of the waters, and the long shadows of the mountains thrown across them, till they nearly touch the hithermost shore; at a distance were heard the murmurs of many waterfalls not audible in the day-time. I wished for the moon, but she was dark to me and silent."

But we have been looking here across the lake only. From Friars Crag proper at the end of the walk, a rocky promontory, furnished with some ancient and stately fir trees, it is given one

Derwentwater.

to see right down it, to its upper end three miles away, where the rugged outlines of the "Jaws of Borrowdale" seem to be always dark and frowning, however serene the atmosphere and however bright the sky. But I really cannot describe Derwentwater. It is more familiar to me than any English lake, and the better one knows it the more futile does such an effort seem. To catalogue the crags and hills and mountains in whose bosom it lies, is but a barren business, and brings one no whit nearer to the conception of their infinite beauty and wonderful grouping. To enumerate the leafy islands that seem to float upon the lake's bosom, and descant upon the nature of the woods which in such profusion and with scarcely a break deck the shores, would be an idle waste of words. Are not all these things written in the many excellent works devoted to the local topography? one of which, at any rate, I trust the reader who likes to have his peaks in order, for private use, as I confess I do, and his islands clear in his mind, will not omit. Let it be mine rather to recommend him merely to take boat, if the day be kindly, and paddle leisurely about, and judge for himself if he thinks there can be anything upon earth more fair. And there is no better lake anywhere for boating than Derwentwater. It is hardly large enough to often put up seas, in summer time at any rate, that are dangerous. There are no steamers to knock you about, nor yachts to run you down, nor anything like the number of craft that ply on Windermere. It abounds in leafy bays, in snug coves where the water laps against rocky promontories on which pine-trees murmur and bilberry bushes covering the ground give completeness to a foreground that carries one's fancy away for a moment to far Canadian lakes. But not in Canada certainly, nor anywhere oversea, is there that velvety, that mellow perfection of foreground such as only a British atmosphere acting on a British soil seems able to produce. Nor do I know of any other land where mountains of such modest altitude are so boldly fashioned and so assisted by the kind delusions of soft skies as to be well able to challenge comparison with many beside whom they are but pigmies.

There are perch in the lake too in plenty for those who affect this peaceful branch of sport, and one so admirably adapted to family use. There are pike for the more vigorous and unsociable; while for the really serious angler the Derwentwater trout, tolerably numerous, exceedingly capricious, but when captured of most admirable size and quality, afford much scope for skill and patience. I do not think many strangers go to Derwentwater to catch trout, and in this they perhaps exercise a wise discretion. Not but what there are plenty of them; short, thick, lusty, well-fed fellows too, the best probably in all the Lake Country—though it would not do to say so to a Windermere man—and they will average moreover something like a pound apiece. They commence their somewhat fitful attentions to the artificial fly in early April, while their ardour culminates of course with the advent of the May-fly, called here the "Drake." After this dissipation they refuse to have anything more to say to flies of any kind, and sulk about the lake bottom amid the admirable provender with which nature has in Derwentwater provided them, and with such a lavish hand. The local enthusiasts, however, are quite numerous; and any May day when there is a breeze you will see half-a-dozen boats at least drifting slowly before it in the upper reaches between the lead mine on the western shore and Lodore upon the other. The Keswick fly fishers, who largely consist of local tradesmen enjoying a well-earned retirement, are as industrious as any company of Waltonians I have ever met. I do not think they ever miss a possible day from the beginning of the season to the end; and when the good moment comes, and the Derwentwater trout makes up his mind to leave the toothsome things below and shoot up through the clear water for a change of menu, the faithful Keswick angler is quite certain to be there, and he earns his meet reward. His two or three brace of fish weighing perhaps half-a-dozen pounds, will carry him over with contentment several days of scantily rewarded toil. And when in the first week of June the May-fly puts in an appearance, better results are confidently and with some justice looked for. During that high festival you may see fifteen to twenty boats every morning drifting in slow procession, and in a row, where the wind listeth: and in each boat there will be two sportsmen, one standing up at either end, and each sportsman will be armed with a two-handed rod, from fifteen to twenty feet in length. Indeed there will be such an amount of energy and back work going on, that a Southerner might well suppose that twenty-pound salmon were the object of pursuit, not one-pound trout. Most people nowadays fish lakes with little ten or eleven feet one-handed rods. But the Keswick angler is a prodigious Tory, and has a belief in his grandfather's weapon that no argument could shake. No one at least can say that he does not toil hard for his sport —working down a salmon pool, for reasons obvious to the initiated, is indeed child's play to it. I have myself both caught and eaten Derwentwater trout, and whether on the end of a line or on a plate want nothing better. There are beyond a doubt too half hours when the May fly is well on that will bear comparison for pleasure and profit with brief periods on almost any water.

In no way do I regret, however, many hours spent on the bosom of Derwentwater, that, so far as trout went, were often blank ones, when the neglected flies trailed aimlessly on the ripples, and the ripples sang with soothing monotony against the keel. It is not easy to have too much of a good thing, and the surroundings of this Keswick lake form a very good thing indeed.

I wonder too how many of those who take their pleasure on Derwentwater in their various fashions ever give a thought to the gallant but unfortunate family who were once its lords. At a remote period the Radcliffes seem not only to have owned the lake and valley below it, but a large amount of territory stretching towards Cockermouth, which afterwards passed with one of their ladies into the Dacre family. The somewhat shorn Radcliffe of that day then more than made up for the loss by himself marrying the heiress of those great Northumbrian and Durham estates that dwarfed his patrimony about Keswick, and made his revenue in 1700 larger, it was said, than that of the Electorate of Hanover! They still, however, kept their mansion on Lord's island yonder, now but a mass of foliage, with small traces of the old house; and from here the last Countess of Derwentwater is asserted, though with doubtful accuracy, to have journeyed to London to intercede for her gallant but injudicious husband, lying under sentence of death for his leading share in the rebellion of 1715. No other family, I fancy, lost its head (in both senses) in each of the two risings. The last and third Lord Derwentwater was twenty-six years of age when he joined Forster of Northumberland in that rash and luckless business. His younger brother Charles, fresh from a continental education and close association with the exiled Stuarts, was with him heart and soul, if not indeed the more fervent of the two. Both the young men showed conspicuous gallantry, and were throughout opposed to those fatal and vacillating councils that ended, not merely in failure, for that was inevitable, but in the capture of the leaders at Preston. Nearly a hundred of the rebels suffered death; Lord Derwentwater alone of them all being granted the distinction of dying by the axe. His brother Charles was several times respited, but kept in close confinement at Newgate. Getting tired at last of his prison life and feeling doubtful of ultimate pardon, he escaped one night during a feast given by his fellow prisoners, and after eluding his pursuers for some time in London, managed to slip away to the Continent, where he lived at the French Court on an allowance made by his nephew, who had succeeded to part at least of the estates, though the title had lapsed.

As an instance of Charles Radcliffe's tenacity of purpose a story is told of how, after proposing sixteen times to a well-dowered widow, Lady Newburgh, and denied further access to her presence, he descended the chimney of her apartment, and making his seventeenth appeal won her admiration and her hand by the novel audacity of his method. On the death of his nephew he assumed the title of Comte de Derwentwater, but when over forty years of age he seems to have been unable to resist the temptation of visiting old scenes and friends in England, though still under severe proscription. No doubt he came to Derwentwater, but he lay perdu for weeks in the neighbourhood of Gilstone, and haunted at evening and after dark its now deserted and neglected grounds, being taken by the natives for the ghost of the decapitated Earl, and left in consequence most severely alone. Charles Radcliffe seems indeed to have been something of a humourist, and to have much enjoyed his ghostly character. On one occasion he chased a bailiff, who fled from him in such terror as to strike his head against a branch and drop unconscious to the ground : the bailiff, when he came to himself, swore the dead earl had thrown his head at him, and petitioned for his recall ; whereupon another was sent, who vowed he would put a bullet through any ghost that crossed his path. The chance of proving his courage was soon offered him, for the supposed phantom met the bold bailiff crossing a ford, and taking his horse by the bridle hurled him over backwards into the water. This settled the question wholly in the ghost's favour; and the terror grew such on the Gilston manor that no one would come near the place, and the tenants even refused to till their lands. A party of soldiers was then sent down, and as Charles Radcliffe at that very time took advantage of a favourable opportunity for crossing to Holland, they got the credit of laying the uneasy earl's ghost.

Radcliffe then entered the service of the French king, and when the '45 broke out drifted naturally into the movement, but was captured with his eldest son and others at sea by a British frigate and sent to the Tower. Here he was kept for a year, the difficulty being that he was a French officer ; and so long as he persisted in refusing the name of Charles Radcliffe, and speaking of himself only as the Comte de Derwentwater, it would remain with the government to prove that he was the same man who had been convicted thirty years previously. Witnesses had at last to be brought from Gilston, who swore to his identity to the satisfaction of a jury, and he was finally sentenced to death. His demeanour throughout his captivity and trial was haughty and contemptuous. Just four months after the famous executions following on Culloden, this last Earl of Derwentwater, if we may so call him, was led brilliantly apparelled through lines of life guards and executed with great solemnity on a platform wrapped in black cloth. He died with unflinching courage, as became his situation, in the fifty-third year of his age, professing with his last breath the utmost devotion to the Catholic faith, to Louis XV. and the first Pretender. "I am but a poor man," said he, as he handed the executioner ten guineas, and begged him to do his work well. The latter earned his fee, for the axe went through the neck at the first blow and stuck in the block. The present lord of the manor of Castlerigg and Derwentwater is a member of the Marshall family, whose wide interests in the Lake Country we took note of when at Ullswater.

The humours too, if you may so call them, of my boatmen have sometimes in idle half hours upon the lake, when all hopes of trout have temporarily fled, caused me no little entertainment.

I asked a clear-eyed long-limbed young dalesman who was out with me one day whether he often rowed foreigners about. To which he replied that he took a "gey few of them" on the lake. I then asked him how he liked Americans. He said he liked them well enough; but countered my query by asking another as to the fishing in America, and then went on to say that he supposed the waters there must be either choke full of fish or else that there were none at all.

"What makes you think that?" said I. "Well, sir, because whenever I take a party of Yankees out they get in a tur'ble way if they don't catch a fish about every two minutes. So I supposed they had either never had a rod in their hands before, or else were accustomed to catching fish as fast as ever they could haul 'em in."

I discovered also the interesting fact that only a week or two before this, Hercules had been engaged for several days by a French family straight over from Paris. I asked him if they could speak English.

"Aye," said the young waterman drily, "they cud gabble what they ca'd English."

"Did they talk to you?" said I.

"Aye, they crack'd wi' me a bit."

A little more encouragement and I was favoured with some of the conversation, which must have been of an entertaining nature, and have given the Parisian matron, her son and daughters, who made up the party, a rare notion of Cumbrian amenities. To shorten matters as much as possible, it appears that this good French lady had conceived the notion that the British working class were what is called pro-Boer to a man.

"She asked me," said Hercules, "if I wasn't sorry for the poor Boers—dom'd if she didn't. I told my lady that if I had the handlin' of the business I'd cut t' last one of 'em into little pieces, and wouldn't leave one o' t' dirty blackguards above ground."

"And what did they say to that?"

"Oh, well, t' young leddies tittered like, and the old ooman looked a gey bit queer. They then axed me," said Hercules, growing communicative, "whether I wouldn't like to live in France, an I tould 'em that maybe I'd like t' country better nor t' people!"

"There was a young chap too, a civil enough feller, but jest a lile nipitty Frencher like, an' he thought he could pull an oar, and was for ever teasin' o' me to row a race wi' him. Lor, I wasn't goin' to fash myself racin' wi' such as 'im (Hercules, I may remark, is the champion sculler of the lake); it 'ud be like stannin' up to wrastle wi' a lile gal. However, he kept botherin' me, so I said t' last mornin' I'd give 'im a 'alf mile spin. Lord, it ain't worth talkin' about. I left 'im stannin' still a 'corse; an' then I asked 'im if he'd had enough, and told 'im that a Frenchman couldn't no more row than he could fight. All 'e was fit for was to holler and make a noise."

"Well," said I, "I shouldn't think you saw much more of your party after that?"

"Oh, aye, I did tho'. The very mornin' as they went away, the lady come down to the boat landing, and asked the governor to send for me; and she thanked me for my attention and give me three 'alf crowns, and said if all Englishmen were as obstinate as I was she was not surprised as Lord Roberts was getting nigh Pretoria."

I don't think Hercules, who is a really admirable and trustworthy young man, had any notion that he had been discourteous. I think too that forgiving French lady must have been worth knowing.

From the upper reach of the lake too Lodore, when swollen by rain, shows finely as it leaps from its woody height; and its hoarse roar rising and falling with the breeze is a pleasant accompaniment to the gentle gurgling of the ripples beneath the drifting boat's keel. The sprouting ferns and the brilliant green of the all-pervading bilberry bushes give the nearer hills upon the Catbell side a delightful freshness beneath these June suns; and in the woods the oak leaves still wear the golden flush that precedes their full maturity, and show curious patches of almost autumnal colouring amid the rampant greens of sycamore and beech. Nor are there many woodlands in the Lake Country that show their foliage to more exquisite advantage than those which spread upwards from Barrow Bay, enveloping the cataract of that name to the foot of the noble ridge of grey cliffs which find their summits in Wallow and Falcon crags.

A hundred and odd years ago, in the earlier part of the long war with France, the inhabitants of Keswick and its neighbourhood used to amuse themselves and nurse their martial ardour with mimic sea fights upon the lake. Islands used to be taken and retaken by flotillas armed with muskets and artillery, and an immense amount of gunpowder consumed, while the *élite* of the neighbourhood applauded the actors from rows of gay marquees pitched upon the shore. A contemporary account of one of these naval functions lies before me, and would, I think, amuse the modern reader if space allowed such inconsequent quotations. There were "terrible cannonades and dreadful discharges of musquetry, which filled the ear with whatever could produce astonishment and awe, and impressed on the awakened imagination the most lively ideas of the war of elements and crash of worlds." One can well believe this when the local chronicler goes on to tell us that the noise was heard at Appleby, thirty miles away, and through two or three ranges of high mountains. It is pleasant too to know that what was left of the combatants and the spectators were capable of dancing till the small hours of the morning in a ball-room erected for the purpose; and Keswick streets resounded in the dawning day to the clatter of chariots bearing the exhausted families of squires and leading yeomen towards the rutty roads which led to Cockermouth and Carlisle, to Ambleside and Penrith. Country folk in those days were contented for the most part. There were no feverish longings for distant splendours, or at least not many. Their horizon was practically fixed, and within it they no doubt succeeded in extracting as much enjoyment out of life as their railway travelling descendants. I would undertake to say that winter in the Vale of Keswick was livelier in 1780 than it is in 1900.

Mr. Fisher Crossthwaite, who has told us much of old Keswick, gives us a vivid picture of the excitement caused there during the early years of Elizabeth's reign by the advent of a large number of German miners, whom the enterprise of the thrifty queen had imported to open up the minerals of the country. Two German experts were given a free hand on all the royal manors, and "the best copper in England" was reported to Secretary Cecil, after a year or two of investigation, as having been found in Newlands. It seems that three or four hundred of these foreigners were brought into the district, with the inevitable result of a conflict with the natives. Even the gentry seem to have viewed the movement with suspicion; the Derwentwater family doing something more than stand aloof from it, while the Earl of Northumberland had great disputes with the queen, who seems to have worked his land as well as her own without so much as a " by your leave " or a hint at compensation. Her Majesty's policy however prevailed, and beyond a doubt brought much prosperity to a poor country, in spite of the racial jealousy that most naturally found vent in blows, in a region whose chief trade was war. The Germans, however, eventually settled down; and our authority, besides giving us the after history of many of these families, a matter only of local interest, gives a long list, which he says is but a fraction of the German names upon the Crossthwaite registers, the word "Dutchman" being written after each entry.

But we have idled away already so much time on Derwentwater there is none left to say a word about Saint Herbert and his isle. For we must get back to the boat landing, consult one of the many weather prophets there, who surely ought to be sound ones, seeing they have such ample leisure for studying a very capricious type of it; and so back to Keswick, with a view only to leaving it.

Vale of Newlands.

Crummock Lake.

CHAPTER V.

I WOULD advise no one whose legs and lungs are adequate to the task to omit the ascent of Skiddaw. It is rather the fashion of some guide books to sniff at this noble mountain, because the accomplishment of its ascent is such an easy matter. I can understand a cragsman taking up this attitude, as I do not think it would be possible to break your neck anywhere on Skiddaw; but to the ordinary climber who follows the ordinary route, no mountain in England presents any difficulties worth mentioning, and their relative degrees of simplicity do not seem to me to be very much to the point. The view from its summit at any rate will compare with that from any other mountain top, while the outlook towards Scotland and the Solway is not unnaturally the best of all. For the same reason Skiddaw possesses a distinction when seen from Carlisle or Dumfriesshire that I do not think Helvellyn or Scafell with their unquestionably finer details of outline enjoy from any distant point. Skiddaw forest too, which spreads away from its farther or western skirts, a wild wilderness of open grouse moor dark with heather, is a feature not characteristic of many mountain view in Lakeland, and one that has a peculiar charm when bathed in sunlight, and looked down upon through a veil of whirling mist.

I purpose in this chapter to compass the journey to Buttermere, which, though but fourteen miles away, lies over the roughest and steepest pass that the coaches surmount anywhere in the north. But first we have to traverse the length of Derwentwater as far as the mouth of Borrowdale by the lakeshore road, which, though charming from a scenic point of view, is as deficient in others as are most of the Cumbrian highways. Westmoreland by the way prides itself on being much ahead in this respect of its neighbour; but both seem to observe the vexatious custom of deferring their repairs till May and June, and executing them even then with such uncompromising completeness that not so much as the width of a plank is left for the hapless cyclist to pilot his machine along.

After passing over the Lodore beck and within sight and sound of its famous falls, we run almost into the grounds of the fine hotel which for choice of situation has to my thinking an advantage over all others in this region. The wooded cliffs and crags that overhang the spot are in themselves so beautiful: from their readily accessible summits such a gorgeous panorama of Derwentwater and its surroundings can be enjoyed, while over the mountain plateau beyond, of which they are the outer wall, such numerous expeditions suitable to every grade of physical capacity can be so conveniently undertaken.

But I shall never pass the other hotel, a little further on at the mouth of Borrowdale, without recalling a most delightful Irish waiter, whose presence contributed no little to our entertainment while quartered there for a few days. It was at a time when most hotels were empty, and Pat had nothing like enough to occupy an all-consuming energy, which found vent in strange performances. He was very big and very stout, and sleek of face, and was clad of course in the orthodox uniform of his profession; but he was a Tipperary boy and country bred, and the ruling passion of the Irishman was so strong within him that you might hear betimes the rush, as of a whirlwind, past the window, and if quick enough might catch a vision of white socks and flying coat-tails and streaming hair as our fifteen-stone patriot, clinging to the bare back of an unemployed omnibus horse, sent him down the stony road at a murdering gallop.

A patriot I have called him, for he was an ardent Home Ruler, though who was to do the ruling was problematical, seeing that priest, landlord and politician were all equally taboo in his scheme for the Irish millennium. He was very eloquent, however, when encouraged to debate. But his professional gifts were what called forth my special admiration, and caused it to be borne in upon me for the hundredth time how magnificently superior the Irishman can be, when he so chooses, to any other white man in this capacity: at any rate, how infinitely more acceptable, how cheery, how imperturbably good-natured, how smilingly tolerant of criticism on soup and fish, that the average waiter resents, in his face at any rate, knowing the fault to be none of his; how lavish of small attentions that are not perhaps necessary but pleasant to receive. No one surely in these accomplishments can touch the capable Irishman (who has not been in America) as a table attendant. That very familiarity, which is part of his solicitude to make you happy and comfortable, is so wholly inoffensive, while the smiling philosophy, which receives the sixpence with the same demonstration of gratitude as the half-crown, challenges one's admiration.

Pat was a past master in all this; and when a coachload of, from his point of view, most unpromising lunchers turned up, I used to take note of how his good-humoured assiduity never for a moment flagged. And he had no interest in the house whatever, being in fact but a stopgap waiter. He was not, I believe, regarded as such a treasure behind the scenes; and it is certainly true that when not riding the 'bus-horses, or talking politics, or fetching something for somebody, or cleaning his plate, he used to tinkle on a fearsome instrument that I had never seen or heard before and do not remember the name of, not being a musician. He was gifted with a powerful imagination too, for one day during the distractions of dinner, he found time to slip a small cutting from the morning paper on the cloth by my plate in mysterious fashion, with a stage whisper, "Me brother, sorr!" I found on examining the slip that it contained a list of some troopers of a Colonial corps who had been wounded in attacking a Boer post, and was sorry to see underlined in pencil the name and initials of a youth of my acquaintance in that regiment. The name was a not uncommon one in both England and Ireland, and it happened to be Pat's. I did not, however, give him away.

He disappeared amid the convulsions of joy with which Keswick very properly celebrated the relief of Mafeking, and was never heard of in Borrowdale again. His brother's presence in the victorious army and his sufferings in Britain's cause no doubt made Pat himself the unique combination of Parnellite and Imperialist he seemed to be. Long life to him! He was a very first-class waiter, and much more.

But I did not come into this country to talk about Irish waiters, and by the same token we are now well round the corner and through the gateway of Borrowdale. The broad level pastures through which the Derwent ripples gently for a mile or so above the lake, and in wet weather sometimes submerges, narrow down where the first bridge crosses the river, and the ancient hamlet of Grange with its little church stands at the entrance of the gorge. One can well understand why the eighteenth century writers fling their most strenuous epithets at Borrowdale, and speak of it, though with much ignorance and poetic license, as a land of unknown terrors and fearful possibilities. Gray positively declined going any further. He had already crept along from Lodore in silence lest the crags above should fall and crush him; and here he gave his shaken nerves repose in a farmhouse whose owner entertained him with an account of the annual destruction of eagles' nests which was then a part of the regular programme of the Borrowdale farmer. Beyond Grange the rugged hills draw together, and through the narrow vista of rock and wood ahead of you,

The Bridge at Grange.

the upstanding cone of Castle crag rises against a dark and high and mysterious background of mountains made grimmer in June by lingering patches of snow. Birch woods, tender, fresh and graceful, clothe the steeps upon our left in exquisite profusion: upon the right the river, pent in a narrow channel, frets upon its rocky bed or slumbers just long enough in some deep pool by the road side to show the infinite transparency of its waters, even in a land where all waters are clear. A mile or two further and the passage opens, the overhanging heights fall back, the river leaves us, and we are in a tract of level meadows hemmed in on every side by mountains and drawing rapidly towards the hamlet of Rossthwaite. "A truly secreted spot is this," says old West, writing in the time of the French revolution and twenty years after Gray, "completely surrounded by the most horrid romantic mountains that are in this world of wonders."

Borrowdale must indeed have been an outlandish place in ancient times; a cul de sac, without any outlet at the back save by rough pony tracks over wild mountain passes. This, perhaps, would have no special interest but for the fact that some of its yeomen families have lived here upon the same lands, so far as the most competent judges can tell, since a period prior to the Norman Conquest. The manor, which included most of the district, was granted by a Derwentwater to Furness Abbey, and at the dissolution fell to the Crown, in whose hands it remained till James the First, doubtless after his great quarrel with the border tenantry, sold it to two Londoners. These gentlemen, however, and with somewhat significant alacrity, parted with their rights, for less than a single year's revenue, to the occupants. The list of those who, from holding under border or customary tenure, thus became freeholders in 1613 is practically the same as that which appears a hundred years before on the roll of Furness Abbey tenants, and thanks to the labours of a Keswick antiquary lies before me now. The main addition is that of a small group of gentlemen headed by Sir Wilfrid Lawson of Isell and Lamplugh of Lamplugh, who figure in the contract (known as the Great Deed of Borrowdale) on account, no doubt, of mining rights that they had acquired in the Elizabethan "boom." Birketts, Youdales, Fishers and Braithwates are the most prominent names, and all of them still flourish in the district. Some are in Borrowdale itself even yet, and there can be no doubt have lived in it since time is worth taking any account of.

All the world knows that the last half-century has seen quite a *débâcle* among the Cumberland and Westmorland statesmen. The reasons are as varied as they will be obvious to any one who gives a thought to the matter. These small properties, mostly between 30 and 300 acres, were not divided at death, but went to the eldest child, boy or girl, often charged for the benefit of the rest of the family. The origin of this custom was in the obligation of each small property to provide one or more men-at-arms, according to acreage, for service against the Scots, and subdivision would have caused endless complications. An over fondness for ardent spirits is reckoned among the causes of this decline, while the rise in land, often in this country to a fancy price, before a steady inroad of wealthy buyers for fancy purposes, added to unprecedented opportunities for engaging in commerce and going out into the world, made a change from the old conditions inevitable. It was a picturesque and happy state of society, however, this old one. The farming freeholder with a fairly generous holding and attached by blood to the soil, goes to make perhaps the ideal rural community. Besides the holdings, too, there were the great common lands on the mountains where sheep and in those days stunted cattle also roamed free. But you could not keep such men on the land nowadays. Primogeniture for such a class would be of course ridiculous. Yet once begin charging or dividing small estates, you create intolerable burdens on the one hand, or reduce them on the other to peasant holdings which, are quite another affair. Great numbers of statesmen's descendants, it must be remembered, are now living as tenant farmers either upon or adjacent to the lands their forbears once owned, and the nature of this ownership and their relationship to the Lords of Manors varied so much as to be best left severely alone in a work like this.

I spoke just now of James the First and his quarrels with the border tenantry. The fact is, that after the union of the two Crowns in his illustrious person, the over-canny monarch, thinking with some justice that the terms of military service against the Scots, by which the border tenants held their lands, would be no longer necessary, fancied he saw an excellent chance of turning an honest penny. Now the Crown tenants were very numerous on the western border, and the King gave out that all holding their estates from him were to surrender their titles, and that fresh ones would be issued, subject, of course, to money fines and rents. A roar of indignation arose throughout the country from Morecambe Bay to the Solway. Men whose ancestors had fought for their farms for generations, in this once wild and lawless country, could little understand the equity of paying a money rent, more particularly since, unlike the King, they suspected that their fighting days were by no means yet over. At any rate, they mustered to the number of 2,000 at Ratten Heath, between Kendall and Stavely, and there passed a unanimous resolution to the effect that " they had won their lands by the sword and were quite able to retain them by the same." They then bound each other by such strenuous oaths to resist the imposition to the very last drop of their blood that the King was alarmed and dropped the scheme like a hot coal.

The rudeness and simplicity of life in regions like Borrowdale till quite recent times must by all accounts have been astonishing. A great measure of independence and obstinacy among mountaineers bred in this fashion, and dwelling for centuries in what was practically a democracy, was inevitable. A parson who had gone from the South as a young man to an adjoining dale some thirty years ago put the matter one day in a laconic but complete fashion. He had been viewed, he said, with much suspicion on his arrival, as a stranger and potential innovator. "You can't drive dalesmen," screeched an old dame to him in significant fashion on his first parochial visitation. "Oh!" said the other, not greatly moved by so familiar a platitude. "And you can't lead 'em," she shouted after a brief pause and in still more strident and menacing tones. "Ah!" said the new vicar taking a more serious but still hopeful view of the situation. Five and twenty years of effort to do one or the other, he went on to declare, had convinced him that the old lady had never said a truer word in her life, for you could do nothing with them at all by ordinary and recognised methods!

But this small group of stalwart Borrowdale yeomen have sent out many successful men into the world, even if those who remained at home are somewhat conspicuous for their toryism. The managership of a mine, for instance, is the last situation in which you would look for continuous heredity, but in Borrowdale even this phenomenon might have been found; for in the famous black-lead mine at Seatoller I am told that the Dixon family had at no distant date held that position from father to son for 150 years! This lead, I may remark, is reputed the finest in the world for pencils, and tradition says that it was beneath the roots of a great ash torn up by the wind it was first discovered. The mine was first worked in Elizabeth's reign, and by the end of the eighteenth century had grown so valuable that a special Act of Parliament was passed to make the picking of wad from the dump-heaps a felony; for Jews were in the habit of coming to Keswick for the special purpose of dealing with these pilferers. The mineral was all carried direct to London in a six-horse waggon guarded by an armed escort and sold monthly at the company's warehouse. A building too was erected over the entrance of the mine in which guards slept at night with firearms beside them.

Even this sequestered spot was not free in the Civil War from the tramp of armed men. Sir Edward Radcliffe, of Derwentwater, was up for the King, and Borrowdale contributed its quota to his troop. Sir Wilfred Lawson of Isell headed the Parliamentarians, who stored their munitions of war on St. Herbert's Island, destroyed the Radcliffe mansion on Lord's Island, and among other exploits, rode up Borrowdale and over Stake Pass to Rydal, where they sacked Rydal Hall, even tearing up the floors in seach of treasure.

It is only fitting that the cuckoo should call merrily from

more than one hill-side as we enter the ancient hamlet of Rossthwaite, for a legend runs that the dalesmen of old were so simple as to believe that the spring would last for ever if only they could keep its winged minstrel in their valley, and with this in view they actually commenced to build a wall at the mouth of Borrowdale, whose remains I have no doubt could be produced if sufficiently insisted upon. We must not, however, linger at Rossthwaite, with its old-fashioned nooks of ancient cottage masonry and grey moss-grown roofs, its barking collies

Honister Pass.

and soft, swishing sound of travelling sheep; though the snug hotel beyond, set in a charming garden above the Longstrathbeck may well tempt us to do so. Rossthwaite is an admirable centre for hill walking and climbing. The Stake and Sty-head passes are handy to it. The Scafell and Great Gable group of mountains can be readily ascended and can be seen as we continue our road. Glaramara towers close at hand: Thirlemere, Grasmere and Dungeon Ghill may all be reached by mountain routes that give the moderate walker a long day of such scenes and such air and altitude as he would wish for. But we, who in this narrative, at any rate, have to stick for the most part to the road, are bound for the Honister pass and have yet, near a thousand feet to climb before we are over it. And Seatoller here may be accounted the foot of the actual ascent; a cluster of old buildings whose remarkable grouping against an overhanging background of tall trees, illumined by the flashing of a mountain torrent, is one of the best bits of the kind in the Lake Country.

Once through the wood above Seatoller, our way, enlivened by the almost continous cataracts of Horse Gill, emerges upon the wild fell and a road that is rarely rideable winds up the deep mountain hollow to the summit of the pass. It is not well that rain should fall while making this ascent, for there is nothing bigger than a bunch of rushes in the way of shelter; but it is well perhaps that it should have lately fallen and filled the fountains of the hills and stirred into activity the slender cataracts that hang like silver ribbons against the grey face of the mountain, upon our right and left. You will often turn in the toilsome climb to get breath and at the same time to look back over Seatoller and Rossthwaite to the Armboth fells, and the fine mass of Helvellyn towering in the background. But the wildness that of right belongs to the top of the pass is somewhat qualified by the sheds connected with the quarry which has riven the savage face of Honister Crag into shapes that in gloomy weather rather add perhaps than detract from its natural grandeur.

As we begin a descent so steep as to make the journey from the other side almost impossible for vehicles, one of the most striking scenes in the Lake country bursts into full view. For Honister Crag, a rugged and gloomy mass of precipice and screes, fills the whole foreground to the left, soaring up to a height of near 2,000 feet. Between this and the opposing shoulders of Dale Head we may look down through the narrow vista to the Buttermere road, trailing along a wild valley far beneath us. The descent with a cycle is tiresome in the extreme, while it causes timid females on the top of a coach to grip each other in spasmodic fashion and wish themselves well home again. But the steeper the grade, the quicker, after all, one is down, and we may sail away over an unfenced moorland road, with a beck roaring and growing beside us for a couple of miles, till Buttermere spreads its shining surface across the narrow valley and another mile or so of easy road through the charming woodlands that fringe its banks lands us at the hamlet itself.

This last consists of a farmhouse or two and numerous outbuildings, a diminutive church, though larger than its predecessor, a parsonage and three inns, two of which are comparatively modern, while the third, appropriately called the *Fish*, is quite a venerable tavern and of some note in early Lakeland travel. These buildings cluster chiefly upon the neck of land which divides the head of Crummock from the foot of Buttermere, amid a pleasant network of meadow and pasture through which the little river connecting the two lakes prattles merrily. It is a quite ideal spot, and gives a greater sense of seclusion from the world than any haunt of tourists we have yet been in. There is, of course, no escaping from the fact that a certain number of vehicles, every single week-day during the summer, make the twenty-four mile round from Keswick, coming, as we have done, by Honister and returning over Buttermere Hause and the Vale of Newlands, undoubtedly one of the finest and probably the heaviest coach drive in England. But except for the midday hours, largely occupied by visitors in feeding, and I daresay for the August holidays, Buttermere is a marvellously quiet spot considering its fame. I have myself been, in May, the only visitor at the three inns, which is equivalent to saying in all Buttermere, and again, in mid-June, but one of a small company of cheerful but unsuccessful fishermen.

Now Buttermere and Crummock lakes, together with the strip of land that parts them, completely fill a narrow, trough-like valley of something like five miles in length, and not often over half a mile in width. On the hither side only, where runs the road, a narrow fringe of fenced enclosures and belts of woodland straggle a short space up the mountain foot or hang above the lake. Upon the further or the western side, for nearly the whole distance of both lakes, the mountains, in various shapes and clad with varied natural growths, fall almost abruptly to the water's edge. Above Buttermere particularly is this the case, High Crag, High Stile and Red Pike all 2,500

Crummock Lake.

feet or thereabouts, forming a stupendous wall of green, not very rugged such as can be seen of it, but none the less imposing from the very vastness of the natural curtain that catches the sun so early on its downward course. The fine effect of this silent, overhanging steep, too, is greatly heightened by the cataract of Sour Milk Gill which for hundreds of feet falls like a thread of shimmering light, with sound unheard, but instinct with life and movement. It is immediately opposite the village, leaping suddenly into sight from the rim of a lofty ledge, and you would almost guess from the look of the hollow between the summits of High Stile and Red Pike that the stream issued from a tarn within their shadow, as is, in fact, the case, its source being in a lonely shallow lakelet full of ill-fed trout, and but a few hundred feet from the summit of the range. No sojourner at Buttermere should by any means, if favoured with good weather, neglect to ascend Red Pike, since the climb, though steep, can be quickly made, as it springs sharply from the lake shore and pauses nowhere.

Looking up Buttermere.

Buttermere too, like the other lakes we have seen, has its own characteristic charms. A single country house, buried in luxuriant and long planted woodland on the eastern shore, is almost the only touch of outside humanity about it. It is wild and natural without being savage like Wastwater. In still weather the marvellous purity of its waters, the clean silvery nature of its strand and bottom in the shallow bays; the dry, white shingle of its shores contrasting with the bright verdure, not only of bordering strips of meadow but of the reflected mountains, give Buttermere, to my thinking, at any rate, a character all its own. Yet I am not sure if a quiet dull day after a stormy season, when the immense green walls between which the narrow lake sleeps are all spouting with white waters hurrying downwards in strange contrast to the motionless and glassy surface, is not as good a moment as any for loitering by its shores. Honister Crag, so prominent an object, is, beyond a doubt, best suited to a gloomy sky. The rocky heights above the lake-head known as the "Haystacks" match well, too, with a sombre background. When I recall, however, the look of the valley as it appeared to me one sunny morning in June last from the lower ledges of Red Pike a thousand feet above it; the brilliant blue of the lake ribbed by the light breeze and catching the shadows of the passing clouds, the green woods of Hassness blowing along the further shore, the bold heights of Robinson and Buttermere Moss, of Whiteless Pike and Grassmoor, shifting their moods every moment with the changing sky; when I recall the infinite beauty of that scene, and in the midst of it the peaceful cluster of old buildings, embowered in foliage with its carpet of green meadows spread around it from lake to lake, I am inclined to repent and think the mood that would favour the gloomy sky is the least happy one, and that the most complete and enduring enjoyment is after all to be found in the other, and the sunnier aspect. Yet I am sorry, too, for the lover of nature, if there be any such, who is insensible to the influence of her more sombre or more savage moods.

Nowhere is one more forcibly reminded than at Buttermere, particularly when one wants to get out of it, of the "starfish" nature of the Lake Country formation, and of how much road travelling in proportion to the actual area has to be accomplished before every main valley has been exploited on wheels of any kind. Ennerdale for instance, lies just over the high ridge before us, an hour's walk perhaps for an active youth, but to get round there by road means a circuit of a dozen or fifteen miles. Wastdale, further on again, can be easily reached on foot in three hours by mountain paths, but to get there on wheels means a circuit of half Cumberland. I shall venture, therefore, by way of variety, to take a day in the mountains, and gossip for a few pages along the steep track which leads from the head of Buttermere over Scarf Gap into Ennerdale and thence over Blacksail to Wastwater, wildest of lakes. This is a matter of some four hours each way taking things very easily, which in a long summer day leaves ample time for rest and refreshment at the inn at Wastdale Head, and even for deviations from the track should such seem tempting. This, indeed, is one of the most striking walks in the Lake region, and though from start to finish traversing a perfect solitude, need have no terrors for any but the hopelessly short-winded. You may save two miles, moreover, at the beginning and end of the day by riding up the shore of Buttermere and leaving your machine at Gatesgarth beneath the shelter of Mr. Nelson's roomy waggon sheds.

The homestead and enclosures of this farm, somewhat famous in Herdwick genealogy, fill what is left of the narrow valley beyond the head of Buttermere. A typical mountain sheep farm it is too, reaching out upon every side to the limit of vision, or, in other words, to the rugged crests of High Stile and the Haystacks, of Fleetwith Pike, Dalehead and Robinson which form a horse-shoe round it. Many a prize ram and ewe has been bred upon these fells, and such sprinkling as you may see of the three thousand and odd sheep now carried on the run will no doubt possess some measure of the blood of a long line of cup-winners. Plantations of beech and oak and larch, screen the homestead from the north-west winds that are said to rage up the narrow lakes in winter with tremendous fury. A beck courses through the yards beside the grey farm-buildings of unmortared stone with cheerful and harmless prattle under a June sun; but as the present occupant once observed to me, if the builders of these old homesteads had only realised what a tyrant a beck could at times become, they would, even at the sacrifice of some convenience, have gone a little further from their banks and a little higher up the hills. Through the flat of fenced enclosures that forms the floor of the narrow valley, the infant Cocker and the Warnscliffe beck hurry to the lake amid unmistakable traces upon either bank of their propensity to misbehave. An oat-field or two, some meadows promising a late hay crop, some fresh sown turnips just entering on their struggle with the fly, a few milk cows and some playful colts comprise the home industries. But the important part of Gatesgarth's live stock are away now on the Fells, some of them you can see flecking the velvety slopes of Fleetwith, others are cropping the short turf of Hindscarth, some are lying in the shadow of rocks and boulders beneath High Crag. An inevitable few again will be huddling in remote nooks and crannies under the torture of the relentless maggot, while the small force of the farm men and dogs with shears and salve pots are probably at this moment hunting for the patients over the ten or fifteen square miles of their wild and rugged holding.

When you have climbed under a hot sun, and by a rough path, to the high shoulder of Scarf Gap, you will have stopped many times to look back, over the glassy stretch of Buttermere, lying so beauteously in the bosom of the hills; but you will have been glad also to take breath and perhaps even to mop your face. And when the thousand or so feet are accomplished it may perchance be borne in upon you that this is but a little fraction of the hill farmer's daily task in busy seasons, in winter snow or summer sunshine, in rain or storm, in youth or age. And when you have reminded yourself that the compensating picturesqueness and romance of the business is the creature of your imagination and has little part in his, the thought may possibly occur whether with wool at 8*d.* and fat wethers, at such late season as mountain sheep are ready, at thirty shillings the hill-farmer's life is all that poets and summer tourists paint it.

The Gatesgarth fells are no longer "stinted pasture" or common land. The landlord, here again a Marshall, has fenced the boundary, a not uncommon proceeding nowadays and of infinite convenience to the farmer. For though the mountain sheep on commons like the Helvellyn and Matterdale ranges acquire an hereditary instinct for keeping to their own beats that is wholly marvellous, a certain amount of straying is inevitable. This very custom of a common grazing ground, to which each valley-farm has a recognised but unrecorded right to send up so many sheep, has maintained, and indeed necessitated, a usage that is quite unique in England—namely, that of the flock being the landlord's property; a fixture, in fact, of the farm, and calculated in the rent paid, if not, indeed, the principal factor. The origin of this is that only sheep bred upon the mountain know the range. A strange flock would give such trouble for so long a time that an incoming tenant would be almost compelled to purchase of an outgoing one. Hence the sheep, by a natural process, become part of a property that without them is useless. They are valued to the tenant and periodically appraised, the difference at his death or outgoing being due from the one party to the other. The farmer, therefore, under this system, is in literal fact a shepherd working on the profit system with his landlord, though the annual payment in the shape of rent is a fixed one. Gatesgarth, though now fenced in, is held upon these lines, the father of the present occupant having been a noted breeder and prizewinner. So curious a custom will interest, I think, any one connected with country life, and to those of my readers who are not, I offer my sincere apologies for the digression.

I will only add that these boundary fences, such as the one we have now to go through on the ridge of Scarf Gap, with a very necessary request posted on it to shut the gate behind us, consist of iron posts let into the rock and connected by strands of plain wire. They have sometimes to climb the summit of the loftiest mountain, and to traverse the brink of the most savage cliffs. And even with the efforts made to give them stability, it is astonishing to see how in exposed spots at great altitudes the wires have been torn away and crumpled up by the winter gales, and lie about in tangled heaps among the rocks, droning dismal airs to the touch of the summer breezes which play among them. There is indeed little other sound up here on the fells but the plash of the rill just broken from its boggy spring which leads our path-way down into the head of Ennerdale.

The greatest enthusiast on Lakeland will not deny the remarkable absence of bird life among its mountains. We sadly miss the cluck of the startled grouse, the wild whistle of the curlew, the plaintive cries of the lapwing. There are no skylarks here even in the valleys, and the white-backed wheatear with its chirruping note is the only bird whose company we may safely count upon. The ring ousel, the crag starling as it is here called, that shy haunter of high places, that lover of lonely glens and silent uplands, sometimes gives us a pleasant surprise as he dashes with startled cry from some stunted rowan tree on whose future berries he has set his heart. The stone-chat, for which one might fairly look, I have never to my knowledge seen here. But turning for a moment from lesser to greater things, eagles were common enough in Ennerdale, as in Borrowdale, at the close of the eighteenth century, and the destruction of nests was a regular spring function. The same rope that was used in Borrowdale and kept there, says a local writer, was passed on, when needed, to Ennerdale and Wastwater, these three localities containing the most precipitous cliffs in Lakeland.

Indeed we are already face to face with some of the most notable ones. As a faint track through rocks and bog grasses leads us down into Ennerdale, we see beneath us a wild trough-like valley untouched by civilisation, and threaded by the windings of a silver stream. At the head of it the Great

Gable closes the outlook, while away down to the right the waters of Ennerdale Lake gleam between the thrusting shoulders of the hills. But immediately in front, forming, in fact, the opposite wall of the valley, is the pile of screes and crags and precipices which prop the long back of the Pillar Mountain. Though the brilliant sunshine seems to flood everything else, it wholly misses at this hour the savage northern face of the Pillar which lies wrapt in deep shadows that are all the gloomier and the more sombre from the contrast. Though much less than a mile away, the details are so effectually shrouded as to give the whole face of the mountain the appearance of a vast and gloomy precipice. The outline of the famous Pillar Rock, though right in front of us, is literally undistinguishable against the shadowy background, while wandering rays of sunshine that here and there succeed in kissing some outstanding crag add further mystery to the contrasting gloom.

The Pillar Rock enjoys much reputation among cragsmen, for by a false step you may achieve an unbroken fall of something like seven hundred feet. There are numerous routes, too, up the face of it, involving various degrees of peril, as one may well believe from its appearance. Young men of more ambition than experience have been compelled ere now to spend the night on the summit from their inability, or want of nerve, to face the descent. The sad story of the elderly clergyman who twenty years ago was found dead near its foot on the morrow of his seventieth birthday is no legend but a comparatively recent fact. The old gentleman, a Dalesman bred, I think, lived at St. Bees and used to come once a year on his birthday, to climb the Pillar. On this last occasion the physical strain is supposed to have proved too much for him; for on being missed and searched for, he was found lying dead underneath the cliff, not from a fall, as is sometimes related, but from exhaustion or heart-failure after achieving the descent in safety.

Now no one can have been in Keswick, Ambleside, or any

of the Lake towns without admiring the great number of really beautiful photographs upon a large scale of the surrounding scenery. Among these the most difficult, or at least the most notable, crags which the serious climbers affect are always prominent, the Pillar and the Needle Rock, which is near the Great Gable, being the most familiar in shop windows. The latter, as usually photographed, with figures clinging to the side or perched on the narrow summit, has a truly awesome appearance and is calculated to make one's very blood run cold. A young townsman who is an expert and somewhat of a leader in this crag climbing business told me an amusing incident bearing upon it. It so happened that an American, by no means in his first youth nor yet slim in the waist, was fired with ambition to attempt some of the ascents he had heard of in Ennerdale and about Wastdale head, and applied to my informant to superintend his maiden efforts. While a plan of operations was being discussed, the two walked round one of the photographic studios, the Englishman pointing out those particular views which bore in any way upon the subject in hand. The stranger's zeal, his companion noticed, grew unmistakably cooler as the inspection proceeded, and when at length they stood before the Needle rock, which, I have before remarked, is as usually depicted a really gruesome looking thing not unlike a Cleopatra's needle with a crack or two across it, the stout American remained mute for a long time, apparently fascinated by the prospect before him. At length he broke silence:

"What's that thing?"

"The Needle Rock," replied the other.

"And who in thunder's that d——d fool on top of it?"

"That's me," replied his proposed conductor.

"Christopher Columbus!" according to my informant, was all the American said, but a world of meaning may be thrown by an American into the mere name of the discoverer of his country, when fervently invoked.

The matter, it is needless to add, went no further.

We have to follow up the lonely valley for quite a distance, before a deserted cabin, the only sign of man, within it marks the spot where an almost invisible track up a craggy ravine leads to the summit of Black Sail Pass, whence a long and steep descent drops down to Wastwater. Ennerdale, like most of the country round belonged in ancient days to Furness Abbey. In the eighteenth century it was a deer forest, and one is not surprised to hear that even in September the desire for better fare made the stags so bold that they would raid the harvest fields in the lower valley before the very eyes of the farmers and carry off the oat sheaves from the stooks. This is favourite ground too of the Fell foxhunter, and is within the radius of a pack that is kept in Wastdale and of another at Loweswater. But the most exciting sport that was probably ever known in Ennerdale was in pursuit neither of fox nor stag, but of a wild dog whose career reads more like some weird German legend than a simple narrative of English pastoral life.

Sheep-worrying dogs have, of course, been for all time one of the terrors of the sheep farmer, but the performances of "t' girt dog of Ennerdale" in 1810 puts everything else of the kind that I ever heard of entirely into the shade. The late Mr. Dickinson, the well-known writer on Cumbrian life and character, published a full account of the incident some forty years ago, carefully collected from contemporary evidence, added to his own personal recollections. We have nothing like space here to do justice to an incident which, told in detail, is about as thrilling a chapter of sport and mystery as in modern days ever stirred an English country-side, but here, at least, is the outline of it.

The leading figure in the drama was a large, smooth-coated dog, of a tawny colour, with dark, tiger-like streaks upon his hide and supposed to be a cross between a mastiff and a greyhound. He first appeared in Lower Ennerdale, from whence no man knew, in May, and was not killed till September.

For nearly the whole of the intervening period the ravaging brute was the object of unremitting pursuit by the inhabitants of the entire district, with horse, hound, gun, and every artifice that the mind of man could conceive; the sole subject of conversation in cottage and farmhouse, the wonder of the old, the terror of the young.

No sooner had he appeared than the mysterious stranger began operations. The true sheep-worrying dog is rarely considerate enough to kill a single animal and make his meal off it, but mangles maybe half-a-dozen, taking bites out of the living sheep and drinking the warm blood from the jugular vein. The Ennerdale Vampire in his long debauchery of rapine, surpassed his kind in wanton devilry and fiendish epicureanism as much as he did in strength and cunning.

The ordinary proceedings usually followed in such cases were useless, for the strange dog never attacked the same flock on two successive nights, and the range of his depredations spread over miles both of low country and fell. He hunted, as a rule, by night only, lying low by day, and was never known to utter any kind of sound. With the skill of a butcher, he picked the plumpest sheep from every flock, and none that he touched was ever known to recover. He was once seen at early dawn to run·down a fine ram, which is not usual with his kind, and without killing it, to tear out and swallow lumps of living flesh from the hind-quarters of the tortured animal as it crawled forward on its fore legs.

The shepherds often saw the brute and chased him with their collies, but this was futile, for no ordinary dog dare touch him. One day he would be disturbed in a ditch at Lowes Water, another in a wood at Lamplugh: the mysterious beast seemed positively ubiquitous. Men with guns lay round by dozens on the fells at night, but the object of their search, with surpassing cunning, always managed to snatch his bloody supper at the one point that had been left unguarded. The men, says Mr. Dickinson, got worn out with night watching. The women grew tired of cooking meals at all hours for stray parties who were out on this protracted and futile dog hunt. The children feared to go to school by day, or to pick flowers in the fields, and shook or screamed with terror at every sound which broke the night lest it should be "t' girt dog." But this diabolic fiend pursued his remorseless course in spite of every effort to get even with him and nothing else was talked of at the church door or in the market, by the fireside or on the road. Many of the farmers kept a hound or two which they clubbed together for fox-hunting. This scratch pack was laid on to the sheep-killer several times but it laughed at them, running before them till it had had enough and then quietly facing the foremost of the long straggling pack and giving it such a lesson that it fled limping and howling back, to the intimidation of those behind. Poison was tried, but was quite useless, for the brute was much too fastidious to dine off cold meat. It had taken its meals smoking hot for weeks and continued to do so. Ten pounds reward was now offered by a wealthy absentee sheepmaster to the man who should kill the dog, and every one who had a gun took to the hills, including many a lazy loafer to whom such work was thoroughly congenial, particularly as a further fund was raised to supply refreshments to the pursuers. One Willy Jackson, of Swinside, had in the meantime a great opportunity of earning both the fame and the money, for as he was walking, like everybody else in the country at the time, with a loaded gun in his hand, the vampire suddenly appeared within thirty yards and gave him an admirable shot. But the gun, as rustic guns a century ago were apt to do, missed fire, and the brute careered away with his charmed life, to perpetrate further ravages.

June and July passed away, and it was calculated that over two hundred sheep had already fallen victims to the scourge. On one occasion the dog was surrounded in a field of corn by thirteen men with guns, and running out within five yards of one of them, Will Rothery, so frightened him that he forgot to fire, and leaped out of the road crying "Skerse, what a dog!" A deaf old man too, named Jack Wilson, was gathering sticks near by in blissful ignorance of the excitement around him, when the quarry bolted between his legs, which were notoriously crooked. The veteran turned a somersault and to his dying day swore it was a lion that had upset him.

One of the regular packs of hounds was now brought into the country as a supreme effort to put an end to the terror, and if they did nothing else they had some amazing runs. The details of several are given at much greater length than we have space for. One morning, for instance, two hundred men turned up with the hounds on Kinniside Fell above Ennerdale, started the quarry there and ran him to Wastwater and thence through Calder to Seascale on the coast, where night stopped the pursuit. Another time he carried them twenty miles to the Derwent. On a third occasion he was viewed away on a Sunday morning from the high fells, and the chase went thundering down past Ennerdale Church during service, sweeping with it as a matter of course the congregation, including, it is said, the Reverend Mr. Ponsonby, who followed as far, we are told, as his strength would let him. This run ended near Cockermouth in a storm. The pursuers got a sad drenching, but the dog escaped. On another occasion this phenomenal beast actually carried the chase from Ennerdale Lake to St. Bees, where he hid in a garden and was seen trotting quietly away after the weary hounds and hunters were well started on their long road home.

At last, on the 12th of September, he was marked into a cornfield: a large muster of guns and hounds was rapidly collected, and the beast wounded by a lucky shot. This enabled the hounds to keep on level terms with him when he broke covert, but not one of them durst tackle him. When the huntsmen caught them up again the dog was coolly bathing in a pool in the Ehen River near Stockhow Hall, and the hounds splashing about at a respectful distance, afraid to come to closer quarters. A man named John Steel was the first up, but durst not fire on account of the hounds, and the exhausted quarry making a last effort dashed from the river and headed for Eskat Woods. Here after much halloing and beating, Steel, whose gun was loaded with small bullets, got a near shot at the vampire, bowled him over, and became the hero of the day, and, still more, the winner of the ten pounds reward. The campaign had lasted over four months, and no dog out of fiction

Buttermere from near Gatesgarth.

has ever perhaps caused so much and such continuous agitation. The carcass weighed eight stones, and the hide was stuffed and set up in a museum at Keswick with a collar round the neck inscribing the sanguinary achievements of " t' girt dog of Ennerdale."

The rough ascent by the side of the torrent to Black Sail Pass out of Ennerdale has been the subject of much exciting description. One cannot help thinking that the "hardy pedestrian" sometimes writes himself down as a most verdant and melodramatic person, or that the author of some guide books must regard him as a most prodigious old woman. It was not till I had walked over from Buttermere to Wastdale and back for the first time that I became aware from perusing a well known work on the Lakes that I ought to have taken a guide with me! As a matter of fact, and by an accident, I had not even a map, but by taking the bearings from one before starting I found no difficulty whatever in keeping the track of what is certainly as delightful a walk as it is a wild one. Indeed, twice traversed once in May and once in June of the past year, I did not meet or even see a human being between Buttermere and Wastwater. It was therefore surprising to find that "the hardy pedestrian with very minute directions might succeed in finding his way over the mountains, yet every one who has crossed them will be aware of the danger of the attempt and of the fatal consequences attending a diversion from the right path." The hardy pedestrian to whom death was the penalty of losing the track on Black Sail would be something more than an old woman—he would be a suicidal maniac, for he would have to climb the Pillar or Kirkfell mountains, which rise on either side of the pass, for the precipice needful to the tragedy. Even in the worst of thick weather he would hardly do this, while the path down Mosedale into Wastdale is very plain and easy, offering grand views of the precipitous sides of Scafell with the smooth steep slopes of Yewbarrow on the right and Wastwater sleeping in the hollow beyond. For a novice to get befogged on the summit of, say, the Pillar, the Great Gable or Scafell mountains is of course both unpleasant and dangerous. But really in the valleys and passes of this country, so long as streams run down hill, it would require something more than ordinary stupidity to come to very much grief. However, I have before me a printed letter from two gentlemen who declare that Black Sail should not be crossed without a guide, giving as the reason that they had the preceding day done so in a north-east wind and rain storms, and owing to the delay in picking out the track grew so benumbed that death seemed imminent, and nothing in the writers' opinion saved them but an opportune flask of brandy! These gentlemen must surely have been tender plants. A wild day's grouse shooting on the hills or loch fishing in fierce weather would by such standards have finished either of them, and Black Sail should not on that account be credited with such imaginary terrors.

If the skies are clear it is in truth a delightful walk along the broken and extended ridge leading to the summit of the Pillar Mountain, which is but just under 3,000 feet. From here you may see to much advantage the precipitous heights of Great Gable, Scafell and Scafell Pikes, all close at hand, and behind these again the savage outline of the Langdales. All about here is the region most beloved by the amateur cragsmen. These daring souls foregather greatly at the inn down at Wastdale head, which is a convenient point whence to attack "the best bits of work." Here, too, I am credibly informed, you may listen to a jargon as mysterious to the un-initiated as even golf was in the times when there were any un-initiated and the acrobatic feats of the day are illustrated, they tell me, by ardent souls at night, on the smoking room furniture amid a most conspicuous absence of whisky and tobacco. The late Mr. Wynn Jones, who was killed in 1899 on the Alps, has written an admirable book on climbing in the Lake country which will interest even those who have no mind to follow in his perilous steps.

There is more, however, to be seen from the Pillar Mountain than these noble haunts of the cragsmen, since you may look away to the sea and the Solway and to much besides; and in descending to Ennerdale on your homeward route to Buttermere you may save a long tramp and indulge in a little mild excitement by clambering down the screes, near the Pillar rock, keeping a sharp look out always that such stones as you may loosen in the descent leave their resting place before and not behind you. For there is one thing the traveller who climbs alone amid these mountains out of the holiday seasons will do well to remember—to wit that a broken leg, or even a sprained ankle, may possibly be worse than a broken neck. Except on two or three of the more frequented mountains, a crippled and helpless mortal might shout and whistle to the passing wind for all such help as he would be likely to secure from a fellow wanderer, within a reasonable period.

Furness Abbey

Approach to Buttermere.

CHAPTER VI.

In the old Fish Inn once dwelt Mary Robinson, the famous "Beauty of Buttermere," and I use the epithet advisedly, for Mary is no faked-up heroine enlarged and embroidered for the tourist appetite. Indeed she was no heroine at all in the literal sense of the word, but the victim rather in a somewhat tragic story with which all England at the opening of the last century rang for a brief space and remembered for some time. If Mary had not been a village belle of something more than village notoriety, and if the villain of the play had not been a very prince among his kind, it is probable that the incident would have been but a nine days' wonder in the county of Cumberland, its details being of a time-honoured and familiar description. As it was, however, the Press of all England rang with and revelled in the story which appeared in dramatised form on the boards of more than one theatre. Wordsworth celebrated it in verse, and De Quincey has left us an account of it in prose. The former, in addressing Coleridge on one occasion, reminds him of the "Artless daughter of the hills, wooed and won in cruel mockery," and of how greatly they themselves had been "stricken by her modest mien" or in plain English, by her good looks, for De Quincey tells us that the two poets admired her prodigiously. He himself, who also knew her well, is more critical, analysing her claims with much precision and wholly rejecting her title to any remarkable beauty. Large and fair, with a fresh colour and regular features and a touch of distinction in her carriage, sums her up according to the prose writer, and he ridicules the notion of her being comparable to many women he could mention in the matter of beauty. But Buttermere, and the world that visited Buttermere, agreed that Mary was a beauty, and if, as De Quincey hints, she was not quite so artless as the poet fancied, this is of little consequence, for her virtue at least was beyond reproach.

The drama opened at Keswick in the summer season of 1805, when a handsome travelling carriage drew up with a flourish at the door of the "Royal Oak," and deposited a sufficiently good imitation of a man of rank and fashion, who seemed to clinch the matter by writing himself down, on his visiting cards and elsewhere, as the Honourable Augustus Hope, M.P. This was followed by a candid admission of the soft impeachment that he was a brother of Lord Hopetoun. The distinguished visitor soon showed that he had come to stay. He was delighted with his quarters, with the scenery, and with the people, while the latter were equally pleased with him, visiting cards and attentions of all kinds being showered upon him by local society, whose members fairly tumbled over each other in their eagerness to do honour to the Honourable Augustus. Not quite all of them, however. Here and there a doubt was expressed that he was a little too dashing, a little too affable. Coleridge said that even his grammar was at times shaky, but when it was known through the post office that he franked letters, unworthy suspicions vanished, for forgery then might mean death, and after all it was not an unprecedented thing for even the brother of a peer to be deficient in taste and careless of elocution. At any rate, such subtleties were far beyond the discrimination of a village maiden of nineteen, however versed she might be in innocent flirtations with passing tourists, or in the more uncouth badinage of rural swains. For the Honourable Augustus came in due course on a fishing excursion to Buttermere and the innkeeper's daughter who waited upon the guests found such favour in his eyes that he prolonged his sojourn for several weeks, and laid regular siege in open and honourable fashion to the lovely maiden's heart. Who could doubt the result? Whether he won her heart or not, he won her hand, and I have no doubt that the fair Mary's vanity as well as that of the parish of Buttermere, saving always its eligible swains, was greatly flattered.

So the happy day was fixed, and the smallest church in England with its single bell did the best it could under the circumstances to ring out the triumph of the Beauty of Buttermere. The knot was tied as fast apparently as Church and State could tie it. Admirable excuses were forthcoming for the absence of the remainder of the noble house of Hopetoun at the ceremony. What the many ardent friends of the Honourable Augustus in the Vale of Keswick, one of whom, De Quincey relates, had christened his son and heir after him in wholesale fashion, thought of his matrimonial enterprise history does not say. But it was quite evident that the happy bridegroom was in no hurry to introduce his rustic wife to that world of fashion in which he was accustomed to revolve, for the newly-married pair do not seem to have extended their honeymoon rambles very much further than Keswick. Suddenly, however, like a bolt from the blue, the law swooped down upon Augustus and carried him off from Mary's arms to Carlisle gaol, there to be tried on a charge of forgery, which, alas! turned out to be but the least heinous of his many sins. Far from being Lord Hopetoun's brother, he proved to be a person of plebeian though respectable birth, son, in fact, of a

Devonshire tradesman named Hatfield, and the Hopetoun fable had commended itself from the fact of his lordship being stationed abroad. But I must here condense what is in fact a long and somewhat thrilling story of fraud and trickery. Mary proved to be but the last of several victims, mostly her superiors in station, whom with singular adroitness and cunning the prisoner had treated in similar fashion. Coleridge, among other people, had a sight of the villain's papers and read the letters from these despairing and only half-disillusioned women, wives as they thought or had recently thought themselves. "The man," wrote Coleridge under deep emotion, "who, when pursued by these heart-rending apostrophes, and with this litany of anguish sounding in his ears from despairing women and from famishing children, and yet found it possible to enjoy the calm pleasures of a Lake tourist, must have been a fiend of that order which fortunately does not often emerge amongst men."

Hatfield was prosecuted on the forgery charge by the Post Office, condemned, and left for execution, his heartless treatment of Mary Robinson and villainous former record putting all thoughts of the recommendation to mercy by that time usual on the part of juries in forgery cases of a minor kind.* Mary went back to the Fish Inn, from which indeed she had never wandered far, and to her former duties. If she had been an object of passing interest before, she became now an object of pilgrimage. Compared, however, with her unrecorded predecessors in Hatfield's affections, her cross was a light one. She had no children; her rustic neighbours never thought of the word shame in connection with her misfortune, and the world came to gape at her as a sort of melodramatic heroine. There is some evidence that if her heart had been much engaged in the business the wound was effectually healed by her indignation. She ultimately married a respectable farmer of Caldbeck, away East of Skiddaw Forest, and her dust now

* Hatfield was hung at Carlisle.

reposes in the same picturesque graveyard as that of a neighbour whom accident too, in a different fashion, has made still more famous, namely, John Peel of foxhunting renown.

Buttermere is still as sweet a spot as there is in all Lakeland, and enjoys a natural seclusion of which even that nightmare of Lakists, a light railroad, could scarcely rob it. Save for a couple of modest inns and a diminutive new church, it is practically the same spot as that in which the villain Hatfield wooed the Maid of Buttermere, and Wonderful Walker, during his early ministry, spun wool and taught school within the altar rails. Only in the holidays and on high days, at the hours when the passing coaches dump out their loads, will the Solitary have any cause to complain of the pressure of his fellow creatures. Indeed I doubt if the whole parish could furnish fifty spare beds. The outlook over the valley from a few hundred feet up the rugged breast of Red Pike, which forms its western wall, is, on a sunny morning in May or June, one of extraordinary charm and infinite peace. The little hamlet itself with its old barns and farm buildings and big shade trees and stretch of meadows laced with hedge-rows lying between the lakes, looks so unconscious of its celebrity and so wholly indifferent to the outer world. Even the two inns at such a moment might almost be suspected of cultivating a philosophic resignation to the absence of the tourist. Men come and go at Buttermere in their thousands, but in the long intervals between whiles the relapse of this happy valley into its pristine quiet is complete.

The stroll through the meadows, too, from the Fish Inn to Crummock Lake on such a day is delightful. Herdwick ewes with their comical black and white lambs are everywhere in evidence, bleating back defiance at bustling, yapping collies who go about their duties with a conscientious energy and a desire to give satisfaction that is so very human, and indeed so very superior to the average humanity. An old foxhound or two, summer boarders from a neighbouring pack, look on at the hubbub in contemptuous apathy, and callow puppies whose feet have not yet pressed the wintry fells upon a fox's scent sprawl about in the paddock.

How charming too is the clean gravelly shore at the head of Crummock when you get there, visible so far out beneath the lake's pellucid waters, and the cheery voice of the beck as with one final plunge over the stones it ceases from troubling in the quiet depths it feeds. And you will do well to have the key with you of one of the boats that lie moored here beneath the gnarled, stunted oak trees, and pushing off

Crummock in Stormy Weather.

into the sunny ripples that dance outside the shelter of the little bay, paddle at your leisure down the centre of the lake. Many people, though to be sure they are mostly fishermen and prejudiced, maintain that this is the best vantage point for a true appreciation of the valley as a whole: looking as one does from here right up the heart of it, over the long trough where Buttermere, though unseen, lies sleeping, and away beyond to the rugged heights of Honister and the Haystacks. Crummock itself is nobly guarded by commanding heights, by Whiteless Pike and Rannerdale Knotts on the east, and Grassmoor, with its precipitous sides, washed red and bare a hundred and fifty years ago by a long-remembered waterspout. On the western side the descending ridges of High Stile and Red Pike leap up again to the two crests of Mellbreak, and in wild weather when the fountains of the hills are loosed, the thunder of Scaleforce with its hundred and sixty feet of sheer fall can be readily heard upon the shore.

Though holding pike, these two lakes have always been noted for their trout and char. The "laudator temporis acti," however, is much in evidence just now, and that either the trout are not there in such numbers or they do not rise so freely as of yore is the prevalent opinion of old *habitués* with whom I have cursorily talked or fished. That very poor form of amusement, night trolling, seems more successful than the fly, and I have seen more than one trout over a pound taken this way after dark by sportsmen who have flogged the lake all day with fly under propitious circumstances with much less result. On Buttermere only one boat is allowed; on Crummock the inns have several: but there is really nothing to choose between the lakes. Three to the pound is the average weight, and I am afraid three fish to the day is not far off the average catch, though there of course will be notable exceptions. These lakes are quite famous for char, but the char lurks and feeds in very deep water and is caught only by deep trolling. As to the trout, it seems a pity that the riparian rights of netting are still exercised in this country by lords of manors and innkeepers. They cannot be of great value, and if the practice does not cause serious depletion, it is a shocking bad example to poachers and potential poachers, who cannot be expected to regard the netting of trout so seriously as in a district where the act itself is tabooed among owners.

The natural proceeding for the visitor coming to Buttermere as we did is to return to Keswick by Buttermere Hause and the Vale of Newlands; another wild mountain pass and another beauteous valley at its foot. The native, however, when the calls of business or pleasure take him into the outer world, finds his natural outlet by the longer course of the Cocker which drops down from his own lakes through the delightful Vale of Lorton to Cockermouth, there to mingle its waters with the broader streams of the Derwent.

But for us there is no call to scramble back to Keswick; we have to break out of the mountains to the sea-coast so let us take the easier of these two routes and slip along the level road which skirts the shores of Crummock. After rounding a few obstructive craggy headlands and then trending inland through meadows and growing crops, we turn sharp to the westward at the lake foot where the fresh loosened Cocker goes roaring through the hanging woods of Scalehill. Birch and larch, oak and ash, sycamore and beech, mingle here in fine confusion the fresh glories of their June dress. On the breast of a leafy ridge we leave behind us with some compunction the snug hotel, more attractive in itself, perhaps, than those at Buttermere. A mile or two of undulating road and we are skirting Loweswater, as we skirted Crummock. A warm west wind is ruffling its sunny surface, and whitening the rich woodlands which mantle upon its further shore and climb the green foot of Carling Knott. A charming little lake is this, lying so snugly in the lap of hills and woods; famous for big pike and holding trout too, as a couple of boats drifting rapidly along the further shore bear witness to. At the lake head a long and weary climb brings us to the top of the ridge, whence we may pause for a moment and regard with lingering admiration the vista of hill and wood and water so lately traversed. With interest of another sort we may look down on the low country as to the eastward it rolls away towards the sea past Cockermouth and Workington, where tall chimneys and hovering wreaths of smoke stand out against the distant glitter of the Solway.

Here we must leave our highway to descend into prosaic

lowlands, and ourselves turning southwards strike out along a lonely looking byway that keeps the ridge and leads, so says both the map and quite a spruce finger-post, to Lamplugh. It is going of the best, though a lonely looking road as well as a lofty one. In a moment, as it were, we are off the track of the tourist and as much outside Lakeland, though we are treading on its very heels, as if we were in Durham or Yorkshire. The grey, untravelled, limestone road shoots forward in long straight undulations between straggling hedges, thickly dashed with the white blossom of the May and waving, wild, uncared-for locks of bush and brier in the riotous sea wind. Cold snipy-looking commons prolific of rushes and the wild cotton flower alternate with pastures not long reclaimed, where the bird life, so silent on the mountains breaks out once more in the clamour of the pewit and the lone cry of the curlew. Rusty wires hum on black peaty banks and strips of pine wood roaring loudly as we pass give out their tribute of startled cushats. The green fells stretch away inland on our left, to terminate in the familiar mountains we have just been climbing, while on the right there is nothing but the soft sea wind, beating on the ragged foreground, for no glimpse of the low country is permitted to us here. More luxuriant conditions, however, greet us as we run down into Lamplugh, a place that, having been already mentioned, might therefore be supposed to enjoy some measure of outside fame. On the contrary, I do not suppose that any guide book does more than note its name, if that. But in purely local annals and in a homely racy fashion Lamplugh is a place not without repute. I had certainly myself read its praises, not, I fear, in the polished metres of Wordsworth, Southey or Coleridge, but in the rollicking vernacular of one of those local bards who painted the Cumbrian rustic as he was in everyday dress, not as he ought to have been and in his Sunday best.

> " Lampla' an' Loweswater, lang men an' lean
> Hos roags an' thieves fra Branthat' an' Dean."

This is enigmatical and not over complimentary. But it is a fragment of a poem which was written at any rate with knowledge and humour, ingredients for which we may be thankful when the Cumbrian peasant is the subject of a theme. There is a fine stone gateway opposite the church, which banishes the libellous jingle for the moment, for on the arch, together with a coat of arms, is inscribed the name of John Lamplugh and the date, 1591, commemorating another relic of Tudor building activity. Through the iron gates may be seen an ancient manor house now evidently fallen in the social scale. I know not when the race of Lamplugh of Lamplugh became extinct, but its doings, matrimonial and otherwise, are thick upon the Cumbrian chronicle for long after this old gateway was built. While trying vaguely to recall some of their doings which are not perhaps important enough to inflict upon the reader, we come suddenly upon the Lamplugh inn standing alone at a cross road a mile or so beyond. Here the traveller of simple tastes, who like ourselves is bound for St. Bees, would do well to refresh himself, and here, too, a large hand-bill crackling in the wind proclaims the fact that the morrow is the annual festivity of the Lamplugh Club. Now Lamplugh Club day is an almost classic event in the local calendar, being much more than a century old, and has been celebrated in prose and verse of a highly entertaining and realistic kind. Indeed if you happen to be familiar with that notable prose idyll of Dickinson's, "Lamplugh Club," you will find yourself regarding the modest interior of the inn while discussing its homely fare with some interest though with doubtless small inclination to order Lamplugh pudding, a delicacy composed of biscuit soaked in hot ale, with seasoning and spirits according to taste. Though the time-honoured revelry, with which various cases piled high by the door, threaten for the morrow, may be but child's play to what it was in the time of the third George and of Oald Jobby o'Smeathat, and Banker Billy and Johnny Braythat there is still no lack of innocent diversion out of doors, as is evident from the programme.

It has been given to me while on my travels at this season of the year to peruse the play bills of a score or two of such Cumbrian gatherings displayed upon the walls of post office or public house. There is nothing like them in the South for comprehensiveness. Imagine a rural meeting that begins with a welter handicap and ends up with a waltzing competition! I was once rash enough to indulge in some gentle banter regarding so singular a combination while being ministered to at a country inn upon the Solway. But the young person, who on that occasion was the ministering angel, bridled greatly, intimating that this particular event, the waltzing match, I mean, was her special perquisite. Every taste and every form of activity is here catered for, and with, I think, much good sense. Horse racing on the flat and over hurdles, pony races and trotting matches are on the card of events; sprinting for young men and old men, races for girls under ten and women over fifty, with wrestling, of course, and tugs-of-war. A hound trail is usually a feature, and as I have said, a waltzing competition with various entertainments of a similar kind that have slipped my memory. It would be interesting to know if any country side in the world can show so liberal a spirit in the matter of its outdoor entertainments.

The good folks of Cumberland and Westmorland have been ardent sportsmen since time began. In the days of the Merry Monarch, the country squires were wild about racing. The Sandford MS. tells in quaint language of a great match on the "famous horse course" at Langwathby between the "Earle of Morrayes wily horse ffox," and an English horse called Conqueror. But "the Conqueror conquest him and won the money though the night before ther was the terriblest blast ever blowen; churches towers, trees, steeples, houses all feling the furie of the furies thereof. The devil a stir whether of England or Scotland I cannot tell but the English horse got the prise. The great stores of woods was so blowen done across the way as we had much adoe to ride thorow them yet not so bad a blast as usurping Oliver had when the devil blew him out of this world, God knowes whither."

A Cumbrian antiquary who has concerned himself with this important phase of country life in bygone days gives a long list of local racecourses in full use in the seventeenth century, Langwathby or "Langanby Moor" being always the premier gathering. Among other things, the Sheriffs were excused from entertaining his Majesty's Justices of the Peace on the condition of presenting a fifteen pound plate to be run for in the county. The programme for the coming racing season seems, in fact, to have been officially arranged at Quarter Sessions, where Penningtons, Musgraves, Lawsons, Hassells, Briscoes, Huddlestones, Aglionbys and a host more, whose names are still familiar in the land, represented the justices, who formed, as it were, the Jockey Club of Jacobean Cumberland. "Brave gentile gallants and justiciers, great gamesters, never without two or three running horses, the best in England."

Some, we learn, "galloped themselves out of their fortunes." But Mr. Joseph Thwaites of Ewanrigg Hall, seems to have combined business with pleasure, caution with frolicsomeness, to quite a wonderful extent; for he was "one of the wittest brave monsieurs for all gentile gallantry, hounds, hauks, horse courses, boules, bowes and arrowes and all games whatsoever; play his £100 at cards, dice or shovelboard, if you please, and had not above £200 per ann., yet left his children pretty porcions; and dyed beloved of all parties."

Stag hunting too was much in vogue in bygone Cumberland, and even before the Restoration there was a club known as "The Cumberland Gallants," who conducted "a hunting progress," or, in modern parlance, met at the chief deer preserves in turn.

It is near a dozen miles from Lamplugh to St. Bees, and for nine of them, as far that is to say as Egremont, the road traverses a brick red country, greatly scarred by the working of iron ore. There is no need to linger over the dreary rows of sordid houses that chiefly compose the little towns of Arlecdon and Frizzington, of Cleator Moor and Egremont. Every man, we are assured upon all sides, is in full work at seven shillings a day. The cottage interiors in this fine summer weather are in full evidence: so are all the population who do not actually

St. Bees.

labour in mine or quarry or smelting works. And one may be permitted perhaps to wonder why the standard of domestic comfort, taste and cleanliness among these people is so much lower than that of their neighbours in the hamlets of our recent journeyings, who look so trim and tidy on half the income. It is not poverty, that is very certain, or over-crowding, that has made slatterns of them. For the breezy open country is all around, though disfigured here and there by tall chimneys, or huge dump heaps, or the uncouth outlines of machinery.

The backs of the Lakeland mountains are rolling parallel with us as we travel south, and the mouth of Ennerdale, where the green fells part to let out the river Ehen, seems close at hand, while upon the west we are trending nearer and nearer to the sea. Here and there a pugnacious looking dog scowls on the roadway, or a basket of carrier pigeons is being borne to the station, while the public-houses have everywhere an unmistakable air of prosperity, thick as they stand. Rabbit coursing, too, is a leading pastime in these communities, and the passing traveller would assuredly draw the inference that neither church nor meeting-house was the factor here that they are in Welsh or Cornish mining life. Irishmen, as is natural, flock hither in considerable numbers, and another importation is that of Spanish ore, which is largely taken for smelting along this coast. There was a great exodus of miners to the Transvaal between 1894 and 1897, their families for the most part remaining in Cumberland. Such men as these, unaccustomed even at home to look beyond the moment, and who in South Africa were getting big wages paid out of European capital, were used, it will be remembered, very freely as witnesses by those whose interest it was to minimise the grievances of the Uitlander. If this strip of iron ore country, running into coal as it nears Whitehaven, is a sad blot upon the land from an artistic point of view, it has, at any rate, been of immeasurable service to an otherwise backward region, for many a fortune has been dug out of it, and thousands of human beings have here made a good living for the better part of a century.

The ruins of the famous Castle of Egremont rise grimly up amid the somewhat murky atmosphere of an unattractive though ancient little town. It was a Norman fortress originally, passing by death and marriage through many illustrious stocks. The de Lucy's owned it when the incident occurred which gave rise to Wordsworth's poem "The Horn of Egremont Castle." This notable instrument, it will be remembered, hung over the Castle gate, and was so deeply saturated with the honour of the de Lucy family that it refused response to any lips but those of a rightful Lord of Egremont. When the owner and his younger brother, however, were away on a crusade, the latter was overborne by a desire to own the family property, and hired some rascals to drown his brother in the river Jordan. Believing the nefarious job completed, he hurried homeward, and took possession of the broad estates appertaining to Egremont Castle, prudently refraining, however, from

Egremont Castle.

any attempt to play upon the family horn. But soon after this, while celebrating his succession by a great banquet, he suddenly and to his horror heard the loud blast of a horn at the gate. The usurper did not wait for further developments, but fled incontinently out of one door while the rightful owner entered at the other. Years afterwards he returned to Egremont to crave forgiveness of his injured brother, which obtaining, he retired into a convent to repent him of his sins.

It is now but three miles to St. Bees; and it is singular how abruptly one leaves the smoky belt of Cumberland behind, for in ten minutes we are running smoothly down a red lane, deep sunk in a rich hollow, fair and fresh, warm and green as South Devon. Precocious crops of potatoes and grain are flourishing upon ruddy hill sides, and a merry brook is tinkling by the roadside, amid a perfect carpet of bluebells, or playing hide and seek among lush thickets of alder, willow, and briar rose. Out again in the open, and the sea-breeze hits us in the face as the road goes dragging up through bleak pastures to a bleak skyline. The windy ridge surmounted, St. Bees shows plain below us, a straggling, grey-roofed town, in a narrow valley opening to the sea. A queer old-fashioned place it seems, too, as we descend upon it, cut off to all appearance by high ridges of treeless pasture from the outer world. As a matter of fact, however, a small railway wriggles in here from the south by the coast line, and wriggles out again through the hills to Whitehaven.

St. Bees is very emphatically a village, though a large and attenuated one. It might be a thousand miles from coal and iron; some travellers given to metaphor might say from anywhere. Its single long street comes climbing out to meet the approaching visitor, and carries him gently down through half a mile of plain, old-fashioned cottage houses to the level meadows in the valley, where amid an oasis of stately timber may be seen those venerable buildings which have endowed the place with such measure of fame as it enjoys. Perhaps it was the contrast with the mining villages so recently traversed, but St. Bees struck me on a first acquaintance as the most delightfully drowsy place for one that claimed to be almost a town I had ever seen. I was labouring at the moment, too, under a trifling misconception, which may have somewhat unduly emphasised this seeming repose.

For, like everybody else of ordinary acquaintance with such matters, I had all my life been familiar with the name of St. Bees as a prolific nursery of north country parsons, and as the best known perhaps of all those gateways to the Anglican ministry which are somewhat invidiously known as "back-doors"; I had in fact come there on purpose to see the famous College. On riding down the village street I marvelled greatly not so much at the absence of all sign of student life, since that might readily be accounted for, term-time though it should have been, but at the dejected air of so very small a place, which for several generations had been in its way a University town. I looked long for any signs of life, till after a while a tired-looking individual, smoking a pipe near an open door, broke the solitude, and of him I inquired the way to the College.

"T' College! Thear's nae College here."

"Well then, the University."

The native looked vacuous, and shook his head.

Then the light of intelligence gleamed from his eyes, and he waved his pipe northward.

"I racken ye means t' grammar schule."

"No, I don't; I mean the College."

"Thear's nae College here."

This was too much; and I rejoined, with some heat, that it was the only thing there was there. But at this moment an imperious demand from a red-armed lady in the adjacent doorway broke up the interview prematurely, and my friend vanished.

There was no one else in sight, so I pedalled slowly downwards.

A baker's cart then drove rapidly by, and a sudden thought struck me.

"Is this St. Bees?" I shouted to the whirlwind as it passed.

The man of loaves was probably taken aback by the absurdity of such a question, and if he answered at all it was when out of range. This was certainly the quietest University town by a very long way I had ever seen.

A trustworthy looking matron now came along carrying a pie, and to her I applied for the whereabouts of the College.

"There's no College here, sir."

"Well, then, the University."

"There's no——" At that moment there was a loud clangour of bells and a small cloud of scorchers dashed down on us out of the solitude. We ran for safety, and when the turmoil was over the lady with the pie had vanished.

A small urchin was playing on the side walk

"Look here, my boy, is this St. Bees?"

"Aye."

This was at once reassuring and perplexing, but the little railway station now hove in sight, so I made straight for it, discarding several possible sources of information on the way. Here at least this exasperating conundrum would be finally solved.

The daily train was evidently due, and the little station was quivering in anticipation of it with a crowd of a dozen passengers and all astir. The stationmaster was of course much in evidence, and now at any rate I should know the worst. "Stationmaster," I said, "would you be kind enough to direct me to the College?"

"The grammar school, I suppose you mean, sir."

This was worse and worse; it was impossible that one could have been the victim all one's life of so monstrous a hallucination.

"Look here, stationmaster," I said, "I won't detain you a moment, but you have got an establishment here that has been turning out parsons with blue hoods by the hundred since a long time before you and I were born. Now, where is it, please?"

The stationmaster looked at me, I fancied pityingly, for a brief moment, when suddenly up went one arm above his head, and the other with his whistle to his mouth, and he was across the line in a moment. Fate was against me! The train was approaching.

There was still a porter on the near platform, but I was now in no humour for long speeches. "Porter," said I, "have you got a College here, and, if so, where?"

The porter was a very sharp man, and did not seem pressed for time, and from him I learnt at least the bare fact, familiar doubtless to many of my readers, to wit that the College had collapsed some three years previously. There was nothing surprising in such an incident escaping the notice of an uninterested layman in the far South. But that an institution so comparatively venerable, and, to judge by the number of its alumni that one meets not only in the North but all over the

Whitehaven.

world, so prolific, should have suddenly snuffed out was quite outside ordinary calculations.

I had much cause, however, to be thankful for the mistake that had brought me there, for St. Bees is well worth seeing. The ecclesiastical settlement in which all its interest is centred stands out by itself on the further side of the little valley. The old buildings of the grammar school, which has taken out a new lease of life and is doing good work, are quite charming, and form three sides of a square. They suggest at first sight certain Cambridge Colleges in miniature, though their ruddy tint comes from stone in this case, and not from brick. Just across the road, amid a grove of ancient trees murmurous with the congenial clamour of a rookery, other buildings of academic aspect cluster round the beautiful old abbey church of red freestone, presumably occupying the site of the original foundation of the Celtic saint, St. Bega. The aloofness of the neighbourhood itself from the world, and the further isolation of this group of venerable buildings from even such life as throbs here, takes hold at once of the imagination. Whether the movement which gathered divinity students here for nearly a century was desirable or not for the Church of England is no concern of ours. But he would be a dull dog— and many such no doubt came here—who was insensible to the peculiar fitness of such a place for such a purpose. From an artistic point of view one can have nothing but regrets that it no longer serves it. As at the Welsh St. David's there is something peculiarly suggestive of the early Church about the whole atmosphere of St. Bees, and student days spent there must, on minds receptive of such things, have left cherished and lasting impressions. The academic spirit certainly broods amid the shade of the limes and sycamores that wave their tops over the beautiful roof and massive tower of St, Bega's spacious church, and the now deserted lecture halls and other relics of its eighty years' collegiate existence. Pleasant walks wind about amid the shade, and the mellow red freestone of the ancient walls shows to much advantage between the scaly trunks of the sycamores, the moss-green columns of the limes, the shining pillars of the beech. The sough of the sea comes faintly from the shore not a mile away, and mingles with the stir of leaves above. A deep clangour of bells from the hoary tower strikes down through the green flickering roof; an answering note sounds from the clock tower of Archbishop Grindale's grammar school ; and the rooks, as if they too by long association shared in the daily programme of the settlement, grow clamorous, and give a finishing touch to a scene that is wholly charming.

At the distribution of Church property after the Reformation one Thomas Chaloner received a grant of the cell, manor, and rectory of St. Bees. Though a descendant, we are told, of the seventh noble tribe of North Wales, what was very much more to the purpose, even in those days, he was a wealthy mercer of the City of London, and took his name from his trade. He rose to great distinction as a courtier and diplomat in Elizabeth's time, and, like all the new owners of Church and Crown lands near the border, had much friction with his tenants, who had been accustomed to regard themselves as legal fixtures, and forced their new overlords in the end to come down to their point of view. The Chaloners seem to have been glad in no long time to dispose of their manors to a Wyberg, who, being presumably a native, understood better what he was about, though the Wybergs in due course gave way to the all-absorbing house of Lowther, who endowed the College with the living. What there was of St. Bees Church settlement in the ninth century was burnt by those Danes who, with the Norwegians, came in by the west coast and got a permanent footing. Mr. Ferguson has clearly shown too how strong and at the same time how distinct from the other was the Norwegian element in Cumberland; the latter, as the Norse place names, the innumerable thwaites and garths, show, settling for the most part among the hills; the former, as similar evidence attests, squatting in the valleys. The present church of St. Bees commemorates the Benedictine Priory founded by William de Meschines about 1130.

From St. Bees itself, a short mile of grassy valley leads you down to its little bay, whose north side is sheltered by the bold headland which also takes its name from St. Bega; the only high bit of coast in fact between the Solway and the southern Esk. It is a cheerful cove-like little bay, marking the site, geologists tell us, of a submerged forest, but, what is more to the point, displaying firm clean sands, on which all the children apparently of St. Bees, bare-legged and rejoicing, disport themselves. Its only noticeable claim to be considered a watering place is a solitary hotel of dazzling whiteness, and severely simple but comfortable construction; a rigidly nautical building, in short, owing nothing whatever to shore-going fripperies. You crunch up to its doors on deep sea-side shingle, and a full-rigged marine flagstaff completes its character. To ardent lovers of salt water it should appeal as suggesting residence in a lighthouse or a coastguard station, without their disadvantages—for it is not only clean and fresh, as I can testify to, but most comfortable withal.

Egremont from a distance.

But we have dawdled too long in this sleepy hollow of the coast, and must get back to the village and climb the long hill once more towards Egremont, turning sharp to the south, however, before touching either that town or the mining belt. Hence it is some six miles to Calder Bridge, through a pleasant undulating country, devoted apparently to the breeding of Cheviots and border Leicesters and the grazing of shorthorns, though big, thrifty, dark-coloured Galloways here and there form a pleasing variety upon a soil that looks everywhere admirable. An old stone bridge carries us across the Ehen

River, which, fiery with the tint of iron works, tumbles with much commotion between bosky banks. A venerable native is lounging against the parapet, and on slight provocation develops a talent for reminiscence that has doubtless but few opportunities for display. The time-honoured lament over the change of times, and above all the passing of land from its former owners, both squires and statesmen, are the burden of his talk. These things are not without their attraction in the original with the help of a pipe and the accompaniment of a rushing Cumbrian stream, but they do not lend themselves to reproduction. So travelling still southward and leaving Beckermet, which means in Norse, I believe, "the meeting of the waters," on the right, a broader and more travelled road leads us at a higher level towards Calder Bridge. From up here we have a far wider outlook. To the right over a strip of green rolling country, sparsely sprinkled with homesteads, the Irish Sea lies blue and sparkling beneath the touch of a light breeze and the glow of a summer sun. The little watering place of Seascale, where bathers and golfers congregate in moderation, can be just seen breaking the long and somewhat unknown shore line with a touch of the outer world, and the white puff of a train is slowly crawling through the fat and peaceful pasture land towards St. Bees. To the left the fells of Lakeland, between Ennerdale and Wastwater, roll their rounded shapes along our route, all aglow in the bright sunshine, while straight ahead of us, but still far away, is Black Combe, which seems to spring with amazing suddenness from the hitherto level coast line and fill the sky with its huge humpy form.

The woods hereabouts bear ample evidence to the fury with which the winds lash this western slope of Cumberland; for the beech and sycamore plantations that here and there brush the road crane their tops eastwards so low as to form a thick flat roof of interlacing leaves from which startled birds break with most untoward commotion. A sharp descent now drops us into Calder bridge, where an imposing gateway opens up an imposing avenue. The stag's heads which surmount the pillars recall the fact that this was the home of the Cumbrian Stanleys, who, if memory serves me right, came in the first instance from a small manor in Eskdale. A charming village is this of Calder, expanding outwards by degrees in two rows of irregular old-fashioned buildings, till there is space between them for a rustic green, and beyond this again a fine old

Calder Abbey.

freestone church looks down on the clear streams of the Calder which churn below amid rocks and leaves.

An old-fashioned hostelry, the "Stanley Arms," across the bridge, completes the picture, and does something more than a roadside business. For a mile or so up the narrow valley of the Calder stand the ruins of the famous abbey, which, next to Furness, was of chief importance in north-western England. What is left of this beautiful Cistercian house, founded in the twelfth century by Le Meschin, son of the founder of St. Bees, now adjoins a small country house which is in no way out of harmony with its more venerable and long dismantled neighbour. Of this latter, the beautiful pointed arches supporting the central tower, and the walls of the south transept and cloisters are still in a great measure perfect. And a wealth of ivy and creepers has clambered up the ruinous walls, till it mingles with the spreading tops of beech and ash, whose leaves flutter where a high-pitched vaulted roof once echoed to the notes of chaunting monks. The warm red stone of arch and pillar and cloister wall shows in charming contrast to the green lawns from which they spring so gracefully, and form an ideal framework for the glimpses of woodland, fell and sky that show between. The hawthorns in the park too are a blaze of pink and white, the chestnuts in the splendour of their bloom. The silence of a summer afternoon could hardly brood over a spot more eloquent of monastic peace. The neighbouring house is empty, the garden quiet, and there is not a sound in the air, save the cawing of the rooks in the tree tops, and the plash of the Calder, which but a stone's throw distant, comes tumbling from the wilds of Copeland forest over red limestone boulders and glittering through avenues of over-arching woods.

From a retreat so snug it is natural enough that we can only escape by the same road we entered it, and joining the main highway again at the village, there is an easy run over the undulating country between sea and mountain to Ravenglass. Gosforth is passed with its ancient cross, Holmbrook with its winding streams, the outlook upon every side assuming in the meanwhile a grander phase. The Scafell group looms wild and high in the west, and the dark fells beyond Muncaster and the Esk look us in the face as we drop down into the small harbour at Ravenglass, where the last named river, together with the Irt and the Mite all meet the tide amid a waste of tossing sand-hills.

The cyclist who is indifferent to brake or pedal. will be precipitated into Ravenglass with much velocity by the steep country road which rushes down past a handful of modern villas and cottages under the railway arch, and terminates apparently in the water itself. Indeed, if you are not duly careful in shooting the arch you will be very apt to finish your journey in the harbour instead of the town. But these are grand words--there is not much of a harbour and very little of a town. The bar has silted up since the days when large Roman fleets rode here at anchor, and but a few small boats laden with manure and such like now crawl up with the tide to what is left of a once famous place—to wit, a single street of slate-roofed white-washed but mostly ancient houses that, lying

Near Calder Bridge.

just above high-water mark, mutely tell as plain a tale of vanished consequence as you may wish to read. Ravenglass during the Roman occupation was the chief port in north-west Britain. The inland and the sea-coast road from Chester to Carlisle met here : many acres of buildings clustered where now there is green meadow, and large fleets gathered in the then ample harbour. But it can scarcely be the glamour of the Roman period which causes the modern map-makers to write Ravenglass in such big capitals, to the unfeigned surprise of the few strangers who drop in there, and to the undoing perhaps of some of them. Not, by the way, that there is any lack of homely accommodation, for the inn is I believe excellent. The general air of the place, however, is that of having outlived its mission in life and its hope of usefulness. No doubt, every soul inhabiting the double row of queer old-fashioned tenements is usefully and worthily employed, in some way or other, but not, I take it, after the manner of their predecessors, for smuggling is writ large all over Ravenglass, and it has a delightfully wicked appearance, though it does nothing, I believe, more reckless nowadays than gather mussels.

Its reputation as a haunt of lawless and irregular characters was in former days considerable, and even in its respectable and reformed old age one might well fancy that there yet lurked here some persons of original and primitive habits. It looks twenty-five miles from a railway station, though it is not in fact two hundred yards. It has no architectural pretensions whatever, but only a wealth of expression and much pathos in its quiet, bygone, passed-over and forgotten look. It would stimulate the fancy, I think, of a writer of marine fiction, who might spend a week here profitably among such stray artists who rummage in obsolete harbours and love the skeletons of old boats, the shimmer of wet sand and the white wings of sea-fowl.

Once upon a time a church dignitary from the far south, who was spending his holiday in the lake country, came over to take the Sunday service at Ravenglass. It was a case of good nature in a sudden emergency, and the reverend gentleman, gauging Ravenglass, like the rest of us, by the measure of its type upon the map, took with him a sermon suited to the mayor and corporation, to the black-coated and top-hatted, to the befeathered and befurred intelligence of a thriving provincial town. His surprise was great when he found himself in the ancient little church, so charmingly set amid the Muncaster woods, which serves the worshippers of Ravenglass. It was still greater, and was not unmingled with embarrassment, when his unaccustomed eye looked down upon the score or so of Ravenglass natives who on that occasion and at that particular season made up his temporary flock. One thing at least was quite clear, and he folded up his manuscript with much deliberation, put it in his pocket, and when sermon time came met the emergency in extempory fashion to the best of his ability and no doubt with success.

Now, no one passing through Ravenglass in the early summer should omit to visit the gullery, as the spectacle is not one to be seen everywhere nor every day. The stranger will do well too to seek the guidance of the veteran boatman Farrant, whose two boats lie off the spot where the far end of the village street jumps into the water, and constitute, so far as my observation goes, the mercantile marine of modern Ravenglass. It is well to follow this course, not merely because the quickest route is by water, but on account of the venerable pilot himself, who is highly intelligent, and has a good knowledge of everything that flies over the sea or swims in it. The little estuary, by which the three mountain streams which mingle their waters here in the harbour escape to sea, is about a a mile long, dividing as it were two vast sand barrens. The one upon the north side stretching towards Drigg, and nearly cut off from the mainland by the tidal portion of the Irt, is some two or three miles long, and perhaps one in width. A large portion is the breeding-ground of thousands of gulls and terns, protected from molestation by Lord Muncaster's keepers, who have charge of the rabbit warren adjoining it. The birds return regularly to lay their eggs and rear their young amid the bent-clad sand-hills. The ground seems to be divided out between black-headed gulls and terns, and the border line more or less accurately observed. It would be an experience, I think, to most people and something of a revelation to walk for half a mile or more, literally picking their steps among the dark forms of half-fledged gulls scuttling like young chickens or pheasants in every direction, while a vibrating canopy of shrieking parents turns you giddy with the ceaseless movement of their wings, and almost drowns the sound of your companion's voice with their ceaseless and strident clamour. Nests lie in clusters, half-a-dozen together, amid the bent grass. At this season some few still contain unhatched eggs. In others the shells lie around recently broken, and the late inmates scuttle like fluffy balls around our feet, while the earlier hatched birds race up the sand-banks and through the grass like coveys of running partridges. The whole ground over many acres seems literally alive with them, till passing out of the gull colony with its deafening clatter, we emerge on the domain of the terns, whose sharp cries and scantier numbers give, by comparison, a sense of almost silence. The tern will be recognised as the graceful hawk-shaped member of the gull tribe, pure white in colour, swift and nimble as becomes a bird of prey. They are later breeders than the black headed gulls, and though the nests, full of bright coloured, deeply blotched eggs, are as thick upon the ground as those of their neighbours, scarcely any young birds are as yet hatched out. The tern will tolerate no busybodies, and will savagely attack any winged intruders, striking them with its sharp beak upon the head with singular accuracy. My guide related how he had himself seen them kill partridges in this fashion with a single blow, who had ventured within their territory. Passing out of this sandhill country of the terns on to the barer flats, some oyster catchers, an odd sheldrake or two and a few plovers disport themselves at a respectful distance from their neighbours; though by the same token it may be remarked that the bays and estuaries of this west coast are nothing like so well furnished with wild-fowl proper as the shores of Northumberland and Durham on the North Sea.

As we paddle back over the half-mile or so of flowing tide toward Ravenglass we listen to the now too-familiar tale of scarcity of salmon, and the decrease in the numbers of fish which with the summer floods ascend the Esk. We fall into gossip, too, concerning the mysterious ways of the king of fishes, and our boatman tells how, on six occasions during a long life spent on the mouth of a salmon river, fish have jumped spontaneously into his boat. On four of these the latter was lying empty, moored to the bank; on the other two he was in it himself. The memory of one incident even yet causes the old gentleman much amusement, though he lost his fish. For it so happened he was one day rowing a party of servants, chiefly females, from a big house in the neighbourhood near the spot we are now travelling over, and a salmon of some twelve or fifteen pounds leapt into the lap of the butler, who was on the cross-seat facing the boatman. This functionary was so intimidated that, instead of throwing himself upon the slippery visitor, he pitched backwards, heels up, into the arms of his fair friends in the stern, causing much emotion and very nearly a disaster, while the equally astonished fish, giving a vigorous kick, flopped over the side of the rocking boat into his native element again.

On the River Leven.

Ravenglass.

CHAPTER VII.

SLOPING gradually upward from Ravenglass is the block of high and broken land which divides the valleys of the Esk and Mite. The whole western or seaward end of this ridge is clothed with the luxuriant woodlands, or green with the lawns and glades of Muncaster, the most beautiful country seat in Cumberland, where Penningtons have lived, so far I can learn, since time began. At the lower edge of the demesne, long before its beauties reveal themselves, and in fact but a stone's throw above Ravenglass, is the site of the Roman town that overlooked the harbour, where big ships, as ships then went, freighted with the produce of the far south, lay at anchor off its wharves.

But I do not think I should linger by what is now but a bare pasture,—old Ravenglass having been mostly built out of these Roman ruins,—save for the immediate presence of a solitary relic which I rather fancy is a unique specimen of its kind. We have excavated Roman villas in plenty all over England, but I do not know of any that have defied the elements above ground, and at the same time survived the depredations of the local builder and road-maker, save this one at Ravenglass. It stands even yet some twelve feet high, and is fashioned out of that red freestone which the Romans got out in such quantities from the quarries at Gosforth. As a matter of fact, it was assumed with surprising carelessness, till no great while ago, to be a mediæval fortress of some sort, and is even yet known locally as Walls Castle. But when the archæologists got to work upon it the matter was soon placed beyond all doubt. An elaborate system of hypercausts was laid bare by slight excavations, and glass with other material was found in the débris. The sills and sides of the windows are even now fairly perfect, and there is a niche for a bust or image, while over the inside of the walls may still be seen a coating of rose-coloured plaster.

Now, as a mere subject for the play of fancy, I do think a bit of Roman architecture, standing above ground like an ordinary Norman keep, is much more stimulating than any amount of excavated work. The fragment of the basilica wall at Uriconium, near Shrewsbury, the white city of Llywrch Hên, destroyed by the early Saxons, always seems to me so much more suggestive, looming thus mysteriously above the stubbles and turnips of a Shropshire landscape, than all the acres of excavated buildings sunk in the ground around it. How much more then does this Roman dwelling house, perhaps the sole survivor of that wonderful, almost inconceivable epoch of our island story, stir one's fancy to vain endeavours to picture it. Chancellor Ferguson, who if special knowledge can give value to such retrospective tableaux most assuredly possessed it, paints one for us here, and asks us to recall the spot as it was in the year 300 A.D.—with its great fort, its row of officers' villas on the terrace above, its extensive suburbs full of farmers, tradesmen and hangers-on of the garrison. Out of the fulness of his knowledge he touches the deserted harbour with magic wand and fills it with vessels from the Mediterranean and the Bay of Biscay, all busy loading and unloading cargoes, while Spanish and Italian sailors crowd the wharfs bending beneath loads of olives, anchovies, sardines, great amphoræ of wine and other luxuries which the Romans loved and had taught the Britons to love. Outgoing cargoes were here, too, of a far different kind awaiting shipment: large sporting dogs and dejected natives, some going as slaves, others as recruits to fill the wasting ranks of legions on Continental service. The garrison on this coast, all authorities seem to think, were, as regards the rank and file, largely composed of Moors and Spaniards and of other races from the remoter shores of the Mediterranean.

But we must leave the sleepy Ravenglass of fact and the lively Ravenglass of historic fancy alike behind us and push on, either by private drives through the deer park or by the public road as opportunity offers, to the higher ground and the

Muncaster Castle.

green woods of Muncaster. The castle itself lies behind the ridge, perched finely on its southern slope with a commanding outlook both up and over the valley of the Esk, and from the level of the stream below appearing to spring out of a very sea of foliage. From this point indeed it makes a noble picture, though the great square tower is I think the only really ancient portion of the building. Art and nature have indeed had opportunity for combination here that is not often given even to the famous country seats of England. There are woods as fine, and glades as green, and dells as deep no doubt elsewhere. There may also be broad terraces of velvet turf winding round steep slopes clothed with everything that can be coaxed to bloom and blow in this soft western climate. Granted that such foregrounds, beautiful though they are, may readily be matched, it is not likely that they can often form the setting and the frame for such a landscape as may be seen through every break in the foliage, through every opening in the woods at Muncaster. For the whole of Eskdale, with its rich lowlands, its wild bordering fells, its shining stream, opens out to the west; and against the sky just far enough to give

From the Terrace, Muncaster Castle.

the glamour of distance, but not so remote as to dwarf their altitude, the mass of the Scafell mountains lies nobly piled.

Muncaster, like so many ancient seats, has its special heirloom, for Henry VI., when a fugitive from the field of Hexham and a benighted wanderer, was found by some shepherds upon the crest of yonder fell, where a chapel now points its gables heavenwards in pious memory of the event. The hapless monarch was brought down to the castle by his humble rescuers, and there tended till returning health or prudence allowed of his departure. As a token of his gratitude he left behind him a glass cup which the Lords of Muncaster still cherish, and on whose preservation an ancient legend says the good fortunes of the house depend.

A pleasant and well-kept road leads from the foot of the Muncaster grounds up the northern side of Eskdale, but it is private and sometimes locked. So the passing traveller who would see the lower part of the valley must take the public road on the southern bank of the river, and this is not only the worst in Cumberland, but, having regard to the physical simplicity of the route it follows, its roughness takes one wholly by surprise. Perhaps it is of no great importance, still I am sorry for the farmers who live upon it; and those I encountered in my first and only struggle with its ruts, rocks and gates, seemed fully conscious that some meed of sympathy was due to them. As a matter of fact most tourists enter Eskdale higher up by the road from Miterdale, and this implies not only a considerable detour from Ravenglass, but also the loss of the fine retrospective views of Muncaster that so greatly enrich the scenery of the lower reaches of the river. Tourists however rarely visit Ravenglass, but cling for the most part to the mountains, coming down from Wastwater and doubling back through Upper Eskdale over Hardknott, on which toilsome path we ourselves are bound The little mineral railway, too, which runs up Miterdale from Ravenglass and into Eskdale, where the dividing barrier drops for a moment as it were to let it through, is often used, and with it comes the main road, which those on wheels of any kind most usually follow. When this point is reached, the sorrows of the cyclist from Ravenglass by the valley road will be over for a time, and he may drown their memory if he likes at that attractive and old-fashioned hostelry "The King of Prussia." Even in these dales the indomitable Frederick, the ally of Pitt, the hero of the Seven Years' War, was a name to conjure with, no doubt, and to be exalted to the highest honours that a country-side once famous for its thirst could offer to a popular character.

From here to the foot of Hardknott, the most rugged pass that wheels attempt in the Lake Country, is six miles. Till this is reached there is nothing for the cyclist to complain of, and the charms of Eskdale, which are exceeding great, may be enjoyed without let or hindrance. Upon the right is the rugged wall of a wild moorland country which carries grouse and heather, and contains the lake of Devoke, where the most excellent of trout abound, stretching away to the Duddon valley. On the left is a greener, but more broken mass

Eskdale.

of fells, that roll away on either side of the gloomy tarn of Burnmoor to Wastwater and the forest of Copeland. Farms and small hamlets with foliage in abundance, both of wood and hedgerow, form a cheery foreground to the surrounding heights, which grow in stature and in sternness as the valley narrows. The river twists and babbles merrily through sun and shade, growing feebler in its note as its junction with each tributary stream is passed. The sun is bright, the air is warm, and fleecy clouds are moving with slow and stately steps from the east, as far to all seeming above the highest mountain tops as the last are above us. June can be as kind in Lakeland as in Kent or Essex, and when you catch her in such humour it is a treat not to be forgotten lightly. Thrushes and linnets pipe in the thickets; the cuckoo's loud note sounds along the fern-clad foothills, and the corncrake grinds out its harsh but seasonable cry from lush and flowery meadows that await the scythe. Among the most delightful of Cumbrian valleys, Eskdale may assuredly be numbered, and to it belongs the further distinction of bearing its charms unpolluted and almost undiminished to the sea.

A new hotel of some pretension seems the only evidence in the valley that the touring world has a fancy for making any stay in it, while further on the old "Woolpack," a wayside inn of local note, lies snugly set amid shady trees. Somewhere too in the valley the little narrow-gauge railroad is winding its way along, for yonder to the left is its terminus, which rejoices in the euphonious name of Boot. Much pleasantry is indulged in concerning the mild adventures of tourists who take the good intentions of the little line, which after all was built to carry minerals and not men, too seriously. But to the natives of the valley, who no doubt understand its humours, it must be of great service. And from an æsthetic point of view, moreover, it seems to me so entirely unobjectionable. An industrious steam threshing machine would be a fiend by comparison as a disturber of the rural calm. I must confess some inability to sympathise with the indiscriminate uproar that every mention of a new railway in a picturesque country calls out. Neither a railway train nor a stream of beanfeasters on wheels harmonise to be sure with the beauty or repose of nature. I am not sure, however, that I don't prefer the former evil. The tumult is at least all over in a moment and there is peace for an hour or more, probably for more by a great deal between Boot and Ravenglass. But the beanfeaster, to use a southern term for convenience, is with you on the turnpike much longer and much oftener. He hurts much more too, for not only does he actually throw his dust upon you, but his choice and merry jibes as well, if he is very full of beans—or beer. He at any rate does not come to these parts "humbly, Wordsworth in hand," which was the sole condition, said a leading luminary among Lakers, with some surprising lack of humour, on which he would welcome the alien. Now a railway it must be admitted relieves the road traffic immensely; sometimes it even restores it to that elementary and peaceful condition which in our selfishness as lovers of nature we cannot help rejoicing in. At the expense of a shriek and a rumble at long intervals it creates a peace where otherwise there would be no peace from the noisy clatter of *chars-à-banc* and brakes. The Holyhead road, for instance, through the vale of Llangollen enjoys moderate immunity from any disturbing kind of traffic, but it would be intolerable if the Great Western did not whisk the swarming tourists westwards under mountains and through woodlands, which lose, as I have good reason to know, little of their beauty and seclusion by the process. There is surely nothing in the actual track of a railroad, particularly if it be a single one, more intrinsically offensive than in the artificial constructions of Macadam! To the eye of the eighteenth-century recluse, who may have felt as we do on such matters, I have no doubt the wide metal coach road, walled up here and blasted out there, seemed an abomination. Nowadays the very people who grow hysterical at the bare mention of a new railroad, almost cherish the turnpike and are even tolerant or apparently so of the beanfeaster. Such is custom and its subtle but prodigious power. Let any one, in all candour, with a cool head and without prejudice, consider whether the railroad from the æsthetic point of view is not the victim of much ill-considered and unjust abuse. The cunning rabbit, the timorous hare, the suspicious pheasant will tell you I think that for their part they prefer it any day to scratch or scrape or dust themselves up on, to the everlasting hubbub of the turnpike.

Having said so much I feel I have laid myself open to the

suspicion of holding a brief for the perpetration of some monstrous outrage on the Lake Country—a railway up Scafell, or round Derwentwater ; though I am bound in fairness to say that Snowdon has not suffered and thousands have beheld the finest mountain outlook in Britain who could not otherwise have done so.

But we are now mounting a track which is altogether too much for the kind of traffic which carries the beanfeaster and the tripper. The last farm is left, the last gate closed, and we are fairly breasting the open fell with the pass of Hardknott some thirteen hundred feet above sea level before us. It

Near Boot.

seems difficult to imagine that this steep, tortuous track, striking out so relentlessly for the high and lonely fells, was once a great Roman thoroughfare. But before going far one is very forcibly reminded of its old importance by the well marked remains of the fortress which defended it upon the western side. The lines of this same fort, about a hundred yards square, are yet most plainly to be seen, with the traces of a tower at each angle, much of the stone being from the Gosforth quarries. I need not say that most of this has long been carried off to do duty in neighbouring walls and farmhouses, but the mound where stood the tower for signalling up and down the valley remains, and the two acres or thereabouts of green which was the parade ground is plain enough to see near a large cairn about a quarter of a mile off. Experts have been here on and off during the past century and found many curious things, among which were leaden pipes that brought the water from a spring in the hills a mile away. There were bricks too, and tiles baked in the kiln, which with smelting works then existed near Ravenglass—nails, glass, pottery, iron hooks, and a carved stone which seemed to fix the date as that of Calpurnus Agricola, 162-9. The officer in command up here must in truth have had a dreary time from the Roman point of view. Yet this north-west frontier was no doubt the place to see what active service there was going, and one is apt to forget that Hadrian's Wall was something more than a remarkable piece of defensive masonry, and that it meant a busy line of stations and a constant movement of masses of men and merchandise. Cumberland, at any rate in Roman times, was a busy and a stirring country compared to the barbarous wilderness of many centuries later.

But we must hurry over Hardknott with our pen as no man ever hurried over it yet upon his feet or in the saddle, unless indeed it were flying smugglers with the gaugers on their heels for this was the natural route by which the illicit plunder of Ravenglass went inland. What constitutes, however, the real terror of the crossing is the fact of its being a double ridge. For when you have climbed near 1,300 feet it is but to descend again for half that distance with a view to surmounting another ridge beyond of equal height. In the intervening hollow we cross the head-waters of the Duddon, the Duddon of Wordsworth's sonnets, and of much fame for its exquisite scenery, and may see it winding down to Seathwaite, where for most of a long life dwelt a character that has acquired, owing in the first instance to Wordsworth, much fame in Lakeland lore. This was the Rev. Robert Walker, or "Wonderful Walker," though probably the point of the story is that neither he nor his parishioners saw anything wonderful whatever in his performances. Hence the interest of the man, not as an average type perhaps, but at least as an extreme one of an old-time dale parson. To those who have a mania for labelling and docketing every creation of the novelist and the poet, Walker will chiefly appeal as the man whom Wordsworth had in his mind when he drew the somewhat idealised pastor of "The Excursion."

The subject of this unavoidable parenthesis was born in 1709, the twelfth son of a Seathwaite yeoman. Being the weakest of the family he was "bred a scholar," and went through the usual Cumbrian programme of village school-teaching to holy orders, followed by a combination of both offices at Buttermere, where there then stood the smallest church in England. In 1736 he was appointed to Seathwaite, then worth about £5 per annum, where he lived and worked for the remaining sixty-six years of his life. He married early a wife with a dower of £40, the principal of which was never touched. He raised a large family, educated them all well, and left £2,000 and a vast amount of woven cloth to be divided among them. Those who write articles in newspapers upon the problem of how to live on what is now called nothing a year might well feel abashed at the relation of such a performance. Indeed, the reader going only on the above bare facts might fairly object to being trifled with by an arithmetical absurdity.

But this dexterous and indefatigable cleric left no means untried of turning an honest penny. He took out a licence in his brother's name, and turned the parsonage into an alehouse, a proceeding which, on the face of it, does not sound well in modern ears. But its dubious morality seems to have been more than atoned for by the reverend publican's own abstemiousness and his uncompromising attitude towards drunkenness in his scant customers. He taught school for eight hours a day, working his spinning wheel unremittingly, and making a desk of the communion table, while the children sat around him within the altar rails. Every spare day he toiled in the fields as a labourer for wages, besides filling the post, so common then to the clergy of these mountains, of will maker, accountant, and general scrivener to the neighbourhood.

He worked hard, too, at his divinity studies, often till the morning hours in a fireless room, visited the sick assiduously, and even relieved the needy. The family at the parsonage only tasted meat on Sundays, when, with a boiled joint and a mess of broth, the good vicar entertained between the services those of his parishioners who came from a distance. He always preached himself, and that to a full church, and during the whole period of his ministry there was not a Dissenter in the parish. The only relaxation this phenomenal divine allowed himself was an occasional rubber of whist on winter evenings, and I think upon the whole it will be allowed that his epithet of "wonderful" is justified by something more than alliteration.

Many of the old-fashioned Cumbrian clergy added to their pittances by turning regular farmers and dealers. Mr. Sherwen, the rector of Dean, who only died in 1870, was a notable example; he was accustomed to walk immense distances to market, and drive home his bargains, generally good ones, on foot. Like the excellent Walker, "he was economical," it was said, "in small matters that he might be liberal in large ones." And among his prudent habits was that of retiring to a shed to put on his trousers inside out when about to dive into the sheep-pens at market. He made up for his lay avocations in the week by preaching inordinately long sermons on Sundays, and on one occasion, when the phrase occurred "And what shall I say next?" a wag in the congregation called out "Amen." He would go any distance "to visit the sick, set out a drain, or knock out a bullock's wolf-tooth;" a person in short of all-consuming energy. But the inevitable hour arrived when even he had to depute another, his nephew in this case, to fill his pulpit, while he himself played the part of listener, calling out " Hear, hear ! " with some vigour, it is said, when sentiments in his young relative's address seemed to deserve such encomium.

It was another sheep-farming parson of the same type, Mr. Sewell, of Troutbeck, who when once preaching at the little church at Wythburn before its restoration, and when the rickety pulpit yawned away from the wall, dropped his sermon into the crack. After vain endeavours to extract it he gave up the hunt and faced the congregation with this manly apology: "T' sarmont's slipt down i' t' neuk and I

Troutbeck.

can't git it out; but I'll tell ye what—I'se read ye a chapter o' the Bible's worth ten of it."

After crossing the infant Duddon the second ridge is approached by a tortuous valley known as Wrynose, and near its summit the three counties of Cumberland, Westmoreland and Lancashire meet. The spot is marked by the "three shire stones." Hence a two-mile descent brings us to the farmhouse of "Fell Foot," which, with its yew trees, makes a well known landmark. On the right the mass of Wetherlam dominates our road; on the left is Pike o' Blisco, while ahead of us and down below is the Brathay valley, with Wansfell and Illbell showing in the far distance.

But I am here confronted with a sore dilemma in the shape of a network of roads that wind about amid a rare and beautiful confusion of wood and hill and water. This broken and comparatively lower country, which, roughly speaking, lies between Coniston, Windermere and Rydal, and is watered by the Brathay, is more familiar and more trodden perhaps by visitors of all degree than any other part of Lakeland. Roads and paths twist about in all directions and finger-posts are everywhere indicating the proximity of waterfalls and spots of interest that more especially appeal to the capacity of that great majority of tourists who like the four square meals a day, which modern British custom has adopted, and like them all at the place of their abode. I would not advise the cyclist to venture overmuch on these by-roads; the distances are short and he will save himself some vexation if he leave his machine at home. There are fine highways, however, along the valleys of this limited region, as is only natural where wheels of every kind, from the aggressive *char-à-banc* to the private landau or Victoria, roll thick enough, even in June and July. It is all very charming this lake-head district. There are tumbling waterfalls and slow-creeping stretches on the rivers—rocky rapids and sedgy lakelets, full of reeds and water-lilies, which last, though well enough in Surrey, seem somewhat inharmonius here. There is foliage, too, of every kind and colouring, for the outside world have not only been thronging through here this hundred years, but building houses and planting woods. It would not be true or fair to say that they have caused serious injury, while the everlasting hills, which no man can disfigure except by quarrying or planting pine woods, loom ever behind in continuously changing outline, as you wind about the bosky glades below and catch their forms at various angles through the opening boughs. What is a poor prose-writer to say about a region

O

of such beautiful confusion? One cannot go on perpetually painting landscape on foolscap. It is a country for the artist and the sonnet-maker or for essays upon Wordsworth, who lived long enough to see this, his own immediate neighbourhood, become a fashionable haunt. Yet with all the beauty of this region I confess to feeling just a little stifled in it. If it seems to wear a look of being too continually on show, that is doubtless due to a distorted fancy which one cannot expect every one to share, but only wonder how many do. The villa, the shrubbery, the high wall and the planted woods, the regulation pathways and painted gates seem to me too much in evidence. However, it would be ridiculous to quarrel with the inevitable, seeing how beautiful the whole thing is even yet. For myself however I candidly confess I would much sooner be by the Derwent or the Esk than the Brathay or the Rotha. The atmosphere is more natural and more fresh. The woods are not quite so self conscious, the scanty fish, to put it another way, not so accustomed to being stoned by light-hearted cockneys from northern towns.

If I had my way, however, I would turn sharp to the left at Fell foot before reaching this soft and sensuous country, and follow the road that climbs above Blea-tarn and under Lingmoor, and so down into the head of Langdale. There is nothing over luscious or stuffy here in all truth, for many people, and with some justice, regard it as the gem of the whole Lake country. It is always better to ascend a valley than to drop in at the head of it. But once down on the flat, green sward of meadows, through which the wayward Mill beck goes casting its gravel and *débris* on either side, the method of approach may be forgotten, for the Langdale valley does not shrink and climb, and narrow to a green gorge after the usual fashion when it penetrates the hills. But so far as traffic is concerned it ends abruptly in a *cul de sac* of most noble proportions, the valley itself being of ample breadth, and a fine carpet of meadow spread across its level floor. An old homestead or two, with some fine grouping of ash and sycamore timber, gives a further touch of lowland peace and plenty to this sequestered nook, while in striking contrast lofty mountains of a wild and savage character spring high into the air on three sides, and seem literally to overhang the verdant flats below. On the north the famous twin crests of Langdale rugged, knotty, and fierce of aspect, for the higher half at any rate of their 3,000 feet, dominate the valley. The west is wholly filled by the great masses of Bowfell and Crinckle craggs and Pike o' Blisco, which sweep round on the south to the lower but still lofty ridge of Lingmoor. The time of day to be here is without doubt when the sun is drooping westward, for then the rugged majesty of the Pikes is illumined from summit to base by a search-light they can gloriously sustain, while the opposite steeps of Bowfell and Crinckle crags are infinitely increased in majesty by the mysterious mellow shadow that enwraps them and intensifies their dark and broken outlines against the fiery splendour of the western sky.

But I want to get on to Hawkshead by way of Coniston. And there is a road which leads thither also from Fellfoot, turning sharply to the right and travelling by Tilberthwaite and down the secluded vale of Yewdale—a journey of perhaps four miles over an indifferent road, but through charming scenery. How insistent are these Norse names in this north-west corner of England. The Celt, who was the first to print his tongue upon the district has been curiously displaced in this particular. To mention Crinkle crags (Kringle, a circle), Tilberthwaite, Stang End, Yewdale, which has given such a familiar surname to the country, and Berk Howe is merely to take the nearest names that meet the eye. Every *gill* and *beck* and *thwaite* and even *tarn*, which is, I believe, the Icelandic for tear-drop, recalls the thrusting Norseman and the sore straits of the Strathclyde Britons, who fled in such numbers to their kinsmen in North Wales. The local vernacular abounds in words that are used to this day in the Scandinavian countries. Many living

Cumbrians too, remember, when "Kurkgarth" was freely used for churchyard, and the word "gard" in its various forms, being the Norse for enclosure, is found of course in every dale. *Ness* and *force* tell the same story, while *Hause* is everyday Icelandic. The Danish word "toft" for farm buildings was continually used till quite recently in daily speech. A colt is still called a stag, from *stiga*, to mount, while the weakly member of a brood, flock, or family still goes by the name of "Reckling," which is the Norse for "Outcast." Mr. Ellwood, a great authority on Cumbrian folk-lore declares that on his first look

Coniston from across the Lake.

at the Danish language he could read whole verses of their Bible with scarcely any recourse to a dictionary, from his knowledge of the Cumbrian vernacular.

We strike the head of Coniston Lake, in former days called Thurstone (Thor's stone) water, at its upper end, close to the village of that name, which, like Boot, is connected with the sea-shore by a branch line. It was at Coniston that Craig Gibson, after giving up his practice at Lamplugh, spent the next few years of his life, and the last that he was to spend in his native district. And who may Craig Gibson be? ninety-nine out of a hundred readers will most assuredly demand. His portrait figures in no shop windows, nor can his biography in concentrated form be purchased for a penny at the local stationer's, nor is the house he occupied an item in the round of the enterprising *char-à-banc*. Poor Gibson, in short, is not reckoned among the immortals of the Lake Country, by outsiders at any rate, but unlike all of these except Wordsworth, he was a native of it and a product of the soil. Gibson was, in fact, a country doctor, whose practice carried him far and wide through hill and dale, among all classes of people. He had a wonderful knowledge of the country folk, among whom he laboured till he was over forty, and a vast fund of sympathy and humour, which endeared him to all. With this he combined a passion for dialect studies, and some genius for writing poems both of a humorous and pathetic nature. No man who ever lived had such a mastery of the varying dialects of Cumberland and Westmorland, or better knew the inner character and the humour of their rugged people.

The last twenty years of his life were spent at Bebington in Cheshire, where he was prominent in all historical and archæological movements. There he died nearly thirty years ago, and a granite monument in the churchyard commemorates his supremacy as an interpreter of Cumbrian life, and folk-lore. Gibson was a great admirer of De Quincey, but as was perhaps inevitable in a shrewd, observant man to whom the vices and virtues, the everyday life of the dalesman was so familiar, he held up to some ridicule the ideal peasants of the gentle Wordsworth, who had but little inside knowledge of the humble folk above whose holdings he wandered and dreamed. Now there was an old lady among Gibson's patients named Betty Yewdale who lived in a solitary spot above the world in Little Langdale, and is the heroine of several stanzas in the 5th book of the *Excursion*. The wanderer, it may be remembered by those who have read through that moumental poem—(Ah! how many are there nowadays?) gets benighted upon the fell, but is eventually guided by the light of a lantern to the neighbourhood of an isolated cottage.

> A house of stones collected on the spot
> By rude hands built with rocky knolls in front.
> Backed also by a ledge of rock, whose crest
> Of birch-trees waves above the chimney top.

The lonely female is holding the lantern as a guide to her husband, who is due home from his work in a distant quarry. The wanderer enters, and is simply and hospitably entertained by the worthy couple for the night. The husband is away before cock-crow in the morning, and the guest is thus apostrophised by his childless, but resigned helpmate :—

> "Three dark winter months
> Pass," said the matron "and I never see,
> Save when the Sabbath brings its kind release,
> My helpmate's face by light of day. He quits
> His door in darkness, nor till dusk returns,
> And through Heaven's blessing thus we gain the bread
> For which we pray and for the wants provide
> Of sickness, accident, and helpless age.
> Companions have I many ; many friends,
> Dependants, comforters—my wheel, my fire,
> All day the house-clock ticking in mine ear,
> The cackling hen, the tender chicken brood,
> And the wild birds that gather round my porch."

Thus speaks Wordsworth's Betty Yewdale—the Doctor's Betty of real life now comes upon the scene. There had been a big funeral near Coniston, to which all the country had gone, and Betty's husband, sad to say, had remained away all night ! It was Betty's nearest neighbour that told the Doctor the story, for it was to her that the forlorn one came burning with indignation against her truant spouse, and in no good temper with her friend when she found that, though a fellow sufferer in the same degree, she took her affliction with most provoking calmness.

"Won't you laid (seek) him ?" asked the heated Betty.

"Nay," said the neighbour.

"Ye ma' due as ye like," replied the other; "but I mun bring mine whoam as he will."

Betty then set off for Coniston, and this is her friend's account of her return.

"On i' t' efternen she co' back drivin' Jonathan afoar her wi' a lang hazel stick, an' he sartly was a sairy object, His Sūnda' cleeas leuk't as if he'd been sleepin' i' them ont' top of a dirty fluer. Tie of his neckloth had wurk't round till belat ya lug an'l lang ends out hung o'er ahint his shoulder. His hat had gitten bulged in at' side, an t' flipe on't was cock't up beeath back and frunt o' togidder, it wod ha' been a querely woman body at wod ha' teean a fancy till Jonathan that day. Says I, 'Ye hev fund him then.' 'Fund him!' says she! 'ey, I fund 'im. I knot whar ut lait 'im. I fund him at t' Black Bull wi' yower meeaster and a lot meear o' t' seeam soort. They war just gān to git ther girt pan o' beef steeaks set on t' middle o' t'ecable. I meead t' frying pan an' t' beef steeaks flee gay merrily oot o' t' door, an' I set on an' git them sic a blackin as they will'nt seeune forgit. Then I haillt Jonathan oot fra among them, but when I had gitten him out wi' me I shāmt ut be seen on t' roads wi' him. Sike a pictur ye niver see the like of. We hed to teeak t' fields for 't an'as it warn safe to let him climm the t' walls, I meead him creep t' hog hooals (the openings under the stone walls), an' when I gat him in, his heead in an' his legs out, *I dūd switch him.*'"

Many of Gibson's ballads were set to music and are still familiar in Cumberland. He could also wiite and speak the dialect of the Ecclefechan part of Dumfriesshire, whence came his mother's people, and Carlyle wrote of his folk-lore ballads in language which, for that caustic sage, was positive enthusiasm. There have been indeed quite a number of native singers, some gentle but mostly humble, in the Lake Country. Miss Powley, of course, who died not long ago at a great age, every Cumbrian knows, and her dialect poem, "The Brokken Statesman," is quite a classic on the border. The tragic fate of

Sanderson, again, has been told of by Wordsworth. How he lived alone in a cottage, which catching fire burnt up all his manuscripts and fatally injured the unhappy author. Lying under a tree near the burning cottage, he learnt the fate of his works and expired with the remark that he wished to live no longer, and might well have quoted, had he strength, a verse of one of his best poems :—

> And blest are you in early graves,
> For age is but protracted pain,
> A longer strife with winds and waves
> Upon a wild and stormy main.
> My lot has been to linger here
> Till every earthly joy has fled,
> Till all is gone the heart holds dear,
> And gathered sorrows bow my head.

Miss Blamire, Miss Gilpin, and Mrs. Wheeler, all long dead, were celebrated for their dialect songs and sketches, while Robert Anderson was among the most prolific. The blind, fiddling, rollicking Stagg, who flourished early in the century, was in some ways the most spirited and realistic of all. His locally famous poem, the Bridewaine, as well as Rosley Fair, are as perfect specimens of graphic description in vigorous vernacular as could be found.

The first treats of the old-fashioned Cumbrian wedding, the summoning of the country side, the race to church, the mad gallop back again, the feasting and dancing afterwards, the wild orgie of fighting and drinking, and the gradual return of the neighbourhood to its normal sanity after three or four days of revelry.

> At last 'twas gitten wheyte fuor days
> The lavrocks shrill war whusin'
> Wheyte yen by yen, wheyte dairy'd an' deylt
> O'th rwoard t'wards heame are wrustlin
> Some heads an' thraws war stretch'd i' th' nuik,
> An' loud as brawns war snouran ;
> Others wi' bluid an' glore a' clamm'd,
> War leyke stick'd rattens glowran

> The fiddlers they i' th' parlour fought
> An yen anudder pelted,
> Tom Trimmel leyke Mendoza fierce
> Poor Tommy Baxter welted
>   Reeght sair that neeght.

After skirting the upper end of Coniston for a considerable distance, and mounting afterwards a prodigiously steep hill through the thick woods of yet another charming seat of the Marshall family, a fine backward view down the whole length of the lake, most amply rewards the labour. No mountains or

The School House, Hawkshead.

hills of magnitude press near upon the shores, or form from this point any appreciable item in the outlook; no visible islands or bold promontories relieve a certain tameness from which Coniston by comparison with its sister lakes is held to suffer. But no sheet of water six miles in length lying in the lap of English woods and hills, can be otherwise than beautiful: and, after all, this is the wrong end from which to look on Coniston. Any one who would do justice to the Lancashire lake (for we have been in the County Palatine since leaving Fellfoot) must take boat and drop down towards the lower end. Thence across the broad stretch of dancing ripples he will see as fine a mountain background as any English lake could wish for, with Coniston's particular mountain, "The Old Man"—another vulgarism of a Celtic name (Allt-Maen)—showing amid the foremost and the boldest.

The four miles of road from Coniston to Hawkshead are remarkable for little but the perpendicular nature of the grade. We are now in a tamer country, but the little town itself is well worth a visit, if only for its quaint architectural

Newby Bridge.

features and its eloquent suggestions of a bygone state of things, social and economic. Hawkshead boasted once of a great wool market, whither all the wool grown on the surrounding mountains was brought for sale, and of a flourishing grammar school, where the sons of statesmen, parsons, and tradesmen prepared themselves for college or the world. Here Wordsworth was educated, as everyone knows, and the outside of the house wherein he boarded is much inspected from the street by the indiscriminately curious. But the ancient part of Hawkshead is a place to loiter in to much **advantage.**

Around the old wool-market are a great store of quaint angles and archways and narrow wynds and courts, all fashioned in the rude stone and slate which served so well the old-time builders of this Lake Country. There is an ancient church too, set nobly with its green graveyard on a ridge above the town, as becomes the centre of a parish whose boundaries are so large, and whose history is so rich in local interest as that of Hawkshead.

Windermere, or Winandermere, as the old name went, though narrow always, is narrowest at its centre where a steam ferry available for all kinds of traffic plies busily. The road thither

Windermere.

from Hawkshead is not remarkable, though for the mile or so that it skirts Esthwaite there is all the charm that water spreading between green pastures and summer woods can give. At the Ferry a road turns to the right, and the actively disposed with time upon their hands might well be tempted to follow it to the foot of Windermere, and so back upon the further bank to Bowness, whither we are now bound, and can, moreover, reach in ten minutes if we so choose. But I would urge them rather to explore the beauties of the lake's lower end by water. For though it may seem strange that no highway follows the course of this half of the most famous and most frequented sheet of water in England, this is practically the case, for the road, which starts from the Ferry in such promising fashion, carries you through an almost continuous screen of woods, and by steep gradients that for this reason you climb to no purpose. I speak feelingly, having once made this mistake and, though the details of this secluded road have escaped my memory, being in truth somewhat monotonous, the regrettable state of mental heat in which I found myself at Newby Bridge has not. The road back to Bowness upon the other side looks beautiful upon the map: but the lie of the country and the earlier struggles of this same highway to grapple with it which are very conspicuous from across the lake, would certainly confirm me in recommending any one to see the beauties of lower Windermere by boat. Perhaps one ought to know better, but there is something particularly irritating when your object is to circumvent a beautiful sheet of water, and you are thrust inland and set to toil up and down perpendicular lanes, between high hedges or buried amid unpenetrable timber, and hopelessly cut off from the object of your journey. In wild lakes, hemmed in by mountains, you expect no artificial assistance and are thankful for such facilities of transit that are offered, but amid the soft and peaceful and much visited environs of Windermere you do expect some kind of lake shore road and take the omission in no good temper. At the ferry there is an admirable hotel with pleasant lawn sloping to the lake and much frequented by yachting folk on regatta days. For just off here the competing yachts make their start, and a fair sight it is on a bright summer day, the snow-white sails of a dozen cutters flapping or bulging against the wall of green woodland and wooing the fitful mountain breezes with cunning and skilful manœuvres.

Above the ferry, as we cross the half-mile of water, the large wooded island of Belle Isle seems to close up the lake, so narrow and invisible is the passage it leaves on either hand. While downwards for a six-mile stretch between wooded hills of moderate height, the water gleams and glistens to its lower end. White-winged yachts are crawling listlessly on even keels, and two or three steamers plough still whiter furrows through the surrounding calm, their decks crowded with day trippers, for the excursion train takes no reck of the London season or the school vacation. Row boats with brightly clad passengers are wobbling irresponsibly to and fro, and the unsociable angler, though the mayfly is over, may be descried by the experienced eye drifting sadly along the wooded shore.

From the ferry-landing to Bowness is but a step, and once

A Street in Hawkshead.

there, the road leads us for a further two miles of gradual ascent, between hotels and lodging-houses, shops and villas to Windermere railway station, and Riggs' famous establishment, so finely perched three hundred feet above the lake. The right thing to do is to stay here, whether for a meal or for a month, and in either case to make your way up another four or five hundred feet to Orrest Head, and there enjoy one of the noblest prospects in the Lake Country. I will not bore the reader with a list of the summits that on a fine day imprint their varied forms upon the wide horizon away beyond the glittering length of Windermere. Half the mountains in the two counties may from here be seen, and much that is not mountain, but is beautiful to look upon.

It is nearly a hundred years ago since this spot caught the fancy of a young Oxford undergraduate, who, by purchasing some land here, became Wilson of Elleray, and famous to posterity as "Christopher North." Son of a prosperous Glasgow merchant, young Wilson went up to Oxford in 1803 as a gentleman commoner, richly endowed with good looks, high spirits, health, brains, and physical strength, and weighted only with a somewhat unpromising love affair. An Admirable Crichton was he, in truth, if ever there was one. The lady novelist might almost plead him as a precedent for her Double First, who, in his moments of leisure, wins the cricket match and the boat race for his University, and, a much greater feat, makes breaks of three figures on country house billiard tables.

Wilson won the Newdigate, and a most brilliant First-class in the final schools. There were no "Blues" in his day, but he used to jump the Cherwell, and walk to London in a day against time, for sporting wagers. He fought cocks with much avidity, and when his boisterous spirits attracted the notice of the Proctors, he dumbfounded them, we are told, by impassioned extracts from the Ancient and Modern classics. He had bought Elleray during a vacation, as a passing fancy, and when he left Oxford the final collapse of his love affair seems to have turned him from any definite ambitions, and towards a residence in the Lake Country. He built a house, now replaced by a later one, on his property, took up his abode there and became very much of a personage in the breezy country life of the district, as well as an intimate of the more secluded circle of thinkers and writers who had so curiously forgathered there. Rich, popular, full of life and energy, he raced yachts on Windermere; fought cocking mains, not only in public places, but in his own dining-room, which he had floored with turf for the purpose; wrestled with the local champions; danced vigorously at balls and routs, and finally married the belle of the county, who proved herself worthy of his choice. He shot and fished with equal ardour. Indeed, what angler but knows that, if he knows nothing else of Christopher North; and with all this he was the intellectual equal and valued friend of the galaxy of famous men who, each in their way, led such astonishingly different lives from his. Wordsworth, De Quincey, the Coleridges, Southey and old Bishop Watson of Calgarth. What a man he was, and what an abiding object lesson for prigs! "He made others happy," says Miss Martineau, who was then living at Ambleside, "by being so intensely happy himself, so that when he was mournful none wished to be gay."

Ten years later his fortune was swept away through the fault of a trustee. With such a brain and such energy as his, Wilson, still a young man, was at no loss for a living, though hitherto he had produced little but poetry. His loss proved, even to himself, not wholly a misfortune, and, to the world at large, perhaps a blessing in disguise. He went to Edinburgh, and, as every one knows, his brilliant articles were for long the prominent feature of *Blackwood*, and at the same time he filled the chair of Moral Philosophy at Edinburgh. In half-a-dozen years he was back at Elleray again, enjoying himself as much as ever, though in less exuberant fashion, and for the space only of his vacations. At an ever memorable regatta he figures as Admiral of the Lake, heading a gay procession of fifty boats, and doing the honours to Walter Scott, Lockhart, Canning, and other visitors. One may fairly assume that such a man, in his youth at least, was not averse to a practical joke. I have heard or read somewhere of his playing one on an entire bevy of Lakeland luminaries: the scene of which was the parlour of the little inn at Wythburn. Wordsworth, the Coleridges, De Quincey and himself were resting there one evening, previous to returning over Dunmail Raise into Grasmere. The landlord had just come in from shooting, and, after a custom not uncommon in muzzle-loading days, had deposited his unemptied gun in a corner. Wilson, taking advantage of the darkness of the room, got hold of it, unknown to the rest, and pointing the barrel up the chimney pulled the trigger, with an effect that may readily be imagined on a room twelve feet square, and full of people, glass, pewter pots and plate. When one considers, too, the amount of high-strung nerves therein collected, the point of the joke seems sharpened into positive cruelty. Wordsworth, though no lover of guns, was too equable in temperament and too physically sound, no doubt, to be seriously

Hawkshead—Misty Morning.

affected. But poor little De Quincey, after an all-night séance with his laudanum decanter, must have been a sad subject for the perpetration of such pranks, while the Coleridges could have been but little better fortified against so violent a shock. Little Hartley, so runs the tale, was buried beneath an avalanche of soot, which the outraged chimney precipitated into the room. Yet Hartley, one might perhaps hazard a guess, was the only one to laugh.

There is not much that I can say of the village of Windermere except to note its beautiful situation. It grew out of the old hamlet of Birthwaite, whose inhabitants, could they rise from their graves around the much restored old church, would certainly have some cause for wonderment. There are trains which run to Manchester in not very much over the hour, and this perhaps has greatly contributed to giving Windermere the air of the cheerful suburb of a large town. It is not merely a favourite resort in summer nowadays, but an abiding place all the year round of quite a number of people, and if they like the climate, which has both virtues and vices, one cannot wonder at their choice.

The lake shore road from Windermere to Ambleside (six miles) is one of the best and the most travelled in all this region. The traffic along it, though relieved somewhat by the lake steamers, is even at midsummer considerable, and in the holiday season prodigious. It is periodically threatened with an electric tramway, and the threat as regularly produces a perfect storm in the correspondence columns of the newspapers.

Any one unacquainted with the district might well imagine that the solitude of some romantic and little trodden byway was the object of the invading monster, instead of a somewhat congested artery very much alive indeed with the most aggressive form of wheeled traffic. A plain man might be permitted to wonder if a road over which char-a-bancs and the like have rioted in endless procession for the last two generations can suffer very calamitously from the advent of an electric coach which at any rate raises no dust. We can readily imagine there being objectors to the innovation, but the vehemence of their language, when applied to the case of this very much frequented highway, must strike any one as a trifle overdone. Even in June the cyclist riding it has not too much time to look about him, and this one would fain be doing, for every yard of the way is leafy and pleasant, and here and there are charming glimpses of the lake. The hand of man has naturally been busy here, and enviable residences set back in well timbered grounds fringe the road for some distance beyond the village. Nor are all of them by any means of recent date. Yonder, for instance, standing in large grounds near the lake shore, is a roomy house near a century old, surrounded by well-grown and choice timber. And so it should be, for here dwelt the great tree planting Bishop Watson of Llandaff, who by somewhat curious logic held his energy in that particular, to atone, and something more, for his remissness in certain other quarters.

Now I have always known Calgarth, vaguely, as an occasional passer-by knows it, but the bishop is an acquaintance, speaking historically, of later years formed in quite another part of Britain. Everybody in Wales knows Bishop Watson by repute, and yet it is a popular tradition that no Welshman of his day ever set eyes upon him. The Georgian bishops of the Principality are not remembered by the manner in which they fulfilled their duties, for they fulfilled them rarely, but by the various fashions in which they shirked them. Some lived in their diocese for the apparent purpose of absorbing to themselves and their friends and relatives a large portion of its meagre endowments. Others lived mostly in England, and the Bishop of Llandaff holds the record as the most consistent and unblushing of the long roll of absentees. Indeed, I was filled with something akin to emotion when I ran my old friend of other days and other climes to earth in a place so long familiar to my sight. He is known to fame in Wales merely as "the Bishop who lived in Westmorland," the precise details of his residence being naturally a matter of indifference to the present generation in Glamorganshire. Here, however, was his perch, and a most delightful spot his Right Reverence had chosen as the scene of his long and leisurely discontent. For strange as it may seem, he laboured under a perennial grievance, holding that as he voted steadily for the Whigs, or rather did not vote against them, for he seldom troubled himself to go up to London, a fuller share of honours was his just due. I regret to say I was till quite recently unaware that this maltreated cleric was further immortalised by two volumes of biography and correspondence edited by his family, and that his lordship is regarded as a contemporary gossip of some interest. I lost no time, however, in atoning for my shortcomings, not so much for the sake of his episcopal philanderings, but from a genuine curiosity to know how he accounted for his continuous absence of thirty years from the scene of his duties, and whether, in short, he had aught to say for himself. A perusal of these volumes will make it clear to any one that the bishop remained to the close of his life in quite delightful unconsciousness that any justification was required, unless, indeed, a preference he expresses for the climate of Windermere is worth noticing. On the contrary, his letters harp rather upon the text of how scant is the reward of virtue and fidelity to duty as illustrated in his own person. They constitute, indeed, a most interesting revelation of the point of view presumably understandable a century ago, and are well worth reading for that alone.

Dr. Watson was the son of a village schoolmaster in Westmorland. An aptitude for mathematics secured him an entry at Cambridge, where in due course he came out a high wrangler. Quite early in life he was appointed to the chair of Chemistry, though without any knowledge of that particular subject. This deficiency he easily made up for, and indeed as a scientist in early life he was a marked success. There, however, his intellectual ambition and energy ended. All his efforts in future were directed to the improvement of his fortunes and he had certainly a genius for getting everything for nothing. He secured the professorship of Divinity, for which he had small qualifications, though this fact was of little consequence, as he had no intention of burdening himself with its duties. He succeeded, however, in raising the stipend to £1,000 a year, £300 of which he paid to a substitute and enjoyed the balance for the greater part of his life, and he was now only thirty-five. His next triumph was the bishopric of Llandaff, and this achieved he went to live in

Westmorland by way of being handy to his duties in South Wales, bought Calgarth, married a county lady, and settled down to the pursuits of a country gentleman. Here he calmly awaited the further promotion which he sincerely thought he was earning by a consistent profession of Whig sentiments and a steady support of the Whig Government by his vote on those few occasions when he took his seat in the House. Unfortunately for Llandaff, that promotion never came, and the South Wales diocese was saddled with this insatiable Cambridge don for the rest of his life, which did not close till he was nearly eighty. It is commonly said he never saw it. But there is one account at least of a visit there given by himself with a most unmistakable sense of having performed a thoroughly meritorious action. The entertaining part of the business is that the bishop posed before the Glamorganshire squires who then entertained him as a neglected person whose conspicuous services were slighted by an ungrateful world, or in other words an ungrateful Ministry. The Glamorgan folks, he declares, sympathised with him—no doubt the Welshmen wished as ardently as the bishop himself for his promotion. His lordship, however, was an unconscious humorist of a high order, and this, I think, gives much of their value to his letters. His crowning jest, perhaps, was the issuing of a circular mandate to his clergy on the evils of absenteeism, and warning the truants back to their posts. There is no symptom in his own account of this affair that a single muscle of the episcopal mouth twitched as he perpetrated this enormous joke—he was beyond a doubt in dead and solemn earnest. De Quincey, who was, of course, a neighbour and knew him well, declares that though he was quite uninteresting as a man, pompous and heavy-minded, as a character he was a really interesting study from his extraordinary valuation of his own deserts, and his inability to regard his career from any other point of view but that of material advancement. Through his entire correspondence the note of wailing at ministerial neglect sounds loud. In his applications for advancement, even in letters addressed to ministers, there is never a suggestion of "enlarged sphere of action," or a call to higher work or anything of that sort. There was no humbug, at any rate, about Bishop Watson. His income, his estate, the just expectations of his family, his position in the county (not Glamorgan!) and his steady admiration for the Whig party—these were the burden of his importunities.

He had lectured for a short time on chemistry at Cambridge, and written a volume of excellent essays on science, and one or two other books. He had no social claims, for he was a village schoolmaster's son. Yet he enjoyed an income of £5000 a year all told, for most of which he gave no value whatever, and a fine position in his native county where he spent his time in sociability and tree planting. "All his public, all his professional duties," says De Quincey, "he systematically neglected. He was a lord in Parliament and for many a year he never attended in his place; he was a bishop and he scarcely knew any part of his diocese by sight, living three hundred miles away from it; he was a professor of divinity holding the richest professorship in Europe—the weightiest for its functions in England—drawing by his own admission one thousand per annum from its endowments, and for thirty years he never read a lecture or performed a public exercise!" And in spite of it all as evidence of what querulous importunity could do in those days, he actually came within an ace of being Archbishop of York! Lady Holland told Wordsworth that Charles Fox and Grenville had quite decided to offer him that exalted post, which promised to be soon vacant. But the failing occupant of the See just outlived the Administration, which was prematurely dissolved. "Yet what an Archbishop!" says De Quincey. "He talked openly at his own table as a Socinian; ridiculed the miracles of the New Testament, which he professed to explain as so many chemical tricks of legerdemain, and certainly had as little devotional feeling as any man who ever lived."

The banks of Windermere at least have much to thank the bishop for, and I should feel constrained to apologise for having given his lordship such an amount of space if he were not in his peculiar way a historical character and a notable example of what was possible of accomplishment for men of nerve in the brave days of old.

Before, however, dismissing the bishop, who seems to have been a kindly host and well liked among his neighbours, I

Windermere.

cannot forbear the relation of a local incident of which his lordship was, in effigy, at any rate, the hero. Among other property that he had bought in Ambleside was an old tavern called "The Cock." The landlord thinking that some extra distinction might attach to his inn if it were known that the bishop owned it, pulled the old signboard down and renamed the house "The Bishop." To complete the business, he had the new signboard illustrated with a rude portrait of his lordship in all the glory of shovel hat and episcopal wig. In the meantime, a new inn was started over the way which appropriated the discarded name of "The Cock," and to such purpose that it attracted no small share of its older neighbour's custom. The owner of the latter, growing seriously alarmed at the turn things were taking, hoisted up another signboard underneath the portrait of the bishop, beneath which, with more of an eye to business than to the fitness of things and a proper regard to church dignitaries, was inscribed, in luminous characters, "*This is the Old Cock.*"

But Calgarth had a history long before Bishop Watson built his new mansion there. Every one knows the legend of the skulls of Calgarth which no mortal power could banish from their niches in the wall. Wherever they might be thrown, whether into deep lake or black wood, they always, by some supernatural means, reappeared, to resume their grim watch over the fortunes of Calgarth Hall. The Phillipsons reigned in those days along the banks of Windermere, a wild, dare-devil, race, if all one hears be true. One of them in particular, an ardent and reckless cavalier in the Civil War, is well remembered and was known as " Robin the Devil." One Colonel Briggs of Kendal, when the Parliamentary party got the upper hand, was very zealous in enforcing Puritan tenets on a somewhat unwilling people. Phillipson, who was a malignant of malignants, swore he would tolerate such insolence no longer, and rode over one Sunday to Kendal at the head of a troop of horse with the intention of killing the obnoxious colonel in church. The Roundhead officer, fortunately for himself, was not there, but " Robin the Devil " swaggered about the church brandishing his naked sword and causing immense excitement and confusion. The incident is preserved in a local jingle : —

> " The door was wide and in does he ride
> In his clanking gear so gay, .
> A long keen brand he held in his hand
> Our Dickon for to slay."

The casque of this ruffling gallant is still to be seen in Kendal church, and Scott alludes to it in " Rokeby."

At Calgarth, too, we cross the Troutbeck brook on its way to the lake, from the village and the valley of that name, which is so familiar in all Lakeland annals. Hitherto we have been thrust considerably backward from the water, getting occasional glimpses of it only through screening woods; but now the road bends downwards to the shore, and at the "Lowood" hotel, dear to generations of honeymooners, a most lovely scene —with the upper reach of the lake in the foreground and all the Coniston and Scafell and Langdale mountains behind— unfolds itself. One might almost as well try to say something original of the "Star and Garter" at Richmond as of this famous haunt on Windermere: so without seeking for inspiration we will pursue the last mile of road, which, running close to the shore, lands us at the busy scene of Waterhead and in sight of Ambleside.

The Mountains at Coniston.

Windermere.

CHAPTER VIII.

Now Waterhead at the top of Windermere is a very cheerful place, for steamers and coaches here meet each other in connection with the round trips in which the vast majority of Lake tourists so industriously engage. But the animation which on a fine summer's day distinguishes the spot is not, as may be readily imagined, well attuned to Wordsworthian associations, nor to the fastidious eye in harmony with the sublime nature of the background.

So let us on to Ambleside, but a short mile away, and passing between serried ranks of lodging-houses, mount up to its still tolerably old-fashioned and characteristic market place. One might, no doubt, write a whole chapter, perhaps many chapters, on the things that have been done in Ambleside, the things that are to be seen there and near by, and the celebrities who in modern times have shed lustre upon the little town by their presence. But Ambleside does not take my fancy as a place to linger in with this intent: and I shall turn at once to the left, along the Grasmere and Keswick road, and enter the lush and somewhat airless arcadia of the Rothay valley. I know that these two miles from Ambleside to Rydal should be an object of admiration, and in a modern sense are classic ground. I confess, though not without trepidation, that to me even walking through the meadows there seems to be something of the atmosphere of a glorified people's park, gravel paths and wicket gates and notice boards are so very much in evidence. There is even a suspicion of orange peel about, and ginger beer bottles may be occasionally seen navigating the tortuous currents of the Rothay. Villas of the dark grey stone of the country and dating from every period of the nineteenth century, though well embowered in foliage, are almost too numerous. As you crawl along near the wall of the well kept but none too roomy road, heavy-laden mammoth conveyances roar by, emblazoned with the objects of their pilgrimage, which are here largely of a personal nature. How incredible the good Dr. Arnold would have thought it that the scene of his Rugby vacations would ever decorate the panels of stage coaches. But all this is inevitable and really of no consequence. There are a score of valleys in the two counties as beautiful in their foreground details as the Rothay, where there is neither orange-peel nor ginger beer. And as for the mighty fells above, Red Screes and Scardale, Fairfield and Dove Crag, they are quiet enough and silent, this time of year at any rate, while even the accessible charms of Loughrigg on the west, with its modest thousand feet of altitude, seem in no way sensible of any overdue attention.

The literary associations of the Lake Country, one need hardly say, cluster most thickly about this head of Windermere. Mrs. Hemans, Miss Martineau, Wordsworth, the Coleridges, De Quincey and Dr. Arnold were all here within a short walk of Ambleside. But what can I say in brief of these illustrious folk that is not familiar, and to enlarge further upon their lives and works is neither within the scope of my work nor to the purpose. There are books upon the English lakes having a special view to the interpretation of their beauties by Wordsworth. There are other books whose titles do not immediately suggest that purpose, but which practically amount to essays on his poetry. Then again, the patriotic local writer is apt to scatter

Wordsworth indiscriminately over his pages, and I presume it is a truism that if ever there was a great poet who required to be used with care it is the bard of Rydal. But some of his admirers appear to me to do him poor service by the random way in which they cull from his abundant store. Happily, the great man was of a self-complacent turn of mind, and according to his friends, not very keenly alive to the unevenness of his productions. Otherwise he would be oftentimes turning in his grave and vainly calling to be saved, not from his discerning friends who handle him with skill and consideration, but from a number of less judicious writers who seem to use him on the principle of a trump card at whist, and "when in doubt" to "quote Wordsworth."

I confess with trepidation to having been sometimes seized with an impious yearning after this country before it had any "literary associations"—when Grey first saw it, and West first wrote of it, and its unknown beauties first provoked the Muse of Richard Cumberland. This, however, is little short of flat treason under the very shadow of Rydal Mount, for yonder are the gables of Wordsworth's modest house of grey stone standing out amid the trees above the road. We have just passed Rydal Hall too, beautiful in its stately timber, the ancient seat of the Flemings, who are there yet. This old manor, set amid what was once a republic of shepherds, is a pleasant survival among what is now in great part a land of villa-residents.

Wordsworth lived at Rydal Mount for the last forty years of his life, and surely no man of note ever reached four-score so nearly scatheless from all everyday worries and cares. It would almost seem as if Providence took exceptional measures to procure immunity from the ordinary troubles of life for the gentle dreamer. She provided him with two women, very literally a Martha and a Mary, who worshipped him and made his happiness the object of their lives. She supplied him with sources of income ample for his simple needs, and that drew neither upon his time nor strength, though as a young man

The Mill at Ambleside

Wordsworth's prospects had in fact looked tolerably dismal, for he was unpractical enough, and had no mental wares suitable for the market. The poetic note he struck so early, and clung to so tenaciously, not only brought in little money, but for years scarcely any credit. Admiring friends, however, stepped into the breach, as they had a way of doing for poets in those days. The family money too, which had been alienated, was restored and he got his share. Then came the office of stamp distributer, worth several hundreds a year, the duties of which were performed by a clerk, and this made him well off for life. It was so late in the day when his poems became sufficiently appreciated to sensibly increase his income as to be scarcely worth mentioning; but the point is, that his means were ample for his simple tastes without the necessity for seriously connecting his art and his purse.

And yet at thirty-nine Wordsworth looked sixty! He was travelling in a public conveyance, says his friend and near neighbour De Quincey, and conversing with an elderly gentleman on the opposite seat, when the latter, alluding to some possible event in the not very distant future, remarked to Wordsworth that at any rate they two were not likely to witness it. The poet bridled somewhat at this, and asked the stranger how old he took him to be. The latter after careful scrutiny, gave it as his opinion that Wordsworth would never see three-score again, and appealed to the other occupants of the coach, who all of them practically agreed in this surprisingly erroneous estimate. Doubtless when the poet was sixty he looked no more! He seems to have had a somewhat ill-knit, awkward, unathletic frame, with rather stooping shoulders, which was strange for a man who spent his life walking in the open air. His complexion, which had been olive, turned ruddy and weatherbeaten with advancing years. A near relative of the writer's, who as a young man met the poet at Foxhow in his seventieth year, recalls very vividly the first impression made by his appearance in the room as that of a farmer.

But what a curious life was Wordsworth's. Surely unique in his passion for rural life, coupled with such complete indifference to the occupations and amusements that one regards as almost inseparable from it, and that the greatest minds with rural tastes have in some form or other always felt the spell of. Wordsworth, though he lived his whole life among a population who shot and fished and ran foxhounds with much ardour, cared not a jot for any of these things. This fact alone is, perhaps, not worthy of remark; but what does, I think, seem remarkable is that in all his poems these luminous phases of country life are studiously ignored. If the poet had been a Southey, a Coleridge, or a De Quincey in his personal habits; if he had hugged his fire and his books and, like most poets and literary men of that period, at any rate, taken his constitutional walk as a matter chiefly of relaxation or of health, the silence on such topics would be conceivable. But we have De Quincey's testimony that books were a secondary matter with Wordsworth. He had not a great many, and was careless of those he had. Reading for him was a matter rather for wet days and evenings. Nature was his book. He was out of doors, broadly speaking, the whole of every fine day. Every rural sight and sound—the crowing of a cock, the bleating of a lamb, the scratching of a mouse—has, we all know, been dwelt upon by the poet with a minuteness that is the joy of his detractors. But if I remember rightly, the note of hound and horn so familiar then as now up on the fells finds no mentions in his descriptive poems. One would have supposed too that even a poet who walked over sheep pastures and sang of them all his life would have been drawn into a little amateur farming or sheep-breeding—that he would have shared in some form or other the pursuits of his neighbours, one would have thought inevitable in the course of so long a life spent wholly in their midst. Nor was it his lot either to minister to them, or doctor them, or to buy and sell with them, or deal out justice, nor was he greatly given to chaffering or joking or gossiping with them or getting at their hearts and humours after the fashion of men who have a turn that way. Wordsworth dreamed past them mostly, I take it, or looked upon them through coloured spectacles. The peasants of his creation would certainly arouse the suspicions of a country-bred man who had never been north of the Trent, and he would not, I think, require the aid of Craig Gibson's banter to confirm them when he got to Westmorland. Wordsworth's fame, however, does not rest upon such lines as these. It was from nature pure and simple that he drew the inspirations by which he earned it. And if the Lakeland peasant was a somewhat glorified personage as seen through the Wordsworthian spectacles, it is amusing to get glimpses now and then of what his humble neighbours in their turn thought of the poet. His well-known habit of spouting his poetry as he walked, with a view to polishing and elaborating it, was a most natural cause of wonderment. "Well, John, what's the news?" said the over-sociable Hartley Coleridge one morning to an old stone-breaker by Rydal Lake. "Why nowte varry particlar, only āld Wūdsworth's brocken lowce ageean." "These mutterings and mouthings of the poet," says a contemporary, "were taken by the poor people as an indication of mental aberration." On another occasion a stranger, resting at a cottage at Rydal, inquired of the housewife whether Wordsworth made himself neighbourly among them. "Well," said she, "he sometimes goes booin' his pottery about t' rooads an' t' fields an' taks na nooatish o' neàbody; but at udder times he'll say good morning, Dolly, as sensible as oyder you or me!"

De Quincey who had, of course, exceptional opportunities for observing Wordsworth's character, dwells with great emphasis on the poet's "extreme, intense, unparalleled one-sidedness." Of his range of reading, for example, he says, "Thousands of books that have given rapturous delight to millions of ingenious minds, for Wordsworth were absolutely a dead letter—closed and sealed up from his sensibilities and his powers of appreciation, not less than colours from a blind man's eye." The egotism and self-complacency which in a higher form was so invaluable to Wordsworth during the years of neglect which his work suffered at the hands of the public, took on at times an irritating turn in the small affairs of life. To quote De Quincey again, who was an enthusiastic admirer of his friend as a poet, he had traits which seemed almost to forbid complete and perfect friendship. Southey, as we know, till late in life, liked his poems much better than their author. One grievance under which Wordsworth's friends smarted is not without humour, yet surely should procure them our unbounded sympathy; for it seems that the great man would tolerate no opinion favourable or otherwise of a landscape in his presence except from members of his immediate household, who, by some mysterious process, were supposed to have assimilated his magic power of vision. He treated all such expressions, De Quincey tells us, with pointed and contemptuous silence, sometimes going even so far as to turn his back on the speaker as if to emphasise his presumption. One can very well understand that to the author of the *Ancient Mariner*, and to the greatest stylist of his day, both of whom, though essentially book men, found for years their whole relaxation in Lakeland scenery, such an attitude on the part of a friend whom they held in high regard must have been extremely galling. This same one-sidedness prevented Wordsworth, no doubt, from doing even in a small degree for north-west England what Scott did for his native country. It would be unreasonable to expect so peculiar a genius as his to have travelled out of its groove except for the fact that his personal connection with his own region was so long and so unbroken, his opportunities so very great. One may be permitted, I think, some disappointment that Wordsworth seems to have been almost indifferent to the moving pageants of history, the passions, the humours and the pathos of olden days. It is nothing that he wrote a few unremarkable poems on such subjects, or published a guide-book which deals chiefly with landscape detail and breaks ultimately into

Rydal Church.

verse. Nor will the few notes he has left on manners and customs seem of much moment when compared with the ampler evidence of local antiquaries and historians. How much is Wordsworth read nowadays? if such a question in such a spot is permissible. How many of the younger generation have worked conscientiously through the *Excursion*? It might be said that this would be something of a test for the middle aged and elderly who were nurtured when the popularity of Wordsworth was in its zenith. It is not in the least strange that wherever in the Lake Country you find a native man or woman of literary tastes you find an enthusiastic disciple of the Rydal bard, but their pious belief that such devotion is common to all Anglo-Saxondom is more noteworthy. It is almost pathetic, and arises perhaps from being in such constant view of the streams of curious tourists who gape at Rydal mount and pay their sixpence to look inside Dove Cottage. The Americans, moreover, are held in Lakeland to be staunch disciples. It may be so! I have never myself gathered that impression in America, but that is nothing. I should fear, however, that it is only the greater industry exhibited by our cousins in " seeing the whole show " when on their travels. The majority of these enthusiasts, I venture to think, like most of their English fellow-travellers, know just so much of Wordsworth as is quoted in the guide-books, have never read a page of the *Excursion* or even heard of *The Intimations*. The precise measure of Wordsworth's present popularity would, in truth, be no easy estimate. Happily, it is no business of ours to form one.

From Wordsworth's house we are carried along the margin of Rydal Lake with its feathery islands and its quiet surface, for no boats may ply on it. We pass Nab Cottage, where poor Hartley Coleridge lived for so long, and at the head of the little lake rise up above the wooded dell through which the Rothay comes hurrying on its short journey from Grasmere Lake. Looking back from here, there is a charming view over

Rydal, but it is not for the purpose of descanting upon this that I would linger for a moment, but because the spot recalls a wonderful spectacle I once witnessed from it, no less indeed than that of a very well-developed specimen of a " Helm wind."

All regions have their special peculiarities, but I know of no other in England that creates hurricanes purely for local consumption. The phenomenon gets its name of Helm from the cloud that is supposed to hang as a cap or covering above the scene of its wrath. It had its hat off when I saw it and that perhaps accelerated its mad rage. These Helm winds usually occur in late spring, and it was the middle of May when I dropped in for mine. They come from the eastward and the first stage of their manufacture takes place upon the Durham and Northumbrian moors. For the warm winds blowing from the German Ocean across the eastern lowlands of these counties grow warmer, till mounting suddenly on to the moorlands they whistle over some thirty miles of an almost unbroken waste of spongy, boggy upland cooling rapidly, so the scientists tell us, in the process. That passed, they have arrived at the western ramparts of the Pennine ridge and from the summit of Crossfell, which the rustic will tell you is the parent of the Helm wind, are looking down over the valley of the Eden. Here the warm breezes of the west are suddenly encountered and the conflicting temperatures create a rare confusion. Out of the hurly-burly as its product a ready made Helm wind rushes down upon the western slopes of the Eden Valley, bounds up skywards from the impact, and then with a shriek of rage and redoubled force plunges into the valleys of Lakeland. And during all this time the rest of the kingdom may be wrapped in a profound calm!

As I was saying, it was in this case a bright May day which from the morning onward grew windier and colder but no darker. In the afternoon a hurricane was blowing. I had to journey from Grasmere to Ambleside and took a cycle with a view to using it when before the wind. This last was lateral in the open valley, but having been twice blown against a stone wall, I took a hint from the other folks I met in like plight and walked tamely beside my "Swift," hoping for better times and marvelling at the fury of the storm at such a season and beneath so blue a sky. At this entry here into Rydal, where the Lake opens out to the road, the gale struck me in the face and with such fury that all thought of further struggles with it

Rydal.

was abandoned. I was glad enough, indeed, to crouch under the lea of a wall and look over the top of it at the really wonderful sight that there met my eyes. For it is not too much to say that at times the whole surface of Rydal Lake was entirely hidden beneath clouds of driving spray. The agitation of the actual surface was of course great, but that was quite a secondary matter; for it seemed as if the gale in its violent and spasmodic rushes scooped up tons of water into the air and then dashed them with headlong force in glittering and scintillating clouds across the lake from shore to shore.

The brightness of the sky, the brilliancy of the sunshine, the blueness of the lake, immensely heightened the effect. Sometimes the whirling masses of water were flung in showers back to their element, like the play of some vast fountain, flashing rainbow colours in the sunshine as they fell; at other times, these great spray clouds were driven high over the banks and scattered far and wide amid the woods behind.

An old man was breaking stones under lea of the same wall that sheltered me, and to him I naturally made some comment on the belated nature of so fierce a storm, for it was as cold as March.

"I racken it's a Helm wind," said the veteran.

Not knowing at the time what kind of a breeze that might be, I thought that the old gentleman was merely expressing himself with undue emphasis upon the ferocity of this one. My landlord, however, when I returned to Grasmere, put the matter beyond all doubt, and introduced me formally to the Helm wind as an institution. That it comes from Crossfell is a popular truism. The theories regarding its manufacture there, which I noted on the preceding page, are those advanced by meteorologists. I may add, in connection with this particular Helm wind, that when the papers came to hand the next day they told of steady and heavy rain in every part of England except this north-west corner.

On emerging from the short wooded gorge that connects the two lakes, the vale of Grasmere opens out all its beauty. The little lake with its single grassy isle fringes the road and its waters lap against the stony strand beneath a screen of oaks and alders. On the further shore, but a few hundred yards away are the wooded slopes of Red bank, from which vantage point may be enjoyed one of the most exquisite and justly celebrated views in Lakeland. You can breathe in Grasmere, there is plenty of light and fresh air. Though surrounded by hills, they stand well back, and boldly show themselves from their woody feet to their craggy summits. Snugly set between lake and meadows is the village itself, and the old grey church tower, with the upstanding mass of Helm crag that splits the head of the valley, rising finely up a thousand feet behind it. The southerly supporters of Helvellyn are all about us on the right: on the left, are woods and steeps and crags, that lead away and upward to the Langdale Pikes and the Scafell wilderness. As a centre for walking, there is probably none better than Grasmere, as a mere glance at the map will show. The hotels are good, the charming gardens of the Rothay and the outlook from them would give attraction to a much less comfortable house, while those who like the sound of wavelets beating on the shore beneath their windows, will find the "Prince of Wales'" much suited to their taste upon a windy day. But though there is plenty of accommodation at Grasmere, one cannot in truth say the charm of the spot is seriously impaired. There are, to be sure, more villas (to use a comprehensive term) of recent date than there are memorials of the original inhabitants. They are mostly fashioned, however, of the slate-coloured stone of the country. And though I have myself no great fancy for this at close quarters, or for the prevailing method of construction, much preferring the red free stone and more massive mortared masonry across the mountains, it must be admitted that the typical house of the country has the merit of unobtrusiveness to a very high degree. The Lake poets and their friends were accustomed to say, sixty years ago and more, that Grasmere was spoiled, but the term after all is relative. The situation is not only beautiful, but has much character in its air of snugness and aloofness from the outer world, though this, of course, has small significance as applied to the present, since a fine coach road runs right through it. But in the past this isolation must have been very real indeed, and Grasmere as it was in the eighteenth century is a picture I should extremely like, by the aid of some magician's wand, to have a peep at.

Mr. Wilson, whose painstaking excursions into the past of his native country have afforded me both instruction and entertainment, tells us that in the Stuart period there were thirty-nine statesmen in Grasmere holding direct from the Crown, and that by the beginning of the eighteenth century the number had dropped to twenty-six. At the present day there is, I think, only one, and with that cheery survivor I have had many pleasant "cracks." I have already expressed an impious yearning for some good picture of this country before it had any literary associations; for even the local antiquary is apt to break off at his most instructive moments, and quote Words-

Grasmere looking towards Dunmail Raise.

worth in a fashion vexatiously irrelevant to his subject. Gray, to be sure, passed through Grasmere in its virgin state, "not a single red tile," he says, "no gentleman's flaring house or garden breaks in upon the repose of this little unsuspected paradise; but all is peace, rusticity, and happy poverty in its neatest and most becoming attire." But Gray merely cast an academic glance and passed on.

Wheels had never entered Grasmere at that time. A packhorse track over the top of White Moss was the only outlet to Ambleside, and over this the bells that now hang in the tower of the village church were dragged on a sledge; one is reminded, too, that the statesmen, who had mostly large families, could hardly have supported them on their small holdings without the surplus produce of the spinning-wheel and the hand-loom, selling, in fact, a good deal of homespun cloth, and being, as it were, manufacturers as well as farmers. In the same way, the north Welsh farmers of former days sold vast quantities of woollen stockings—the men, like the rest, knitting in their spare moments, just as the northern statesmen spun or wove in the intervals of out-door work. "When the great plague," says Mr. Wilson, "raged in Keswick and all intercourse was suspended, the Grasmere statesmen carried their cloth to Armboth Fell on the further banks of Thirlemere and laid it out on a large stone, where the traders met them and transacted their business. The rock in question is to this day known as the "Webb stone." The introduction of machinery and rise of the manufacturing towns seems indeed to have been one of the many causes of the decay of the statesmen class, as it left them without profitable employment for their leisure hours.

Everything too in the shape of food or clothing was produced at home. As to the first, the statesman lived abundantly. Oat-meal cakes, porridge, cheese and milk, were the accessories rather than the main support, as in Scotland, for meat was generously used, sheep for home consumption being freely killed in the autumn, and hung to cure in the enormous chimneys that were then in vogue. We are shown the women in their linsey woolsey petticoats, long-tailed bedgowns, blue linen aprons, great scuttle bonnets and wooden clogs, and have it on good authority that the first statesman's daughter who appeared in the dale in a printed calico dress created an immense sensation. The men too, of course, wore homespun, usually undyed, in which black and white fleeces were mixed. They had big brass buttons on their coats and on Sundays and high days were resplendent with bows of ribbon at the knees of their breeches and silver buckled shoes instead of clogs upon their feet. Houses were then built leisurely and in massive fashion, being intended to last. Only heart oak was used, and in lieu of nails wooden pegs held beams and sashes and doors together. Lime was dispensed with as hard to procure, and an amusing story is told of the first consignment of it that went into Borrowdale; the bearer carrying it across his saddle bow in a bag. A thunderstorm coming on, however, the lime began to fizzle. Upon this the astonished rustic dismounted and poured water over it, the effect of which so alarmed him that he thought the devil was in the sack and throwing it into the beck, rode for home as fast as his horse could carry him. The stipends of the clergy too, who served these dale churches, or chapels, as they were called in olden days, look quite incredible on paper, averaging about five pounds a year. It has to be remembered, however, that most of these men were peasants bred, that they got their "Whittlegate" or board free from the statesmen of their parish, and furthermore, as we have already seen, followed some trade, such as that of cobbler, or waller, to say nothing of school teaching when they were capable of it.

The schedule of a farm sale in Grasmere, in the year 1706, lies before me, and I think the phraseology of the catalogue would sufficiently astonish a modern auctioneer, while some of the prices are significant of the change in markets and in the value of money. Dubblers, Daw tubs, Throwen chairs, fflawing spades, Gimlocks, Tarr kitts, Gramaces, Gavelocks, Sihreenges, Wimbles, Backshaves, and ffishing pitches are a few of the articles from the list. And from the same source one learns that the approximate value of a cow in Grasmere at that time was about £3, a heifer £2, lambs about half-a-crown apiece and fat wethers six shillings ! It is somewhat surprising too to find the French participle still in local use, above all at such functions. For among the purchasers of these mysterious articles we find Braythwayte de Wrey, Newton de Gillfort, John Jackson de Wythburn, a little comic, perhaps, this last !—and so forth. There is one quite sonorous entry on the account, "Christopher Cowpthwayte one ffat cow," and it has some further interest as a Cowpthwayte (Copperthwaite) is still very much a power in Grasmere, being no less than the proprietor of the two chief hotels.

Grasmere church, though of no architectural merit, everyone, of course goes to see, if only for the Wordsworth graves, which could not be exceeded for their charm of situation amid leaves and running water and over-hanging mountains. Near the

Grasmere Church.

church, too, is the field where the chief athletic meeting of the Lake Country is held every August. From what I have already said of these characteristic gatherings, it will been seen that the Grasmere meeting, though very fashionable, is quite a genuine affair and a true expression of the Cumbrian sporting character, not a survival of half-moribund pastimes for the benefit of strangers or quasi-residents or gate money, as is sometimes supposed.

Dove Cottage is an object of perennial interest to visitors

at Grasmere, and no wonder! For surely no modest cottage ever sheltered two such occupants in succession, the greatest poet and the greatest prose writer of their day. Wordsworth was here for six years, De Quincey for twenty. Son of a well-to-do Lancashire merchant whose widow had a comfortable home at Chester, De Quincey opened his eccentric career by running away from Manchester Grammar School, rather from a feeling of boredom, it would seem, than for the usual conventional reasons. On a guinea a week he wandered about North

Dove Cottage.

Wales indulging his imagination in that romantic country, and fraternising with all manner of queer folk. Shunning his home for no very serious reasons, he then threw himself more or less penniless upon London, concealed his whereabouts from motives of boyish pride from his mother and guardian uncle, and experienced the lot of a homelesss and almost starving outcast in its dreary wilderness. But who that has read *The Experiences of an Opium Eater*,—and who indeed has not?—can forget his account of those extraordinary months and the strange companions of his self-imposed misery? Discovered and rescued by his friends, he was sent up to Oxford in 1803. Careless of the honours or emoluments to be gained there by the orthodox course of study, he plunged deeply into philosophy and English literature, and left Oxford after four years with a vast store of learning, but no further forward in his equipment for practical life, and no scheme for earning the necessary livelihood. De Quincey then ran across Coleridge, by that time sunk into a morbid, irresponsible wanderer, consuming a tumblerful of laudanum a day, but still possessed of that magic power of conversation which took every one captive.

The presence of Coleridge's family at Keswick with Southey was the means of turning the young De Quincey lakewards, and eventually cementing a friendship between himself and the Wordsworths, and keeping him in the Lake Country as a permanent resident. The increasing family and improving circumstances of the Wordsworths had just caused them to vacate Dove Cottage for Allan Bank prior to the later move to Rydal. De Quincey now, in 1809, took their late humble abode and there led for the next twenty years his extraordinary life.

Small, thin, and nervous, a martyr to chronic pains, induced possibly by the superfluous hardships he had undergone, and possessed of phenomenal brain-power, the young philosopher had a poor start in life from a physical standpoint. He was now twenty-four, and already on the high road to that opium slavery he has so lucidly described. He had begun the habit as an undergraduate as a remedy for internal pains, and before he had been three years at Grasmere was drinking the insidious liquor to the measure of five or six wine-glasses a night—a deadly dose in itself to the unseasoned. The decanter of laudanum behind De Quincey's tea-pot is a sufficiently familiar picture wherever English is read, and he drank it, in his own words, "as other men drink Madeira." When it was not laudanum it was tea, and yet this frail little creature with the big head and bigger intellect lived to be seventy-four. Harassed always by money cares and more often than not in the clutches of the fiend that gave him such gorgeous hours at the expense of such fearful awakenings, De Quincey's life at Dove Cottage, outwardly so humdrum, must have been a tempestuous one enough mentally.

Admirable in every other relation of life, and second only to Coleridge in conversation, De Quincey had no lack of friends, and the quality of those who were then his neighbours needs no further telling. At thirty he found a most excellent woman to marry him, the daughter of a yeoman, Simpson of Nab Cottage. Even with her aid, however, his struggles with the laudanum decanter were only intermittently successful, and an increasing family brought increasing cares; for under such conditions of health and isolated residence his earnings were in no way commensurate with his commanding talent. In 1830, necessity compelled him to leave Grasmere for some more central sphere of work, and the whole family removed to Edinburgh, where, incredible as it seems, this tortured, worried weakling lived for nearly thirty years more, fighting his old enemy on and off till nearly the end and just contriving to keep the wolf at a reasonable distance from the door. De Quincey, however, was fortunate in his family, and the last period of his otherwise melancholy life was passed in tranquillity at Lasswade.

For the traveller on wheels there is but one outlet from Grasmere, namely, by the well-known coach road which leads over Dunmail Raise to Keswick. The second of the two horns into which the Helm crag ridge splits the valley is Easedale, and this, though much dwelt in and much walked in, is a cul de sac for all but the pedestrian.

Of the six mountain passes in Lakeland available for wheels, Hardknott, Honister, Kirkstone, Newlands, Whinlatter, and Dunmail, the last is by very far the least, being just 800 feet, above the sea. It is more of a thoroughfare too than the others, forming the main artery of travel between the northern and the southern, the Keswick and the Windermere, sections of the Lake Country. It is three miles to the summit of the pass and one of these at any rate it would be prudent to walk. Nor indeed is there much hardship in this; but only the better chance for looking back down the narrow valley to where Grasmere, all aglow with the bright colouring of its meadows and foliage and its glittering lake, lies in the bosom of the hills. And in the meantime the Rothay plunges down the hollow on our left, dwindling in importance as woods and meadows are left behind, till it plashes, a mere moorland beck, by the side of our highway, now for a brief space on open moorland road.

It is wonderfully quiet and impressive up here in the intervals of passing traffic. We have brushed the feet of Fairfield, and Seat Sandal in our zigzag upward course, and taken note of the track which clambers up between them and finally descends upon the further side to Ullswater. Upon our left is the battlemented summit of Helm Crag, the rugged sheep pastures of Gibson's Knott, and the loftier crown of Steel Fell, which with Seat Sandal opposite forms, in fact, the gateway of the pass. The county line too is traced here by a wall, and near the road side is a great flat cairn, which is supposed to commemorate a fierce and decisive battle fought in the tenth century.

Tradition says it was here that Dunmail, the last king of Cumberland, was defeated and slain, and those who care for such things may like to be reminded that in 924 the Kings of the Scots, the Northumbrian and Strathclyde Britons, had submitted to the Overlordship of Edward, the West Saxon. Twenty years later, however, they became insubordinate, and the Saxon King Edmund took an army into the country and on this spot defeated the men of lower Strathclyde (roughly Cumberland), killing, as I have said, their prince. Edmund then handed the country over to Malcolm King of the Scots, on condition that he should be his "fellow worker by land and sea," or in other words his ally in resisting those invading Norsemen who had been so long the curse, as it seemed then, of both. This fight on Dunmail Raise, made Cumberland for over a century, till the time, in fact, of William Rufus, a dependency of the Scottish Crown. There is a strong impression too that it was a leading factor in the despair which drove the Celtic population of Strathclyde to that second emigration into North Wales, though the Welsh chronicle places the incident somewhat earlier. It was during this period, at any rate, that the Norse influence acquired such distinct predominance over the Celtic and made Cumbria in the main a Norseman's country.

One shrinks in a work like this from the very edge of so vast a subject. But one's thoughts, mine at any rate, seem somehow to roll backward more readily in such a land as this than amid the low stubbles and turnips and sandhills of Danish East Anglia. The old world seems nearer as you look on this side up the long slopes of Helvellyn, and upon that over an ocean of rugged upland on which a thousand years have scarce placed a mark. Some stunted oak woods may have vanished from hill sides as in Wales. Cloudbursts, or riotous becks, may have cut a rent in steep slopes here, or there again old scars have doubtless healed and redraped themselves in crisp turf beneath the sheep's light tread. But the sheep and the turf and the crags were all much as now and the becks played the same music when the din of battle sounded here on the Raise and the Cymric remnant went down for good, and Cumbria became Scottish land. How few of us too remember that the very men who were then swarming into Cumberland were at the same time clustering quite thickly upon the virgin coasts of Iceland, a land one is apt in careless fashion to think of as outside the habitable globe, and wrapped in six months of night and almost eternal snow. Yet what a mine there must be among the seventy thousand folks who inhabit Iceland for the delver in old stocks, both of language and of race! Just think of a work compiled about the same time as our English Domesday Book, and which **may now be** read, giving precise particulars of the 4588

Norwegian heads of families who settled in Iceland from the year 874 onwards, the places they settled in, and yet more than this concerning many of them. There is a list, too, in this wonderful "Landama Bók," of all the speakers of Parliament beginning with the first. Mr. Elwood, who again comes to our help with Mr. Eric Magnusson, the Cambridge Icelandic scholar, tells us among a host of interesting things that many of these Icelandic pioneers were not merely the friends and relatives of those that steered their long ships southwards, but in many cases had themselves beyond a doubt tried their luck on the more temperate but less hospitable shores of Britain. It may seem strange enough to us nowadays that an emigrant should hesitate between the banks of the Solway and the coast of Iceland, but when it is remembered that the first had to be won and held by the sword while the latter was a virgin country, such hesitation will seem less singular.

The exile of some of these adventurers seems to have been induced by political reasons. For at the close of the ninth century, the Landama Bók tells of the sailing for Iceland of "Thorolf son of Ornolf who dwelt in Most-isle, was called Mostbeard and was a great man of blood offerings and believed in Thor." "He emigrated to Iceland on account of the tyranny of Harold the Fairhaired, and sailed by the southern part of the land, but when he was come west, off Broadfirth, he threw overboard the high seat posts, whereon Thor was carved. And he prayed, therefore, that Thor should come to land where the God wished him to settle, and he promised that he would dedicate all the land of his settlement to Thor and name it after him. He took land on the south side near the middle of the firth. There he found Thõr cast ashore upon a point of land which is now called Thorsness on that account."

Here is another settler :—

"That summer when Ingolf and his companions went to settle in Iceland, Harold the Fairheaded had been King of Norway for twelve years. At that time had passed from the beginning of the world 6,073 winters, and from the Incarnation of our Lord 874 years. They sailed together until they sighted Iceland, then they separated. When Ingolf saw Iceland he threw overboard his high seat posts for good luck and took a solemn oath that he would there build, where the high seat posts should come to shore. He passed the third winter at the foot of Ingolfsfell on the west of Olfuswater. This year his men found the high seat posts near the Ern-Knoll beneath the heath. Ingolf went in that spring down across the heath and he took up his abode where his seat posts had come to land. He dwelt at Reykjarvik and his high seat posts are still in the eldhouse."

These high seat posts upon which the Norsemen so strangely staked the future of their race were the pillars of the great chair upon which the head of the family sat, and were invested with special dignity and fashioned after the figure of the god Thor. It is not likely that this custom of casting Thor overboard was greatly followed by the Norsemen when descending on British shores ! The Pict the Briton and the Saxon already in possession would have had much more to do with the shaping of the invader's course than any piece of drift wood, however sacred. What gives Iceland a greater interest to the Cumbrian folk-lorist than other Scandinavian countries is the unchanged character of its language and place-names. Many hold that the so-called Druid circles are but duplicates of the Norse "Doom rings" or judgment rings, within which the Scandinavian law courts were held; but this is contentious ground indeed !

We descend the hill beyond the watershed cautiously, for the road is steep and tortuous and the stone walls on either side of it are not inviting to try conclusions with. Fairfield and Seat Sandal are left behind and Dollywaggon now towers over our right shoulder with the broad flank of Helvellyn, an uninspiring looking mountain from this western side, drawing close upon us. What havoc somebody has played with these old Norse and Celtic names, and what bathos they have sometimes been reduced to! Our English mountains of a truth make a poor show in this particular by the side of those of Donegal, Carnarvon, or Inverness, Causey, Robinson, Fairfield and Dollywaggon, to go no further! What a quartette of names for four fine mountains. They might all be in Bedfordshire, and yet they started well too, no doubt. Fairfield is, I think, conceded to be a corruption of Far-fell, Far being the Norse for sheep.

Thirlmere.

Dollywaggon, I have no doubt, has received due attention from the etymologists. At any rate, it begins with a good Celtic monosyllable—but what a continuation! It is held too, I think, by some that Skiddaw, which sounds Norse-like, is in fact Celtic and a corruption of Cadair, the Welsh for Seat, and furthermore that Saddle-back—the commonplace appellative with which Blencathara has been outraged—is a lapse from Cadair bach; extremely plausible if Blencathara, so obviously an original Celtic word, did not stand in the way of the theory!

It is only a few minutes since we lost sight of Grasmere twinkling to the southward, and now to the north and beneath us the blue waters of Thirlmere lie deep sunk and narrow, in the hollow of mighty hills. The Armboth Fells, a fine patchwork of green and grey and wildly rugged of aspect, rise finely from the western shore of the narrow lake, and from up here we may clearly mark how lonely an upland it is that stretches away to Borrowdale and the heights over-looking Derwentwater. Every one dallies more or less at Wythburn at the foot of the pass and a mile short of the lake; for the "Nag's Head" is a famous little inn and was notable as a trysting place long before Christopher North fired the gun up the parlour chimney and so shook the nerves of his brother poets. It is whitewashed outside and homely within, as an old wayside tavern should be. If you are not thirsty, you loiter on the threshold for a bit and pass the time of day with mine host or the ostlers hanging about with buckets in expectation of the Keswick or Ambleside coach, or you sit in the sun on the wall of the churchyard across the road and smoke a pipe and if you have never done so before take a peep inside the little church which, though much restored, is still a characteristic specimen of the diminutive buildings which served the dalesmen in former days and indeed often do so still. In olden times there was a rival inn at Wythburn called the "Cherry Tree," whose venerable hostess used to boast that she had seen sixteen landlords in and out of the other establishment, which at this day enjoys so complete a monopoly. Now there is bound up with my edition of *West* several sheets of *A Fortnight in the Lake Country*, of date 1792, by one Budworth. That gentleman (they got up earlier in those days, when Prime Ministers held interviews between six and eight) came down to the "Cherry Tree" for breakfast, having ascended Helvellyn from Grasmere, and paid sevenpence, he tells us, for all the luxuries of the country! Perhaps, however, his dinner at the "Red Lion" at Grasmere is still more tantalising in the matter of charge. Fish, fowl, veal cutlets, and ham, peas, potatoes, gooseberries and rich cream, with various etceteras, all for tenpence! Wythburn, I may further remark, is one of the bases from which to attack Helvellyn, though I fancy more people come there after than before the performance of this not very remarkable exploit.

Every one knows that Thirlmere is now the property of the city of Manchester and constitutes its water supply; but it must not be supposed it has suffered on this account to any extent

Helvellyn from Thirlmere.

worth mentioning from the somewhat grimy-sounding connection. It has been dammed at its narrow outlet, and fills the gorge in which it lies more fully than of yore, but this perhaps is an improvement. Its new owners, too, have made a good road along its further or western shore, in the place of the old pack-horse track, an innovation which no one will quarrel with. Thirlmere is the most river like of lakes, being scarce anywhere more than a quarter of a mile in width though over three in length. The Keswick road for more than half this distance skirts the eastern shore, and lifted well above it so that, travelling one's self along the foot-hills of Helvellyn, one can enjoy the striking fashion in which the Armboth Fells, with all their rugged grandeur, their gorgeous colouring and their silvery cascades, dip down into the deep water.

Everything to-day is fair. But one can well fancy that Thirlmere, when the wind is north and the skies are black and snow lies on the fell, can look stern enough, and worthy of the spectral horrors with which superstition has peopled its shores. As our road mounts a steep hill, preparatory to leaving the lake, the old manor of Dalehead lies below upon the water-side. It belonged to the Leathes family from the days of Elizabeth till Manchester bought them out, and indeed Thirlmere used to be known at one time as Leatheswater. The Dalehead ghost does not haunt the mansion but the high road above, and represents the restless spirit of an erstwhile denizen of the place, who, returning home one night with a tempting sum of money in his pocket, was robbed and murdered, his naked body being afterwards found in the lake, with a deep gash on the forehead. An ill-conditioned neighbour was suspected, but no proof forthcoming, there could be no punishment save such as the conscience of the guilty man meted out to him and the black looks and cold shoulders of his neighbours. These in the end proved of themselves too powerful for the wretched culprit, and flying his fellow men he resorted to a cave in the hills, which still bears his ill-omened name, and there, let us hope, repented him of his sordid crime.

Armboth Hall is another ancient abiding place, and lies just across the narrow lake from Dalehead, nestling in charming and secluded fashion amid woods and strips of meadow beneath the fell foot and by the water side. Jacksons seem to have lived here alongside of the Leathes and for the same three centuries. But what these respectable statesmen can have been about to invest their old manor house with such a grizzly reputation in former days, history does not say. There is something about a midnight marriage and a murdered bride, I gather from the local historians. But not so very long ago I am assured that the few people who were abroad here in winter nights used to see sights and hear weird noises when the lonely house was known to be unoccupied; lights flaring in every window, and the sound of wassail and revelry sounding loud across the cold waters of the lake. Among other gruesome guests at these entertainments the Calgarth skulls are supposed to have put in an appearance, being back in their niche no doubt before morning, when Bishop Watson came down to breakfast. I should imagine that the very idea of the Mayor and Corporation of Manchester would be enough to lay any self-respecting ghosts (meaning nothing personal, of course), and since Armboth Hall came to such practical ownership all has, I believe, been quiet. Before Thirlmere was enlarged it was so narrow and shallow at this point that a bridge crossed it of unique and curious structure. My own recollection of it is shadowy, but it was suspected of being, like one in Wales, of Celtic origin and there was much just lamentation when the raising of the waters destroyed so ancient and curious a landmark.

The lower part of Thirlmere can be best seen from the further shore, for at Dalehead, as I have mentioned, the coach road swings away to the right and downwards towards the Vale of St. John. In a very few minutes, however, an old fashioned inn, the "King's Head" at Thirlspot, with every claim that Wythburn has, invites inspection. No properly educated local horse would pass this genial spot. The cyclist may do so if he likes.

Early in the century a noted character and humorist reigned here, one John Stanley. And a composition of his own used to hang under the old sign which is still kept in the house:—

> "I, Stanley, lives here and sells good ale
> Come in and drink before it grows stale.
> John succeeded his father Peter,
> But i' th' old man's time 'twas never better."

The foxhounds come much into this Legberthwaite country, and many generations of the Blencathara pack, after a run over the rough Armboth Fells or the smooth slopes of Helvellyn, have made free with the bar parlour or shambled through the old passages or basked on the door-step in the free and easy fashion of Cumbrian hounds. It is six miles to Keswick by the coach road, while another follows the infant Greta to the right down the beautiful vale of St. John, the scene of "The Bridal of Triermain," and comes out near Threlkeld. After crossing the Greta, there is much laborious collar work upon our route without any special reward till it emerges upon the steep hilltop overlooking the town, when Derwentwater, Bassenthwaite, the Vale of Keswick, Skiddaw, and the whole galaxy of mountains whose acquaintance we made when here before, burst with a grandeur indescribable upon the ravished sight.

On Thirlmere.

Hesket Newmarket, near Caldbeck.

CHAPTER IX.

"D'ye ken John Peel with his coat so gray
Who hunted in Caldbeck once on a day?"

YES, indeed! Who does not ken John Peel wherever English is sung or spoken? He is as well known as Wordsworth himself, his antithesis. If Cumbrian sportsmen claim John Peel, as they well may, for their patron saint and the song that has immortalised him as their particular anthem, they are very far indeed from possessing a monopoly of that famous character. Wherever Anglo-Saxons for the last half-century have been gathered together, not in the three kingdoms only but in America, Canada or the Antipodes, it would be hard to pick out an individual who could not shout the chorus at any rate of John Peel. Yet I have been idly gossiping about Cumbrian bards and have forgotten, nay, not forgotten, but deferred, the mention of Woodcock Greaves. Poor Woodcock Greaves! like the reverend author of "Not a drum was heard," the singer, so far as the world is concerned, of but a single song. Not a very great composition in itself, perhaps, but possessed of a simple pathos which, together with the swing of the music, has touched the foxhunter and thousands who are not foxhunters in a manner that no other ballad of the kind can pretend to. Songs of the chase are legion, swinging and polished verses too, by men of talent as well as of mettle, set to music by notable composers and celebrating famous hunts and famous huntsmen. But where are they all when contrasted with the ever-green notoriety of "John Peel"? —by comparison at first sight a mere nursery rhyme. And then again have there not been "John Peel" waltzes, gallops, polkas, and quadrilles that three generations of youths and maidens around the circle of the globe have followed with eager foot? To a majority of these, the hero of the ballad and the strain is, I fancy, a semi-mythical personage. Only men of a sporting turn, and by no means all of these I am inclined to think, quite realise the actuality of the famous Caldbeck yeoman.

The superior person may say and think what he pleases, but I do not mind confessing that a pilgrimage to Caldbeck, long projected but only recently achieved, excited my fancy no little and stirred within me many pleasurable emotions. Upon my map too, the undertaking seemed a very simple affair, a high road of yellow-ochre and generous breadth running the entire circuit of the Skiddaw uplands from the foot of Bassenthwaite, round again to Threlkeld, taking Caldbeck, so to speak, in its stride. But the real road proved very different from the paper one; nothing indeed could be more unlike.

We have already in these wanderings had occasion to pass by, and to make mention of, the "Castle Inn" set at the foot of Bassenthwaite and some seven miles from Keswick. Two roads at this point go rambling off the tourist track, the one to Carlisle, and the other, as a finger post denotes, to Caldbeck, adding the further fact that the distance thither is nine miles.

It was with a light heart that I turned this corner one day in the beginning of July. The landscape, it is true, glowed with that peculiar brilliancy which in Lakeland is apt to be the presage of a wet jacket, but nine miles under average conditions is no very formidable stretch to place between one's self and shelter before storm clouds have so much as even fringed the blue curtain of the sky. The road, which started with a flourish, as if with some serious intention of living up to its paper character of a great national highway, quickly tumbled to the *rôle* of a Cumbrian byway—and Cumbrian byways are proverbially vexatious. After a mile or two one could understand why the rabbits sat up in the middle of the track and regarded one with as much confidence as surprise, and why the grass in some parts threatened to assume the proportions of a moderate hay-crop. Large stones were broadcasted loosely over the surface, which was mostly of a perpendicular nature, and I was forcibly reminded of that otherwise delectable part of Devonshire known as the South Hams.

After all, if one had to take it easy, there were great compensations, for Skiddaw, I think, looks its very best from this northern side, while the far-stretching heather-clad uplands of Skiddaw Forest, with their green flanks spouting with becks and flecked with fresh shorn sheep, lay all the time upon my right hand. In the narrow vale between were homesteads nestling beneath groves of trees, and the little lake of Overwater twinkled pleasantly amid the verdure of woods and meadows. Here, as elsewhere on the outskirts of Lakeland, one might be miles away from all sign of travel. To-day, at any rate, I had the rugged road wholly to myself. The gorse glowed, and the dog-roses bloomed in the high, ragged, spindly hedges on either hand and the pewits cried on drubbing wings behind them and the curlews called on the long slopes of Binsey Fell.

I wonder, by the way, if people ever ascend this same Binsey Fell? I felt myself irresistibly impelled to the enterprise on this occasion, in spite of threatening signs in the south-west, and did not regret it, though the delay cost me a wetting. Binsey Fell has no particular nobility of outline and is not more than fifteen hundred feet or so above the sea; but then again, it is the outlying sentinel, as it were, of all these Cumbrian mountains and stands out so finely into the low country that the outlook over North Cumberland, and the Solway and into Scotland is almost as fine as from Skiddaw itself and very much more certain of realisation. It was the calm before the storm on this occasion, and a score of villages showed their roofs and church towers, and sometimes, unhappily, their tall chimneys, with ominous distinctness on the rich lowland that stretches from Carlisle to the Solway mouth. The valley of the Derwent starting at our very feet traced its wooded and winding course towards the sea. Away beyond the broad sheen of the Solway the glint of homesteads on the Dumfriesshire hills came and went among the shadows that were now slowly creeping over land and sea. In short, I would strongly recommend the ascent of Binsey; not many hills return so much for so little exertion.

Where the road tops the ridge at the further foot of Binsey Fell it divides, and taking the right hand and most unpromising of the two forks I steadily descended several hundred feet by a narrow lane, to where the somewhat forlorn looking village of Ulldale rises on the further bank of a stream that comes tumbling down from Skiddaw Forest to the plain. It was now raining hard. If Ulldale had possessed average attractions, I might never have reached Caldbeck, and in such case had only the qualified satisfaction of seeing the place where John Peel spent his closing years and died, his chief bit of property and his final home, Ruthwaite, being near the village. But Ulldale was quite hopeless, and though the stony road shot straight up the hill beyond with unmistakable indications of facing the open and the moorland, I elected happily to press forward over the five miles which an unkempt matron informed me lay between us and Caldbeck. A gate across the road above the village was prophetic, as such gates always are, of the roughest travelling. After some climbing I found myself upon a high exposed common over which for several miles, with gentle undulations and Roman directness, ran an unfenced, stony road. Happily, the grass upon either side was tolerably smooth or the pace would have been lamentable, and there was now not a speck of blue left in the heavens. The west was inky black, the east was grey. Rain was falling briskly, and the thunder, which for some time had been muttering afar off, was now crackling overhead or booming in the gorges of Skiddaw Forest. The lightning, no doubt, was in actual reality quite a respectable distance off, but it seemed to me to be playing in unpleasant fashion about the very handles of my bicycle. Beautiful pasture land lay on either side of the open road where Herdwicks and Cheviots, just lightened of their fleeces, with hundreds of hardy piebald lambs, raised clamorous voices to the storm.

I remembered that this must have been the very road over which John Peel's funeral *cortège* travelled in 1854 when he was brought from Ulldale to the Caldbeck churchyard. If his spirit had been of the restless kind and of the wild huntsman type, from which I should imagine it was far removed, this would have been the very day for such ghostly enterprise, over the fells and pastures which *Royal, Ranger, Bellman* and the other canine immortals of the song must so often in life have led the veteran huntsman. And a fine hunting country of the cold, upland sort it seemed too all about here; grass everywhere, fenced and unfenced, drained and undrained, open fell and hard sheep sod, big ox pastures skirted by ragged fences or straggling walls. Windy homesteads, solid and solitary, crowned the ridges at long intervals, gleaming white against the inky background of the skies; unsheltered and exposed, and facing the storm with philosophic unconcern. High Pike, Great Calva, Carrock Fell and the other giants of Skiddaw Forest had hidden their heads in banking clouds and away on the left, shutting out the plain of Cumberland, the lower and greener slopes of Caldbeck Fells opened and shut in the lightning flashes. At Greenrigg, the last farmhouse in the open before the road drops down again to the enclosed country, John Peel was born, and there an aged daughter of his still lives, while another survives in the adjoining homestead which abuts upon the road at the point where a final gate divides this long stretch of high common from the country below.

A mile or so of soaking lane and I was in the village street of Caldbeck, where a gentler rain was falling upon as old-fashioned

Market Place, Hesket Newmarket.

and characteristic looking a collection of habitations as even fancy could have conceived for the environment of so picturesque a personage. And by this I do not mean that there were any architectural gems, such as you may see in some ancient villages in the south, nor would such things have been in keeping with the genius of the place. It was the old-worldness of the north that brooded over Caldbeck, of heavy stone fronts that make their character felt, even through fresh coats of whitewash, of low eaves and old slate stone roofs and heart oak timbers. I must again remark, with renewed apologies to the superior person, that, wet as I was, I felt my blood coursing somewhat quicker as I rode into this remote village, so unknown in itself, and so curiously and fortuitously famous, so familiar by name to me, at any rate as far as memory could go back. There was no doubt about the village inn; it stood alone in the middle of the wide turf-edged space, and looked down towards the church and rectory, while the Caldew sang unseen below. It was just such an inn as I should have asked for and expected at Caldbeck. Snug and comfortable, yet sufficiently primitive, and with no apparent consciousness of the touring public, which a few miles away were such an item on the highway.

A big fire was roaring in the kitchen, for it was ironing day, and I was glad enough to leave the front parlour for later use, and dry my upper garments, at any rate, by the cheerful blaze, while a middle-aged hostess and a more venerable dame discoursed to me on the subject of my pilgrimage. Only the elder lady knew the famous huntsman well, as he died in '54. They were, I think, his connections in some way, as probably were most folks in Caldbeck. "He was just a plain ordinary man," they protested, "one of ourselves." This of course many of us have known well enough, but modern hunting is a conventional pursuit, and we are a conventional people. If John Peel's grey coat and simple habit are overlooked by the vendors of patent stable mixtures, whose artists are accustomed to depict him in the gorgeous panoply of a fashionable M.F.H., it is quite likely that he thus vaguely figures in the fancy of many who crown festive occasions with pæans in his honour.

It seemed quite fitting that a portrait of the local hero should face me as I discussed the homely lunch provided in the inn parlour. It was not a work of art, perhaps, but at the same time had an air of fidelity, which was much more to the purpose, and was painted in oils over a generous space. It represented a benign looking old gentleman, with a longish unwrinkled face, blue eyes, and a most beautiful pink complexion. He wore a very tall and rather wide brimmed beaver hat tilted back on his head, a loosely knotted blue or birdseye handkerchief round his neck, and a long tail coat of brown or grey, while his hand grasped a long-lashed hunting whip. I am quite sure the Hanging Committee of the Royal Academy would not have given that picture a second's consideration, but from my point of view it inspired some confidence, and I need not say much interest, and I drank the health of the original in a bottle of Workington ale, as seemed fitting, for Woodcock Greaves, if I remember right, was a Workington man.

John Peel was not a fell foxhunter such as those we have come across in earlier chapters. Nor yet was he an ordinary low country M.F.H., but something betwixt and between. He hunted a small pack of his own for, roughly speaking, the whole of the first half of the nineteenth century, over the upland grass country which lies between the mountains and the lowland, and as the song implies, rode his own horses behind them. He hunted for his own amusement and according to the Caldbeck folks who remember him was out nearly every day in the week and always, like the fell hunters, at daybreak. His "fields" were of course composed of his immediate friends and neighbours, when they chose to go with him. Mine hosts at the inn talked much, too, of his son, who was known as "Young John Peel" and died at the tender age of ninety not very long ago.

But I was strongly advised to go and see a venerable individual known as "Willie Peel," a nephew of the illustrious John, who had known his uncle well and as a grown man been a good deal with him. This veteran would be delighted, so I was assured, to draw upon his memory for my benefit. And the more so, since what time there yet remained to him was his own and he was "gey fond of a crack." So as the rain had now ceased, I lost no time in seeking out this reminiscent member of the house of Peel, who lived with relatives in a roomy cottage beyond the confines of the village, and found him all that had been described—and more.

It was a plain old-fashioned room into which I was genially welcomed by the veteran's married daughter, and I confess to some satisfaction at finding that my errand was a novelty to both. There was a big open hearth in which a turf fire smouldered, and before the hearth was an oaken settle upon which we sat and talked, or rather my host did, of the days of old. Nothing from an artistic point of view could have been more admirably attuned to the spirit of the theme than this interior, and to sit here in converse with a man still active for his years, as I was to discover, who had hunted with John Peel, I really felt was something of a privilege. I was quite thankful for the presence on this important occasion of a third party of a younger generation. In an early chapter of this book I referred to the lucidity of the Cumbrian tongue as usually encountered in these days. If I did not make reservations I should have done so, and John Peel's nephew may stand for one of them. He spoke the olden tongue in all its purity, of that I am quite sure. Though by no means a stranger to northern vernaculars, he had the better of me again and again though both ears were eagerly cocked, and I was genuinely thankful for an interpreter. If the reader should get a chance to cast his eye over the verses of Anderson or Stagg or Dr. Gibson, he may perhaps get an inkling of what a fearsome tongue old Cumbrian is to the uninitiated when spoken in its pristine ruggedness. I must not linger long over such personal recollections of John Peel as passed on the oak settle by the turf fire. My informant when a young man used to help his uncle in the kennel rather than in the field, and though full of ordinary incidents there is not much to be said in a paragraph or two about a man who hunted nearly every day in the week except Sundays for most of his life.

When he wasn't hunting "he was aye drinkin'," said the free-spoken nephew. But lest I should be accused of smirching the character, even at second hand, of the immortal John, I must hasten to remark that such an implication amounts to nothing in relation to a Cumbrian statesman of a century ago.

John Peel died at the ripe old age of seventy-eight, and was going nearly to the last; and, if like all his neigbours, he was of a convivial turn, we must confess he carried it well. His active career as I have said extended roughly over the first half

John Peel's Home.

of the century. He was very well-to-do as a statesman, owning land which seems to have brought him in from three to five hundred a year in rent, if not more; for, unlike the majority of his class, he did not farm much himself, which perhaps, under the circumstances, was just as well.

Peel spent many years in Caldbeck, and his nephew proposed we should go and see the house where he lived and kept his hounds. This, I need hardly say, had been my fixed intention all along, but I was glad of so well qualified a guide. So we set off for the village again, the old gentleman carrying his four-score years with remarkable agility. The headquarters

S

of the famous sportsman turned out to be a modest house of whitewashed stone by the roadside that I had already passed, and consisted of two small rooms some twelve feet square, above and below, with a 'lean-to' behind. I gathered from the good lady who now inhabits it that I was by no means the first stranger who, doubtless to her vast surprise, had made this demand upon her courtesy. The house has not been materially altered, I was informed, since Peel lived in it. The two diminutive low-raftered rooms, one on either side of the door represented the limitations of the celebrated yeoman's indoor life, and an adjoining wash-house has equal interest as the place where at one time those much-sung-of hounds of his were kennelled. His horses, so said his nephew, were stabled in some buildings still standing across the road. Woodcock Greaves has himself told the tale of how the song was written; while as for his own story he was the son of well-to-do people in Workington, and came to Caldbeck as the owner or part-owner of a small woollen mill, situated in a romantic glen of the Caldew, near the village, which eventually ruined him. He was notable as a *raconteur*, a facile maker of verses both humorous and pathetic, and a hard-riding sportsman. For many years he was John Peel's intimate companion. Long afterwards, alluding to his business affairs at Caldbeck, Greaves wrote—"I was cheated, robbed, and gulled to such an extent by those who ought to have been my friends, that I resolved to go to the farthest corner of the earth. I made a wreck of all; left machinery, book debts, &c., in the hands of a friend to provide for two daughters, while with the four other children and £10 I landed in Hobart Town, Tasmania, in the year 1833."

Here the sporting poet lived to see his family take root and prosper, himself dying at an advanced age within recent memory. Indeed, I very well recollect—and this, too, by way of testimony to the universality of the ballad—reading of his death in the local paper of a remote American town. And by an odd chance a Tasmanian was of the company, and of course had much to say upon the subject, which I have long forgotten. Here, however, is what Greaves himself wrote from Hobart Town, not long before his death:—" Nearly forty years have now wasted away since John Peel and I sat in a snug parlour at Caldbeck; we were then both in the heyday of manhood, and hunters of the old fashion, taking the best part of the hunt in the morning, the drag over the mountains in the mist, while fashionable hunters still lay in the blankets. We had met one night to arrange about earth-stopping and so forth. Large flakes of snow were falling. We sat by the fireside, hunting over again many a good run, and recalling the feats of each particular hound, or narrow breakneck 'scape, when a flaxen-haired daughter of mine came in, saying, 'Father, what do they say to what Granny sings?' (Granny was singing to sleep my eldest son, now a leading barrister in Hobart Town, with an old rant called 'Bonnie Annie.') The pen and ink for hunting appointments were on the table, and the idea of writing a song to this old air forced itself upon me, and thus was produced, impromptu, 'D'ye ken John Peel?' Immediately afterwards I sang it to poor Peel, who smiled, and a tear or two ran down his manly cheek. 'By Jove, Peel,' I said, in jest, 'you'll be sung of when we're both run to earth.'"

The music of the song was subsequently elaborated by a Carlisle musician, if I remember aright, and was first brought to public notice, some twenty years after its composition, by the fact of its popularity among Cumbrian sportsmen. My Peel proved an active as well as reminiscent cicerone. He took me to the Glen of the Caldew, where a modest bobbin mill, almost hidden amid a really striking scene of foliage and tumbling waters, still hums on the site where Woodcock Greaves sunk his money near a hundred years ago in bigger operations. We then worked round again to the village, passing the house where the Beauty of Buttermere, whose woes were recited in an earlier chapter, spent her married life, and followed the stream down to the churchyard, where I paid my respects to the grave of the local hero. This is marked by a plain upright stone upon which is carved a whip, a horn and a hound and a simple inscription stating that it covers the remains of John Peel of Ruthwaite (his farm near Ulldale), who died on November 14th, 1854, aged 78. As we walked back to the inn, my companion pointed out some farm buildings by the roadside where Peel's hounds were kennelled at the time his funeral *cortège* passed down this road to the church. I was assured by my guide, who ought to know, as he was himself a mourner, that as the hearse passed the doors the orphaned dogs within broke into a chorus of canine lamentations and that the village was filled with awe at the nature of the coincidence if, peradventure it was nothing more.

It was full late when I succeeded in getting away from Caldbeck and its entertaining inhabitants, only one or two of whom it has been necessary to introduce here. But the days were long, and I elected to go home round the far side of Skiddaw Forest and Saddle-back, and thus complete the circle to Keswick. I had lost all faith in the paper road, though on the map it continued its triumphant course, regardless of hills and streams and gates and ruts. There is no doubt an excellent road to Penrith, the metropolis, whither the folks of this district in the main no doubt resort. But at Hesket a quaint decayed wool market near Caldbeck, over which "Fuimus" is written in the largest letters, I bid good-bye, to my sorrow, to the Penrith road, and after many miles of tortuous wanderings on rocky or sticky byways, where neither finger-posts nor other travellers nor friendly road-side houses appeared to solve one's frequent doubts, I struck familiar ground at Mungrisdale. Here, beneath the shadow of the eastern slopes of Saddleback, this delectable hamlet sleeps by the upper waters of the Glenderamakin, but two miles from the Keswick and Penrith road and twice as many from Threlkeld. A neat but rustic inn stands above the brawling brook, and suggests a fitting retreat for some solitary who would be in the Lake Country but not of it, in touch with its beauties yet removed from the haunts of men and well off the route of travel.

Road to Keswick.

The Castle and Eden Bridge, Carlisle.

CHAPTER X.

By those who are not indifferent to everything but the actual face of nature, the old capital of this western border land should by no means be left out of any scheme of travel in Cumberland. In former times a tiresome railway journey was inevitable to this achievement. Since the advent, however, of the blessed cycle, it is a simple undertaking as well as a pleasant one to run there from Keswick or from Penrith over admirable roads. The one is about thirty, the other some eighteen miles. Amid days of walking on the mountains or riding on the rougher roads that intersect them, such an expedition makes a pleasant interlude with the railroad too, so handy should strength or weather or machine break down.

For myself, I must say that I do like to approach a town, and above all a town of character and high tradition, upon the roadway; to first behold it perhaps from afar, and to watch the country gradually attuning itself to the neighbourhood of its capital; to mark the old inns and the many still surviving landmarks that in former days cheered the approaching traveller, whether on the coach-top or in lumbering chaise, or on his ambling nag, with saddle bags and holsters; to note the seats of ancient stocks, vanished or still prosperous, whose names are writ large for centuries on the stone of fortress or cathedral or civic hall. When, with such pleasant if inconsequent reflections you have thus passed from country into suburb, and from suburb

market place, or wherever the pulse of your town most
dly beats, you feel already to know something of it, to be in
tter mood at least to learn something, than if you had been
mped out of a railway train you know not where, amid a
stant crowd of busmen, cabbies, hotel-porters and gamins.
From Penrith it is a fine run to Carlisle over the old North
oad by Plumpton and High Hesket with the P   terell on the
left and the Eden on the right, both hurrying to   eir junction

Near High Hesket.

beneath the city walls. But as we have wandered back to
Keswick, it is the longer route we must here pursue, though of
a truth in the briefest fashion, as I want to get to Carlisle as
quickly as may be.

Then let us without more ado, and by way of the familiar,
but ever charming road down the Vale of Keswick and over-
looking Bassenthwaite, transfer ourselves to that same Castle
Inn near the foot of the lake which witnessed our start in the
last chapter for the classic pastures of Caldbeck. Having

there selected the northward of the two routes branching from the coach road, and which leads, so the mile-posts say, to Carlisle in twenty-one miles, let not the traveller be discouraged by his experience of the first four. They are little used, for local reasons which matter nothing here. They are as lonely as the road to Caldbeck, and the abounding coney gambles on your path as confidingly as upon the other. Big pastures, scantily fenced, sweep away on the left to the ledges above the Derwent valley, and on the right trend upward to the fir-crowned ridges of Whitless Scaur. Bothel seems to be perched on the last step of the descent into the plain of the Solway, which lies spread below us, fair and rich as we pass out of the quiet old-fashioned village. Yonder, just in front of us, is Sir Wilfrid Lawson's house of Brayton, conspicuously set upon a leafy slope, with every window glittering in the morning sun. Many another place of note, town and village, hall and church tower, can be marked amid the bright tints of woods and parks, fields and fallows which roll away towards the shining Solway. At Bothel too we strike the main road from Cockermouth to Carlisle, and may bowl merrily along a highway as good as one may reasonably look for in Cumberland, which as a county does not shine in the art of road construction. The generous fields of wheat and barley, just heading out and rippling in the breeze, have a strange look after the cramped enclosures and broken foreground of the mountain valleys. The hay is mostly carried from the big meadows and on the long red drills of ribbed tillage land, the turnips are showing in green and vigorous lines. Shorthorns, are browsing in the pastures and heavy Leicesters share the croppage with the small and more shapely Cheviots. It is a fat country for the most part, this upper lowland. The modest grey and white homestead of the hill yeoman is no longer much in evidence. Large buildings of red sandstone here and there face the highway, but at such intervals as show that a weightier type of occupant is on the soil. Of red sandstone too are the

AN UNEXPECTED CARILLON

labourers' cottages, one-storeyed and massive like those in Scotland, with low eaves and a square window of diamond panes on either side of the door.

We pass the Waver and the Wirger rivers, and leave the market town of Wigton just out of sight upon the left. A carillon comes wildly sounding on the breeze, of a tone and quality most wholly unexpected in such a locality. Bruges, Antwerp, and Ypres rise for a moment to the memory, for such music sounds strange among English fields, and

Wigton.

stranger still when of a sweetness such as this. A timely countryman, however, solves the mystery, which is merely that a neighbouring landowner of wealth and discretion has brought these fine chimes from Belgium and hung them in a private belfrey of his own, to the great delectation of his neighbours. Indeed, a farmer in the neighbourhood assured me that his annual holiday was no longer an unmixed joy, so greatly did he miss the cheery music that at home rang out the passing of his busy hours. We cross the east shore railroad at Crofton and pass the gates of Crofton Hall, where Briscoes have lived this many a long day. Now we are running through Thursby, with a passing thought of the awe in which the great and shaddowy Norse deity was once held along these coasts. Now Dalston (not to be confused with Dalton-in-Furness) is left behind, just off our road (where Romney the painter was born), and further back upon the right lies the present residence and historic stronghold of the bishops of Carlisle. It was early in the fourteenth century that a bishop had urgent reasons for getting the king's leave to fortify Rose

Dalton-in-Furness Castle.

Castle, for it was the sanguinary period following the Bruce wars. But as we cannot visit that stately episcopal pile upon the Caldew it is idle touching on its story.

The entry to Carlisle by this Wigton road is not particularly attractive. The city was of no great account in the mere matter of population till modern times, and its modern features are of an industrial kind and intrude themselves in unromantic fashion on the notice of the traveller from the south-west. But in visiting Carlisle it will be well to forget all this and push straight on to the Castle, and there climb up and take our stand upon the lofty ramparts. With an average imagination and a reasonable acquaintance with British history, border and otherwise, we shall have from this vantage point the best of what Carlisle has to offer, and that best to my thinking is very good. For the old city has played a part more strenuous by far than any other town of note in England, and this distinction, one need hardly say, is due to geographical reasons, and the geography of Carlisle as seen from its castle walls is significant enough to stir the dullest dog. We have seen it again and again during this little tour; the Solway, the Scottish hills, riven with once hostile glens, the fat Eden valley, and the plain of Cumberland, and here above them all the rock around which the tide of battle and the passions of race hatred surged for centuries and the red walls of Carlisle Castle, on which in fancy we have taken our stand.

How placid have been the lives of most English towns, how meaningless their Norman castles, when rated by the standard of Carlisle. Shrewsbury and Chester almost alone can claim something of a kinship in stirring record; but the Welsh March, as such, ceased from troubling three hundred years before life and property was really safe outside the walls of Carlisle. Besides the Cathedral, whose sore vicissitudes of fortune give it an interest like the Castle and a pathos all its own, there is not in truth very much to be seen here. One fancies perhaps a stern hard look about the older streets, as if life for them had been too serious for the arches and gables and mouldings that artists and antiquaries love—just as the corner boys and more demonstrative part of the population are said to inherit a special strain of turbulence from the rude past. But one really does not need to hunt about for Roman arches or the relics of nunneries or Tudor houses in Carlisle, if time is limited, as one might do in cities richer in these things, but poorer infinitely in such records as make it the main story of the Border capital.

We are facing the north, as is only fitting for such a retrospect as I am about to indulge in. Below us, through green meadows, somewhat trimmed and ornamented for the outdoor needs of a modern city, winds the broad and stately Eden. Hurrying from the south to meet it, and thus placing us in the angle of two streams, come the recently united waters of the Caldew and the Petterill, whose infant gambols among the hills which bore them we have looked at in a former chapter.

Before recorded history, says Bishop Creighton, a tribe of the Brigantes had built their huts upon this sandstone bluff, which Nature had so obviously intended for the secure abode of man. But this the reader will no doubt resent, being more than he bargained for. One cannot, however, ignore all mention of Roman times, seeing what a conspicuous part the land of Carlisle then played. It was Agricola with his legions who, about eighty years after Christ, first broke upon the barbarism of these northern forests, and there was nothing tentative or half-hearted in the manner of his settlement. Henceforth the real frontier of Britain was here, and for three centuries the Solway slope hummed with a life more bustling and more organised, and certainly far more cosmopolitan, than would have been found there a thousand years later.

The Roman town of Lugubalia arose therefore on the site of the old Celtic Caer Lywelydd. Agricola built a line of fortresses from the Solway to the Tyne, and forty years later came Hadrian, following the same course with his famous wall, and including in that monumental structure his predecessor's forts. One knows too that a second frontier was formed in somewhat similar fashion from the Firth to the Clyde; but its efficacy was fitful and life between the two walls so precarious that the Tyne and Solway, and the "Roman wall" we know so well, may for practical purposes be regarded as the Roman frontier. Everything indeed connected with Roman Britain seems to require a mental effort. But let us make one brief endeavour to form some idea of this vast defensive work.

Its course was about seventy miles. It was eighteen feet high and eight feet broad, but its actual height was greatly increased by a ditch of fifteen feet in depth on the north side. On the south, a rampart and a wide foss followed the course of the wall as a protection to its rear, in case an enemy should perchance break through. Every three miles, speaking broadly, there was a fortified station garrisoned by 600 men; at intervals of less than a mile were big square towers, with gateways occupied by detachments, while every three hundred yards stood watch-towers manned by sentinels. The civil population that a permanent garrison of 15,000 troops would gather round it must have been very great for the period, speaking relatively, and afforded, no doubt, a strange contrast to the solitude through which one may now trace what remains of Hadrian's Wall. It crossed the Eden on a bridge, just beneath the walls of Carlisle, and it was down yonder at Stanwix, rather than at the town above, that the Romans had their military station. But it was not alone the western end of the great wall that made this "country of Carluel," as it came to be called, so busy. For the coast of Cumberland was low and exposed beyond the point where the wall touched the Solway, and was thickly sprinkled with Roman stations as far as Ravenglass— at which spot, as well as on the cold stations of the Northumbrian uplands, Frisians, Batavians, Spaniards and Gauls shivered in the inclement air. A network of roads covered the country, four passing through Carlisle alone, along which must have rumbled continual convoys laden with the products of the south. Experts have, beyond a doubt, much justification when they tell us that this was for a time one of the most populous parts of Roman Britain.

It was when the Romans had gone that Carlisle assumed some fresh and peculiar importance as a border stronghold, for it was here that the half-Romanised Britons rallied and fought Scots, Picts and Saxons, for a long, vague period in vague and doubtful conflict. With the Arthurian legend we need not concern ourselves. It flourished in the land of Carlisle, as in Wales and Cornwall. But the Strathclyde Britons, stretching roughly from the Ribble to the Clyde, had for a time their centre at Dumbarton, till the Northumbrian Saxons drove a wedge through their centre and cut off Carlisle and its people from their northern kinsmen. Egfrith, the Northumbrian king, seems indeed to have dominated the Cumbrians, while his pious sister, Elfred, founded the monastery in Carlisle and gave the town its ecclesiastical distinction. This same influence seems also to have greatly weakened in Cumbria the old British Church in favour of its Latin rival. But Egfrith in turn was overthrown by the Picts and Britons, while in due course the invading Danes added to the confusion. In 875 they burnt and sacked Carlisle, leaving the district almost uninhabitable. This ended the long period of Carlisle's earlier supremacy. For nearly eight centuries she had been predominant on the north-western border land. First under the Romans, then as the capital of Strathclyde, and even afterwards, when under Northumbrian influences, her ecclesiastical supremacy had remained unquestioned.

We took note when crossing Dunmail Raise of how, after the British defeat upon that mountain pass in 945, the land of Carlisle was granted by the Saxon conqueror to Malcolm, King of Scotland. As an appanage of the northern kingdom it ceased for a time to be a border town, and lost its importance. When Domesday Book was compiled, Carlisle, with Cumberland and part of Westmorland, found no place in it, not being English ground. It was William Rufus who put matters right again, and this with little apparent detriment to the reigning King of Scotland. For Cumbria was then in the virtual power of an independent chieftain, one Dolphin, who ruled over a ruinous town and a district thinly peopled by a polyglot race, in which Norse blood was the prevailing strain. Rufus expelled Dolphin, brought fresh settlers into the wasted country, and built the castle at Carlisle, putting a strong garrison within it. Henry I. created it an earldom of the Welsh Palatinate type—but this was soon abolished as a system of defence not always salutary for the Crown, and the Crown officers introduced. Henry, however, did much more than this. He introduced the Augustine Order and started the struggling Church with various endowments of fisheries, mills, and parish titles. Glasgow and York had hitherto contended for the ecclesiastical overlordship of Carlisle. The King now set the matter at rest by making it a bishopric, and including in the new see most of the present counties of Cumberland and Westmorland. During Stephen's troubled reign Carlisle once more became semi-Scottish, for David of Scotland seized it in the confusion and made peace with Stephen on condition of retaining it as an earldom for himself.

It now became a base for Scottish ravages against England, an intolerable state of affairs which the vigorous Henry II. put an end to once and for all, a proceeding made easier by the youth of Malcolm, his contemporary on the Scottish throne. It remained however for the third Henry to finally extinguish all Scottish claims upon Carlisle, and this he did in peaceful fashion by granting various private manors to his rival of Scotland to be held direct of the English Crown.

Though ravaged during this contentious period again and again by the Scots, there was now no longer any question about Carlisle and Cumberland being wholly English ground. The precise line of the border, however, above the Solway estuary was quite another matter, and one can well understand how little precedent there was for fixing it. It was not like the case of Wales, where Welshmen and Englishmen were of a different race and speech. Who was an Englishman and who was a Scotsman on either bank of the Esk, and precisely what either term meant, would have been a problem to the wisest head in the reign of Edward I. And in the meantime Carlisle was burnt almost to the ground by a terrible conflagration, 1,300 houses and the newly-built choir of the Cathedral being destroyed.

Out of its ashes, however, the border city was to rise to fresh importance, for the strenuous Edward now came upon the scene, who by striving to make all Scotland that was worth fighting for English, settled the matter in unexpected fashion. For the fierce passions he aroused determined for good and all who were Scots and who were English, and created a mutual animosity that it took centuries to cool. One may question the object of the great Edward's statesmanship or deplore the bad fortune that cut him off before its fulfilment, but what chiefly matters here is that Carlisle became for a long period the base of great operations, the scene of martial and courtly splendour: and after Edward's dead body had been carried thither from Burgh-on-Sands, and the barons of England had sworn fealty to his feeble successor, it suffered for it. A bloodier time was beginning for the border than it had ever known, which was saying much. "Carlisle," says Bishop Creighton, "had suffered much for Edward the First, but for a great object; she was now to suffer more." It was fortunate the city had already acquired the beginning of civic and ecclesiastical life. In future they could make but little headway, for Carlisle, became first and chief a great garrison town, and the surrounding country, so far as the eye can range from its lofty ramparts upon both sides of the Solway, became the abode of men who for generations lived for arms alone.

How tell of the dreadful wars of Bruce and Balliol and the stormy period of the third Edward, when again and again the border city was the royal headquarters; of the sieges it stood, and the bloody havoc that raged past it, up the coast to Ravenglass or up the Eden Valley to Appleby? Every man became a soldier, every house that was not a mere peasant's hut a fortress. The independence of Scotland, it is true, was in course of time formally recognised; but the number of English barons who held property there of the Scottish king, to say nothing of the irrepressible fighting instinct of the period, offered a veritable premium on disturbance. But these formal international wars were after all punctuated with quite respectable periods of truce, and in these periods the borderers, lest their blood, perchance, should cool, fought against one another. So fierce and turbulent grew the people and so local the spirit, that mere national hatreds faded into those of tribe and name. The difference between the men on the Annan and those on the Eden might have had interesting distinctions for a student of folk-lore or vernacular, but for all practical purposes they were the same people—a fact which, no doubt, intensified their local hatreds. The borderers became, in time, a thorn in the side of their respective governments. If England and Scotland were united in nothing else, they were cordially at one in contriving restraints and framing codes for these turbulent subjects, whom no ordinary laws could touch; and Carlisle represented all that there was of law and order in this corner of the world, as well as forming the main barrier against Scottish aggression.

Among the many differences in detail between the Northumbrian and the Cumbrian marches was the power of a great earldom, a great feudal house, the Percies, on the east; whereas, upon the west, Carlisle under a Crown officer and a minor bishop was in direct touch and under the direct control of the King. In a former volume of this series I had to relate how the Northumbrians marched under the Percies to the bloody field of Shrewsbury. But though the Cumbrians were as strong partisans of the second Richard as their neighbours, Henry, through his officers at Carlisle, had no trouble in overawing them. The wars of the Roses, again, which gave the mass of Englishmen then living their first sight of blood spilt in serious action, was a mere change in the venue of the war-seasoned borderers, though they were the means of bringing Richard of Gloucester to the north, as we noted at Penrith.

He was also governor of Carlisle for some time and warden of the marches, about which famous office and its duties a few words are necessary.

Both kingdoms, as I have said, were at one as to the urgency of some special laws for the marches, and a system was devised that would almost suggest to us, in its ceremonial, the days of the Druids, and indeed the local civilisation was perhaps well suited to the primitive forms of that dim period. Three wardens were appointed upon either side to preside over the eastern, middle and western marches respectively: the weightiest men that could be found. In war time their duties were obvious, as they represented their sovereign and had almost absolute power. In time of peace however they were more curious and delicate, the chief of them being to confer with the warden of the opposite side and make the customary arrangement for the redress of grievances. They appointed a day for a court to be held, to which all who had grievances were invited to resort, and these complaints it is needless to remark were mostly in connection with four-footed stock. All intending litigants, however, had previously to lay their charges before their warden, who forwarded them to his fellow official across the border; the day of meeting being in the meantime posted up in all market towns upon either side.

The rendezvous was usually at a cairn on the open moorland in that strip of country which had been long claimed by both nations, but at length by tacit consent was regarded as belonging to neither, and was known as the "Debatable land." It lay just north of the Solway, extending to the junction of the Liddell and Esk, and was for long regarded as an international grazing ground between the hours of sunrise and sunset, though at a later period it became the haunt of ruffians and outlaws of every type; it was moreover only distant some eight miles from the walls of Carlisle. Hither in solemn procession upon the day appointed rode the two wardens. The Buccleuch perhaps from the Scottish, and a Dacre of Naworth from the

English side, attended by a great retinue of knights, gentlemen and commons. At their respective edges of the " Debatable land" both parties halted, and four English horsemen pricked out across the neutral territory and demanded from the Scottish warden an assurance of peace till the next day at sunrise. This granted, four of the Scottish party performed a like service for their own warden, and then the two great men moved forward to meet each other at the head of their people, lifting up their hands as they drew near in token that all was well. Proclamations were then made to both parties warning

The Market, Carlisle.

them to abstain from those acts of violence which must have been sorely tempting to many a fiery soul, thus brought in close contact with some hated, personal enemy. Six Scots were then chosen by the English warden and six English by the other, to form a jury. The wardens and their clerks then examined the cases presented and decided on the order of proceedure. The method of trying cases seems to have been cumbered with difficulties. Space does not allow of our entering here into these mysterious rites. It is sufficient to say that a complainant got no satisfaction unless he could produce a witness of the opposite nation—no easy matter, and it is needless to add that

He was also governor of Carlisle for some time and warden of the marches, about which famous office and its duties a few words are necessary.

Both kingdoms, as I have said, were at one as to the urgency of some special laws for the marches, and a system was devised that would almost suggest to us, in its ceremonial, the days of the Druids, and indeed the local civilisation was perhaps well suited to the primitive forms of that dim period. Three wardens were appointed upon either side to preside over the eastern, middle and western marches respectively: the weightiest men that could be found. In war time their duties were obvious, as they represented their sovereign and had almost absolute power. In time of peace however they were more curious and delicate, the chief of them being to confer with the warden of the opposite side and make the customary arrangement for the redress of grievances. They appointed a day for a court to be held, to which all who had grievances were invited to resort, and these complaints it is needless to remark were mostly in connection with four-footed stock. All intending litigants, however, had previously to lay their charges before their warden, who forwarded them to his fellow official across the border; the day of meeting being in the meantime posted up in all market towns upon either side.

The rendezvous was usually at a cairn on the open moorland in that strip of country which had been long claimed by both nations, but at length by tacit consent was regarded as belonging to neither, and was known as the "Debatable land." It lay just north of the Solway, extending to the junction of the Liddell and Esk, and was for long regarded as an international grazing ground between the hours of sunrise and sunset, though at a later period it became the haunt of ruffians and outlaws of every type; it was moreover only distant some eight miles from the walls of Carlisle. Hither in solemn procession upon the day appointed rode the two wardens. The Buccleuch perhaps from the Scottish, and a Dacre of Naworth from the

English side, attended by a great retinue of knights, gentlemen and commons. At their respective edges of the "Debatable land" both parties halted, and four English horsemen pricked out across the neutral territory and demanded from the Scottish warden an assurance of peace till the next day at sunrise. This granted, four of the Scottish party performed a like service for their own warden, and then the two great men moved forward to meet each other at the head of their people, lifting up their hands as they drew near in token that all was well. Proclamations were then made to both parties warning

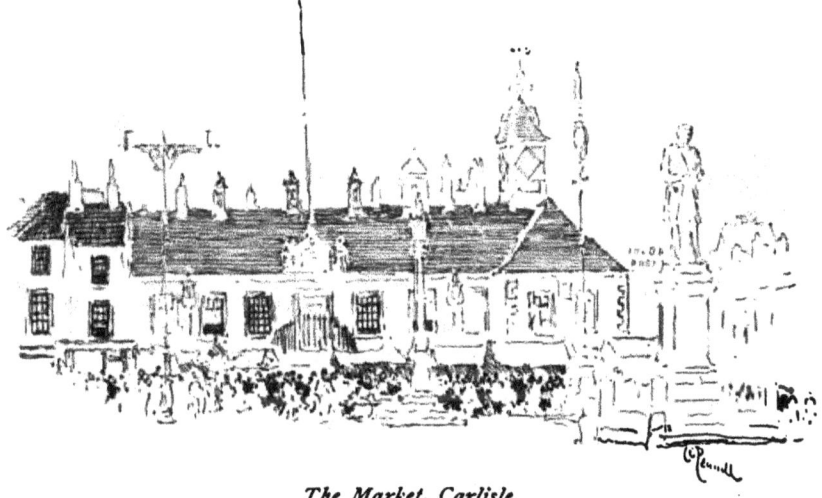

The Market, Carlisle.

them to abstain from those acts of violence which must have been sorely tempting to many a fiery soul, thus brought in close contact with some hated, personal enemy. Six Scots were then chosen by the English warden and six English by the other, to form a jury. The wardens and their clerks then examined the cases presented and decided on the order of proceedure. The method of trying cases seems to have been cumbered with difficulties. Space does not allow of our entering here into these mysterious rites. It is sufficient to say that a complainant got no satisfaction unless he could produce a witness of the opposite nation—no easy matter, and it is needless to add that the jurors, unless the testimony was overwhelming, "went solid" for their own people. The warden himself might acquit a man. "Clear, as I am being persuaded upon my conscience and honour" he might write upon the bill, which was sufficient. In the case of a conviction the warden was responsible for producing the culprit, and had to deliver up a servant of his own as hostage to be ransomed by money if the guilty man was not forthcoming.

When the business was completed the wardens made proclamation of their several verdicts : "We do give to wit that the Lord Wardens of England and Scotland, and Scotland and England, have very well agreed, and agreeable to the laws of the marches have made answer and delivery foul or clean of all the bills enrolled." Then naming another day of truce within forty days they parted with great ceremony.

But these efforts were spasmodic and depended wholly on the will of the wardens. It was not indeed till the time of Elizabeth that really strenuous efforts were made to cope with the disorder in a legal fashion.

Yet when the border was in a mood to be law-abiding it stood on its dignity with immense tenacity. The great case of "Kinmont Willie" has rung down the ages in prose and verse, and no better spot than Carlisle Castle for the recalling of it could of a surety be imagined.

The time was that of Elizabeth, whose zealous new-fangled servants, when there was a really good chance to catch an offender, were apt to be regardless of ancient ceremonial. Though we are anticipating a little in our story, border warfare had by now degenerated into cattle lifting on a lordly scale, and the Armstrongs, who could put 3,000 horse into the field, were conspicuous at this distracting work. Prominent among them was the redoubtable "Willie of Kinmont"—and, perhaps from mere bravado, he put in an appearance at a warden's court at Kershopeburn in 1596, where in perfect security he could thoroughly enjoy the black looks of his many victims from the

English side. But he did not know Elizabeth's "new brooms" and counted without his host. For when the meeting was over Kinmont Willie was incautious enough to separate from the Scottish following, and, though by every sacred law of the warden courts secure from molestation, since he took a road on Scottish soil, the temptation was too great for some of the English when they saw such a notorious marauder at their mercy. So a party of them stole away, and after a smart chase captured the redoubted raider and brought him to their deputy warden at Carlisle, who in his turn could not bring himself to turn loose upon the world again so notorious an offender, and Willie was tucked away safely in the dungeon immediately beneath our feet. But Sir Walter Scott of Buccleuch, Keeper of Liddesdale, glad enough as he doubtless would have been to see this curse of the border brought to the halter by orthodox means, was furious at such an outrage upon border custom, and his soul burned within him. He bridled his choler, however, and wrote curtly to Salkeld of Corby, the deputy warden, demanding Armstrong's release. Salkeld referred the matter to Lord Scrope, chief warden, who told Buccleuch that the case of such a notorious offender must be referred to the Queen. Here was a departure from time-honoured traditions that boded well or ill according as men looked at it! To Buccleuch it seemed outrageous, and he appealed to the English Ambassador at the Scottish Court, who advised Armstrong's release, as did also the Scottish King. But the haughty Queen who had refused her liberty to Mary of Scotland was not likely to soften towards a common bandit; moreover, she had her eye on this border country with a view to its reformation, and she seems to have treated these petitions with contemptuous silence.

Buccleuch then made up his mind to a venture which was as audacious as to all appearances hopeless. And that he had no personal interest in Kinmont Willie—quite the contrary—shows the depth of the border reverence for its code.

Let a justly famous ballad on an episode matchless of its kind relate Buccleuch's sentiments and intentions :

> Now word is gane to the bauld keeper
> In Branksome Ha', where that he lay,
> That Lord Scrope has ta'en the Kinmont Willie
> Between the hours of night and day.
>
> He has ta'en the table wi' his hand,
> He garr'd the red wine spring on hie.
> 'Now Christ's curse on my head' he said,
> 'But avenged of Lord Scrope I'll be.
>
> Oh ! is my basnet a widow's curch,
> Or my lance a wand of the willow tree,
> Or my arm a ladye's lilye hand,
> That an English lord should lightly me ?
>
> And have they ta'en him, Kinmont Willie,
> Withouten either dread or fear,
> And forgotten that the bauld Buccleuch
> Can back a steed or shake a spear ?
>
> Oh, were there war between the lands,
> As well I wot that there is none,
> I would slight Carlisle Castell high,
> Though it were gilded of marble stone.
>
> I would set that Castell in a low
> And slaken it with English blood ;
> There's never a man in Cumberland
> Should ken where Carlisle Castell stood.
>
> But since nae war's between the lands
> And there is peace and peace should be,
> I'll neither harm English lad nor lass
> And yet the Kinmont freed shall be.'

Having thus, according to the poet and in language that leaves nothing to be desired in fire and force, relieved his feelings, Buccleuch proceeded to take action. He ordered two hundred and ten of his most trusty followers to meet him just before sunset at Morton's tower in the " Debatable land," about ten miles from Carlisle. There scaling ladders and breaching tools were braced on spare horses, and in the darkness of the night the whole band crossed the Esk, and avoiding the notice of the Grahams of Netherby, who were the watch-dogs on the English bank, approached Carlisle with much caution, arriving beneath the castle walls about two hours before daybreak. The ladders proved too short, so the pickaxes were produced and a breach made in the wall by the postern gate. All this was done without arousing the garrison, and the sentinels were not alarmed till some of Buccleuch's men had squeezed through the rent and were breaking open the postern. It was then too late. Buccleuch, with part of his men, guarded the approaches to the castle, while the rest rather intimidated than overpowered the garrison by blowing trumpets and raising a great commotion, with a view of creating an impression that a Scotch army had descended upon the castle. Information had been previously gained through spies of the exact place where Kinmont Willie was confined. The door of the dungeon was soon found and as quickly forced, and the celebrated cattle-lifter was borne off in triumph with his fetters still hanging to his legs. The whole party, indeed, got clear away and were riding at full speed for the Scottish border before the men of Carlisle had fully realised the situation.

> They thought King James and a' his men
> Had won the house wi' bow and spear;
> It was but twenty Scots and ten
> That put a thousand in sic a steer.

As there was no time to knock the fetters off the prisoner's legs, a stout moss-trooper named Rowan was deputed to carry him on his back.

> Then shoulder high with shout and cry
> We bore him down the ladder lang,
> At every stride Red Rowan made
> I wot the Kinmont's chains played clang.

> Oh many a time, quo' Kinmont Willie,
> I have ridden home baith wild and worn,
> But a rougher beast than Red Rowan
> I ween my legs have ne'er bestroon.
>
> And many a time, quo' Kinmont Willie
> I've pricked a horse out o'er the furs,
> But since the day I back'd a steed
> I never wore sic cumbrous spurs!

The passage of the Eden was disputed by some of the townsmen, but the mist of morning lay thick on the meadows and the Scots again were able by shouts and clangour of trumpets to create the impression of a strong force. They rode at a great pace through the Grahams' country without spreading the alarm, crossed the Esk, and by two hours after daylight were on Scottish ground. The blacksmith's house between Loughton and Langholme where Willie's fetters were knocked off was shown to Sir Walter Scott when in the neighbourhood.

It was a great performance, and not a drop of blood had been shed. But Elizabeth when she heard of it set no bounds to her wrath, and gave the Scottish Government the choice between war and the surrender of Buccleuch. After lengthy negotiations the bold warden was induced or compelled for the sake of peace to give himself up to her. When he appeared before the angry Queen, a story runs that she asked him how he dared to venture on so audacious and desperate an undertaking. "What is there that a man dares not do?" proudly replied Buccleuch. The wrath of Elizabeth, it is said, was melted by so brave an answer, and turning to her attendants she remarked, "With ten thousand such men our brother of Scotland might shake the firmest throne in Europe."

Once launched, however, upon the sea of border song and story, one might run some risk of remaining up here on the walls of Carlisle Castle indefinitely and forgetting how nearly is the tether of our space run out.

With Henry VII., who gave his daughter to the Scottish King, a brief season of comparative quiet fell upon the border, and to this time some good authorities have attributed much of the minstrelsy which in such quaint but stirring language tells the story of perennial strife. The Scots appear to have been most prolific in this type of song, but such supremacy might partly be accounted for by the fact of the north side of the border having contained more habitable country and carrying a larger population.

After Flodden, where the men of Carlisle did doughty work under a Dacre, Scotland was smitten hip and thigh. Henry

Dacre Castle.

VIII. offered her peace if she would abandon her old and vexatious French alliance. But she refused, and the King, who had treated Wales with the highest statesmanship, turned in fury upon Scotland and swore he would make the marches harmless by depopulation if other means failed. Carlisle became more than ever a place of arms and the normal hatred of the men of Cumberland for their northern neighbours was stirred to frenzy by the King's violent measures. A frightful period of strife and devastation, conducted with devilish energy and method, set in, and the reprisals were of a like nature. The English Government was now sowing the wind, and was to reap the whirlwind. Bad as they had been before, the marches now became in this sixteenth century, when England at large was growing peaceful and domestic, more miserable than ever. The old clans or tribes were swollen by refugees from justice; outlaws and broken men of all sorts who ranged themselves beneath the battle-cries of Scott or Armstrong, Elliot or Græme. All semblance of respectability was erased from border strife. Dacre, who with a handful of men had repelled a Scottish army of 15,000 from the walls of Carlisle, rode with 2,000 men against the Armstrongs, but was defeated. The Scottish warden then attacked them with no better fortune. They became the terror of Cumberland and mustered 3,000 horse.

The Duke of Northumberland was now appointed "warden general," a new office. The measures he took show the desperate state of affairs, for watches were now kept day and night along the frontier, as in the days when Roman soldiery held Hadrian's Wall against the Picts. Every district had to furnish its own quota; while elaborate laws were laid down for the blowing of horns and the lighting of beacons. Every man who crossed the border had to account for himself. No Englishman might speak to a Scot without permission, nor might any Scot live in Carlisle, or even walk the streets, unaccompanied by a native, and, more durable than these fitful and passionate enactments, miles of thorn hedges were planted to hamper the raiding of stock.

Sir Walter Scott in his spirited and inimitable style has given us a graphic picture of the borderer of the Tudor period:

> A stark moss-trooping Scot was he
> As e'er crouched border lance by knee.
> Through Solway sands, through Jarra's moss,
> Blindfold he knew the paths to cross,
> By wily turns, by desperate bounds,
> Had baffled Percy's best bloodhounds.
> In Esk or Liddel fords were none
> But he would ride them one by one.
> Alike to him was time or tide,
> December's snow or July's pride;

Alike to him was tide or time,
Moonless midnight or matin prime:
Steady of heart and stout of hand
As ever drove prey from Cumberland.

It is a frightful picture, and yet this was a bit of Tudor England, the same England that contained the Devonshire of Raleigh and the Warwickshire of Shakespeare! Carlisle was so continuously in the thick of battle it is hopeless to attempt here any serious relation of its exploits. Once it was attacked from the south, for in that futile protest against the conditions created by the Reformation known as the Pilgrimage of Grace 8,000 men of Westmorland, under a Musgrave, rose, and regarding Carlisle as the nearest centre of a Royal authority, marched against it. But the soldiers and citizens of Carlisle were more inured to war than the men of Westmorland, and shattered them utterly, hanging over seventy from the city walls as a warning to reactionaries in general. But, in regard to the border clans, hanging the worst offenders and levelling their peel towers was not the only method of quieting them. Emigration to Ulster, which James I. was busy planting, was largely resorted to, and indeed under the new *régime* of law and order the mere plundering borderers were by no means loth to go. Armstrongs, Grahams and Johnstones flocked over by hundreds, and many a family famous to-day in Ulster has sprung from them, while the wars in the Netherlands and those of Gustavus Adolphus carried away a still greater share of this superfluous and turbulent humanity.

One of Carlisle's greatest triumphs too was of this date or thereabouts, when the garrison and townsmen drove back with slaughter and confusion an army of 10,000 Scots, hundreds of the fugitives perishing in the waters of the Solway. Of grief and this disaster the last King of Scotland died, leaving an infant daughter a week old, the famous Mary Stuart, who in after years when flying from Scotland, as we know, came to this very castle of Carlisle in her rash resolve to throw herself on Elizabeth's hospitality. Yonder, in the south-east angle of the castle, remnants of the tower yet stand which was her dwelling for many weeks. Down there in the meadows below she went hare-hunting or hawking or watching football matches almost daily, being, with her followers, so amazingly well mounted that, as her discontent and distrust increased, her custodians were in constant fear lest the young Queen some fine morning should show them a clean pair of heels and gallop off to Scotland again.

But it must not be supposed that Carlisle was so wholly given over to blood and iron that commerce and religion had no place. On the contrary the merchants did a thriving business, particularly in leather, not being particular, it is said, from which side of the border the hides came or to whom they belonged; while a mayor and aldermen on great occasions went to church in state at the Cathedral as in more commonplace towns. Carlisle took the plague too very badly, and lost nearly a quarter of its population. With the union of the Crowns, fresh efforts were made to civilise the borders, and there is some grim humour in the fact that as King James crossed the eastern march on his way to mount the throne of England a force of Scotsmen simultaneously crossed the western border and raided down the Eden valley as far as Penrith.

But it was King James, after all—or at any rate men acting vigorously under his orders—that put an end to the old border conditions, as we have endeavoured thus briefly to depict them. It was not of course the mere fulminations that he issued to his subjects in what was no longer politically a border country that had this effect, nor his futile attempt to rename Cumberland and Northumberland the Middle Shires, nor even a successful haul of Scottish moss-troopers and a liberal use of halters at Carlisle, which celebrated the first year of his reign. The gentry of the border would have paid but scant attention to the King's commands to pull down their peel towers, or to his platitudes on the utility of agricultural pursuits, if unaccompanied by pressure of a more insistent kind. And this was brought to bear, not violently and of a sudden, but patiently and with a strong hand, by Lord Howard of Naworth, who had married an heiress of the great house of Dacre.

"Belted Will" is of course one of the heroes of border history and fiction. But the character of a heady, merciless, hard-riding, iron-fisted administrator, with which legend and Sir Walter Scott have invested him are wholly fanciful, and partly due, no doubt, to the wild deeds of the Dacres, whose honours and estates he inherited. The real Lord William was a scholar, book collector, and antiquary; a grave and learned person, and, above all, a high-minded gentleman, with an inborn hatred of all that was base or ignoble. He and his lady, the younger of the two heiresses who merged in their husbands the great house of Dacre, had a passion for country life, and Lord William a great talent for rural administration. But his work was done entirely in legal, orderly fashion. Above all, he kept a sleepless eye on those entrusted with authority, and promptly rebuked any sign of weakness or connivance with offenders. The chief raiding clans fought long against these innovations. But gradually the better classes began to call the avocation of the mosstrooper by another name. No fortified houses except those belonging to the nobles and gentry were any longer permitted. Public opinion turned against the old order of things; and in the seventeenth century the business of looting and cattle-lifting was confined to predatory bands of outlaws and broken men, who found little sympathy and possessed no prestige. Lord William, moreover, introduced bloodhounds for tracking marauders, and, among other innovations, made the gentry responsible for the behaviour of their tenants.

When Taylor, the Water-Poet, passed through Carlisle and into Scotland in the seventeenth century, he reflected the views of the day in many lines descriptive of the anarchy that had so recently existed in these parts, and winds up with the unqualified opinion—

> That whoso then did in the Borders dwell
> Lived little happier than those in Hell.

But "now" he goes on to say—

> Since the all-disposing God of Heaven
> Hath these two kingdoms to one Monarch given,
> Blest peace and plenty on them both have showered,
> Exile and hanging have the thieves devoured,
> That now each subject may securely sleep,
> His sheep and neat, the black and white, doth keep."

In this last expression of opinion the excellent Water-Poet was a little too optimistic even still perhaps.

But with this elimination of the border by the Union, and the repression of border habits which followed it, Carlisle dwindled sadly in importance and population. It had always indeed been poor, and of a somewhat rude appearance in the eyes of southerners. In 1634 the Cathedral gave the impression to three strangers of "a great wild country church." It is needless to say that in the civil war Carlisle and Cumberland stood for the King. It sustained a memorable siege of eight months by its old enemies the Scots under Leslie, and after being reduced to the verge of starvation only surrendered at the battle of Naseby.

Three years later it had the remarkable and not very palatable experience of being garrisoned and defended by a force of Scots, then fighting on the King's side, but was surrendered to Cromwell, who placed there two large regiments of horse, one to secure the city, the other to put down the moss-troopers who had become active again during the war. Much of the Cathedral nave and adjacent buildings was demolished by the Puritan soldiers for repairing and strengthening the town defences.

I have dwelt so long on Carlisle, during the ages when in varying fashion it stood unique and alone among English towns, there is little space left for any of its later history when this particular distinction had vanished.

Indeed, Carlisle had never before been quite so small and unimportant as the beginning of the eighteenth century found it, though as a border capital, and a fortified as well as a Cathedral town, mere numbers are not quite a fair test of consequence. The first Jacobite rising, that of 1715, avoided the city, going by way of Penrith to Preston, where we know the motley gathering of Highlanders and Northumbrians met its fate. But in '45 Carlisle played both an ignominious and unpleasant part. A few hundred raw militia comprised the sum total of its defenders when the Highland army arrived before the walls. The Prince had just completed his investment, when news was brought that Wade was advancing on him from Newcastle, and he moved his force to Bramptcn, as a better position for offering battle to the expected marshal. Bad as the situation was within the city, it was not without its humours. For it seems that a fussy grocer, named Pattinson, was deputy mayor, and had given much cause for offence by his officious assumption of authority in the hour of danger. He went so far as to assume that his activity had frightened the Prince away, and was injudicious enough to send a special post to London to that effect.

Wade, as we know, never got to Carlisle. The roads were impassable for artillery, and this fact is instructive of how little intercourse there was in those days between the east and west marches. When Prince Charles heard that Wade was not advancing, he marched back to Carlisle and sat down before it in real earnest. The local militia, who were half-hearted, though under a good officer, and sore at being left unsupported by the government, refused to fight. A few of the citizens courageously proposed to garrison the castle alone, but the lately active deputy mayor was very far from being one of them. However, with the militia intractable, Colonel Durand had nothing for it but to surrender. The mayor and corporation were summoned to Brampton, and there on their bended knees delivered the keys of the city to the Prince, who on the following day entered Carlisle to the shrill skirl of a hundred bagpipes—an accompaniment which seems hard on the citizens in the nervous condition to which anxiety must have reduced them. No harm was done however by the garrison left there by the Pretender while the main body went south, and some one occupied the interval by immortalising the valiant deputy mayor in a still familiar jingle—

>Oh, Pattinson ! ohon ! ohon !
>Thou wonder of a mayor !
>Thou blest thy lot thou wert no Scot
>And blustered like a player.
>What hast thou done with sword and gun
>To baffle the Pretender,
>Of mouldy cheese and bacon grease
>Thou much more fit defender ?

Quite early in our tour we recalled the scenes at Penrith when the Highlanders a few weeks later retreated before the Duke of Cumberland's army toward Carlisle. Everybody knows how the gallant Lancashire Jacobite Townely remained with a trifling force to hold the city and face, so far as he at least was concerned, almost certain death—a hundred and twenty men of his Manchester regiment, twice as many Highlanders and a few Frenchmen remaining with him. A few days of bombardment sufficed to deliver Carlisle into the Duke's hands on his own terms. The Prince's garrison were confined in the Cathedral of all places, to the great indignation of the clergy, but a fortnight after were taken south, the officers mounted with their feet tied under their horses' bellies, and each horse fastened to the tail of the one in front. The common soldiers marched two and two, roped together with their arms pinioned; as melancholy a procession of a surety as ever tramped along the Penrith road !

For the three months preceding the battle of Culloden

Carlisle was charged with the maintenance of a large garrison, and great was the outcry from all classes. · After Culloden, the castle was packed tight for a long time with nearly 400 prisoners, who endured much suffering through the heat of the summer months. Ninety-six of these were condemned to death and the rest to transportation. The executions began in October and were continued in batches. The grim ceremony always opened in the castle-yard, where the prisoners were pinioned and seated on a black hurdle beside the excutioner. Then, at the demand of the sheriff, they were taken out through the gateway over the drawbridge and escorted in solemn procession to Gallows Hill outside the English gate, where they were hanged, drawn and quartered, with all the barbarity of detail then in vogue, the heads of some being subsequently set on pikes above the Scotch gate, the last instance of that time-honoured and gruesome custom in this country. The story of Carlisle henceforth, how in humdrum modern fashion it grew steadily in wealth and population, yet full of its own humours, its racy northern spirit, its pride in its exceptional place in history, its intense provincialism till modified by the stir of converging railways and abounding travellers—is all interesting enough, but quite beside our object, even if I had not already run to such length of tether on the subject as to put further gossip on it out of the question. Indeed I should perhaps have been all this time conducting my reader round the castle, which in the matter of dungeons, cells, gateways, walls and towers, all teeming with memories, is well worth seeing, instead of philandering on its past.

But for this purpose he will find an obliging and voluble commissioner, whose conscientious eloquence I gladly bear testimony to. Indeed I think it is some recollection of having delivered myself over bound hand and foot, so to speak, at the castle gate on my first visit that prompted me to rush my reader up so breathlessly on to the castle walls. My man was a new broom and swept every shred of sentiment from dungeon, keep and chamber as he trumpeted his way along, reading mostly from his guide-book, for he had not yet learnt his part. Indeed he began outside on the drill ground most vigorously with myself alone for an audience, and I am convinced he greatly tried the decorum of a squad of recruits who were practising the goose-step with a view doubtless to hunting De Wet later on in South Africa. So I really know very little of the internal structure of Carlisle Castle, though I confess that does not greatly distress me. Once out upon the walls however, I was a free man again, and much enjoyed myself. My ex-sergeant was a most worthy person, and has no doubt by this time mellowed greatly as a cicerone, glib enough at his part at any rate we may be sure, and perhaps even passing for an antiquary with bank holiday folk from Leeds or Rochdale—more power to him.

But there is not a spot in England, as the late Bishop Creighton, himself a native, has well said, that yields an outlook so stirring of its kind, so rich in memories for those who love to linger over a landscape for the tale it tells, as Carlisle Castle wall, and this must be my plea. Nor have I left room for more than a passing glance at the Cathedral, which, though small, has like the town a moving story, and to this day carries the scars of Roundhead volleys all over its outer walls. But there is plenty of architectural as well as historical interest in Carlisle Cathedral. Its western end is nearly eight centuries old and was the original parish church, and with some later additions forms the nave and transepts. It is built of local grey stone, while the large choir, built and rebuilt in times of stress and storm during the fourteenth century, is of red freestone. The older part is of pure Norman style, simple and massive, though some of the arches are most strangely pressed out of shape by a lapse in the foundation centuries ago, which must have caused a world of terror at the time. The choir is Early English and of fine proportions, but I must confess what holds my fancy most within it are the quaint mouldings of the capitals on the pillars that support the main arches. On these are carved most realistic scenes from country life. On one is a sower, on another a reaper, on another a man gathering grapes; but the masterpiece of all is a monk sitting over a fire, on which a pot is boiling. The reverend gentleman has taken off one boot, and is holding it out, as well as his bare foot, to warm before the flame.

It would be asking almost too much of a visitor to Lakeland that he should extend his operations beyond Carlisle. But should these few pages of desultory gossip on the Castle wall have stirred in any way his fancy or his curiosity a pleasant half-day's run over good and level roads to the northward forms an admirable sequel to such a train of thought. For from Carlisle to Gretna Green, across the Esk and the Scottish border, is but eight miles. Thence turning eastward for half that distance, you may run through the " Debatable land " and the edge of Solway moss—and recrossing the Esk again higher up at Longtown another eight miles will bring you back again. It would not be easy in all Britain to find another twenty miles so palpitating with strenuous memories. For myself I confess that, as I crossed the Eden and passing through Stanwix set my face towards the Solway, I felt my pulses stirring in no sluggish fashion.

The sun was bright but tempered, and the skies were clear; the wind blew gently, but in its breath was the exhilarating crispness of the sea, as the great plain spread before me to the grey hills of Scotland. A mile or so of long-drawn suburb, of low stone cottages, slate-roofed and white-walled, of public houses, ancient and modern, and the broad road parted. The right hand sped away westward to Longwood, Langholme, and the classic dales of Esk and Liddel. The other finger pointed in laconic fashion to Gretna Green and Annandale, to Lockerbie and Ecclefechan and other places famous in border story—and this last was my outward route. Even those who care nothing for tales of battle and murder, and sudden death, for politics and princes, Romans or Picts, Normans, Danes, or moss-troopers, or old, forgotten far-off things of any kind, might allow themselves perhaps emotions of a gentler sort as they press the dust which has whirled around the flying wheels of so many generations of lovers. It is but some five miles hence to the Border, and how the whips of the postillions must have cracked over the smoking teams as the last stage of the great race lay stretched like a white band across the plain before them. I was surprised to find here even yet so lonesome a road and so

Gretna Green.

poor a land. Cultivation has come apparently with laggard steps. Though no longer a moss, every bit of it tells the tale of laboured reclamation. Even now great strips of heathery bog land spread on either side of the straight highway; and recently cut peats were drying in the summer sun as I passed along. Pastures were pale, and growing crops were thin; banks of sod, crowned with yellow gorse and flanked by ditches of dark peaty water, traced themselves over the spongy, sandy land, so well calculated to drink up the blood that so often drenched it. Thick fringes of native fir woods, sombre and lowering, spread along the middle distance, and over their dark tops the pale grey forms of the Scottish hills rose in curious contrast. Such dwellers as there were along or near this classic highway seemed for the most part of the humble sort, judging from the low-roofed cottages which with whitewashed walls crouched sparsely upon the heath or pine lands, while the smell of peat fires came pleasantly upon the breeze. But all this soon changed : for in half an hour I was standing on the high bridge over the Esk, near the point where it opens into the Solway Firth, and I stood there long. Westward towards the sea stretched a waste of blue water and golden sands twinkling with the white wings of countless sea-fowl and the white crests of breaking wavelets, those cruel tides before which the "Laird of the Solway lake" with his young nephew, the last of the Redgauntlets, rode that wild night race for life. Eastward, a herd of cattle, standing knee-deep in the river, still shallow and stony at the ebb tide, made up a foreground that here at least was something more than conventional. Away behind them lay broad marshy meadows, through which the gleaming river twisted, and beyond and everywhere to the north the green Dumfriesshire uplands. From here too, though near thirty miles away, Skiddaw rose boldly up against the southern sky, while the wide gap the Eden makes between the Lakeland mountains and the Pennine range marked that road to England which for the Scottish raiders had such abiding significance.

Before this bridge was built, some sixty years ago, the Esk was crossed here by a ford only negotiable at certain periods of the tide. Think of this further element of excitement and suspense superadded to the mere question of pace-making when the pursuit to Gretna after absconding or abducted maidens was fast and hot! The alternative then presented itself of taking the road from Carlisle to Longtown, crossing the bridge there and swerving back through Solway Moss for Gretna.

The course was four or five miles longer, and some cool calculation and accurate knowledge of the tides was invaluable to pursuers and pursued, or at least to their conductors. This choice of roads added zest in every sense to these wild gallops of honest lovers or shameless fortune-hunters, for the pursuers were thus enabled at times to head off the chase by taking the Longtown angle, while the truant couple stood chafing on the wrong side of the fords of Esk, cut off completely by the enemy from the goal of their desires and Gretna Green.

This famous village is yet two miles on, across the "Debatable land," and stands at the top of a gentle slope at whose foot rolls the Sark, a trifling stream, though now the actual boundary of the two kingdoms. Gretna Green consists of a few old-fashioned cottages of pleasant and leafy appearance clustering round a four-cross road, a venerable looking kirk and a small country house standing in its own grounds and known as the Hall. It was at this last that very many of the marriages were actually celebrated. Much legend has gathered round a certain blacksmith, but as a matter of fact no credentials nor experience of any kind were required of the officiating functionary at a Gretna Green marriage, and almost any of its limited inhabitants were available. Still certain people fell naturally into the habit of being on the spot, and grew no doubt a little glibber than others in the despatch and dignity with which they united applicants and forwarded the necessary documents to Edinburgh. The Hall was the place to which couples of condition, if not pressed for time, would turn. Pennant, however, in 1770 found an old fisherman in a blue coat with a quid of tobacco in his mouth, the most active matrimonial officer of that day. As fees were given, competition was probably brisk, and in the humbler ranks, it is said, a gill of whisky was occasionally considered adequate for the amateur parson's compensation. An Act of Parliament in 1857, making a three weeks' residence necessary for all but Scotsmen, knocked the brisk matrimonial trade that Gretna

Green had conducted for about a hundred years completely, on the head, and left it high and dry with nothing but an imperishable sentimental interest to live upon. In the course of a day spent in the neighbourhood, I found many people to whom the memory of these times was of course fresh enough and heard many stories whose narration would not be strictly relevant here. One brief illustration from an eye witness, however, to show that Gretna Green marriages were not always incited by the sterner sex, may be given. My informant was a Scotsman from Glasgow who had been bred at Gretna, and he very well remembered, he told me, being knocked up one morning by an uncle who among the rest turned an honest penny by uniting runaway couples. He was wanted as a second witness, and the amorous couple proved to be a barmaid of the flashy and strong-minded type and an elderly gentleman of education, and doubtless means, but in a lamentable state of intoxication. The motive of the marriage, money, was unblushingly obvious, and the more backward party to the impending compact could not be induced for some time to stand up, apparently because he was unable. At last, however, the perpendicular condition desirable for decency's, if not for form's, sake, was achieved and the necessary question was put whether he took the bespangled person beside him for his wife. "Wife?" said the happy but somewhat inarticulate bridegroom. "Oh, come, I don't know about that!"

"Oh yes, you do!" said the lady, stamping her foot. "You just do as you're told."

And he did, and my informant's uncle read a chapter of the Bible over the blushing pair, a proceeding which was supposed to give some semblance of decency to this monstrous abuse.

Leaving Gretna by the Longwood road, we are soon across the Sark again and upon English ground. English now at least, but of old that dark region which called no man lord and no monarch king, and where no laws even professed to run—the

home of outlaws, thieves and bandits, who, finding refuge in this
"Debatable land" acquired the name of "Batables" and were
abhorred and feared of all men. There was little enough, however, to indicate such sinister memories till the road dropped
down to Solway Moss, and there sure enough was the real thing.
Neither time nor change have touched those miles of rank
heather and quaking bog and sombre fir woods. My road ran
for a mile or so through the edge of it, raised above the peaty
ditches and shaded by the gloomy pines. As far as I could
see to the northward lay the pathless tract round which so
many centuries of strife and crime, such a wealth of legend,
song and story, have gathered. I crossed the Esk again at
Longtown, where with the rush of an inland salmon river it chafes
the arches of the stone bridge which leads into the border
town. I leaned for a few minutes against the parapet and
looked up the shining shallows of the river to the green hills
beyond which rise above the junction of the Liddel and the
Esk, and part the once turbulent dales they water. I gave a
thought of course to Dandie Dinmont and to young Brown
who passed up this way, to that memorable encounter with the
footpads, and to Kinmont Willie too, whose fetters were still
clanking on his feet and hands as the Buccleuch and his two
hundred men passed that misty morning through Longtown.
Hence to Carlisle, as I have already said, is a level run of some
eight or nine miles. I do not know that there is very much to
say about it, unless that in all likelihood it has been in days
gone by more trodden by the soldier and the war-horse than
any road in Britain. I had lunched near Gretna, and an old
copy of the *Lay of the Last Minstrel* was on the inn table. I
picked it up, and it fell open at the scene where Margaret, in
a love-sick dream on the walls of Branksome Castle, is startled
by the sudden lighting of the war beacons. As I rode
smoothly home to Carlisle through the gathering twilight and
the English hills rose in grey masses ahead of me, the once
familiar stanza kept jingling in my ears with an insistency

that in such a place and mood I felt but little disposition to resist:

> Is yon the star o'er Penchryst Pen
> That rises slowly to her ken,
> And spreading broad its wavering light
> Shakes its loose tresses on the night,
> Is yon red glare the western star?
> Oh! 'tis the beacon blaze of war.

Eskdale.

Kendal.

CHAPTER XI

IN the course of this concluding chapter I have to cover the five-and-forty miles that lies between Carlisle and Kendal. This is not, however, quite such a formidable business as it sounds, seeing that for the first stage of eighteen miles to Penrith I shall leave the reader either to take the train or to give himself over wholly to the material pleasures of a fast run over a really fine and comparatively level road. As a matter of fact, on this section of the Old North Road, there is not a great deal to stop for, nor, if there were, should I venture to do so, seeing how much more time I have already spent in the low country than the title of this book may seem to justly warrant. Still, though the route is outside the bounds I have had to set myself, belonging as it does to the Pennine rather than the Lakeland country, I would strongly recommend the traveller bound for Penrith with time upon his hands to make the longer and less comfortable journey up the Eden valley. The roads are tortuous and not always good, but they lead through many scenes that are beautiful and many places that are famed in story, as any one may well believe who is not habitually asleep as he passes over this section of the Midland Railway on the road to Scotland. At Armathwaite, for instance, nine miles from Carlisle, the Eden ceases for a time from troubling, and spreads a broad unruffled surface below crags and overhanging woods where stands the ancient castle of the Skeltons. The Nunnery too, a venerable manor house a few miles further up the valley, is justly famous for the beauty of its walks and woods and waterfalls. Nature, of a truth, has here lent herself in a marvellous way to art, and art has exercised a tasteful and rare restraint.

The ancient village of Kirkoswald, thick with memories of border heroes and Scottish raids, and rich in green foliage and red freestone, lies just beyond, between the moorland and the river. Featherstonhaughs have been here since the Reformation at any rate, in an ancient and mellow manor house that springs from a monastic college, and still bears its name. On the slope above too are the scant remnants of one of the greatest of the Dacre castles. Indeed it was probably the greatest, "one of the fairest fabrics," says Sandford in 1610, though even then falling to ruin, "that ever eyes looked upon, the hall a hundred feet long and the great portraiture of King Brute lying in the end of the roof of the hall." A Dacre had won Kirkoswald by the audacious abduction of its heiress—a Mutton – from Warwick Castle in 1300, just as two centuries later another Dacre secured the barony of Greystoke by precisely similar means. It was from hence that the Dacre of Flodden notoriety marched to that victorious field in which the men of the Eden valley took so forward a part. A beautiful church too of three aisles stands in the meadows at the village end beneath an old rookery, while a venerable freestone bell-tower perches alone upon the green ridge above and contains a bell of which Kirkoswald is justly proud.

I stood one summer evening on the roof of this same bell-tower in company with the ancient sexton whose care it is. Heavy thunderstorms had cleared the air and filled the Eden, which rolled its brimming waters near bank high through the grassy vale beneath. We looked over in the direction of Penrith and the Lakeland mountains, and even yet more particularly to the green swell of the Pennines close at hand upon the east, and watched the evening shadows crawling over the long smooth shoulder of Crossfell.

My companion was a stout local patriot, and did not seem to think much of Lakeland and its mountains.—" a Kirkoswald man born and bred, and proud of it," though a most quizzical looking old gentleman of exceeding low stature for this land of " lang-men " ; no " new-fangled scholar," but a clerk and sexton of the good old sort, from the top of his shiny head to the soles of his hob-nailed feet. " Now that's the mountain for me," said he, looking at Crossfell, which I have remarked elsewhere is for its height (2,800 feet) very much the tamest hill in England, and lays against the sky like a Hampshire down. "That's the mountain for me," he repeated in a tone of unmistakable challenge to something I had let drop about Skiddaw or Helvellyn.

" You can ride horseback or drive a waggon on to the top of that mountain."

My thoughts were wandering. They had wandered in fact across that very mountain to the scene of many youthful rambles about the wild sources of the Tees and Wear.

" When the last Maister Featherstonhaugh," continued my companion in a more emphatic key, " came of age he roasted a bullock whole on top of yon mountain."

I could produce no such records as that to the credit of Helvellyn and Skiddaw, so my guide put an end to any lingering doubts I might be still supposed to have as to the supremacy of Crossfell by a final clincher.

" Old Mr. Marshall used to light a bonfire and give two or three thousand folks beer and bread and cheese on top of yon mountain when his man got in at the ' lection.' "

Nothing further could be said after that, and I descended the ladder from the belfry, feeling that my standards of comparison would have to be readjusted.

Just across the Eden too, on the way to Penrith, is Lazonby, once part of the great Inglewood Forest, but which Camden tells us was "deparkt in Henry the Eighth's time, and one Jack-a-Musgrave, a metled man, got a lease of a 100 years of it and planted five of his sons at five several houses in it. This Jack-a-Musgrave was so metled a man, as the country people would say, that if they had a spirited boy he would just be a Jack-a-Musgrave." And there was plenty of scope for heady characters in the Eden valley in the days of Henry VIII,

Great Salkeld.

as a reference to the last chapter will show. But Great Salkeld, a little further on towards Penrith, with its massive fortified church tower and pretty village of red freestone, produced greater men and more eligible patterns to youth than even Jack-a-Musgrave. For no less a couple than Lord Ellenborough and Dick Whittington were born here. They went out however to adorn other spheres, while Musgraves still flourish at Eden Hall close by.

The Great North Road pushes straight through Penrith,

where we may join it again, and passing through scenes dealt with in the opening chapter of this book, climbs steadily up to Shap, which is 11 miles away and nearly 900 feet above the sea.

Not only the old coach road, but the London and North Western Railway ascends this long pull to Shap, a place that from many points of view deserves some special notice. Both passengers and drivers in the coaching days knew Shap—or rather the pass four miles to the southward and three hundred feet higher up which bears its name—only too well, as the

The Road over Shap Fell.

wildest and coldest stage between London and Glasgow. Regarded however as a village within the Lakeland district, which it may just lay claim to be, Shap is a place to itself in more senses than one and quite unique. Delightful otherwise as are most places of sojourn in the Lake Country, they are all, with scarcely an exception, set in a hole. No stretch of imagination could maintain that any of them possessed in themselves a stimulating climate. For those who can get up on the hills this is of little consequence. But such as who from age or inactivity must remain more or less upon the level, may be happy and even healthy, but in summer and autumn they can scarcely attain that desirable condition commonly spoken of as braced up. Now at Shap you are on the very roof of the world, and might well wax vigorous without stirring beyond the garden gate. This monopoly of so huge an advantage has stirred Shap up in the last twenty years—or I should more rightly say has stirred the Lake-going world up to its obvious advantages, for it does not appear to me that the straggling moorland village has greatly risen to the occasion or has yet realised its manifest destiny. Its inns have some venerable traditions connected with coaching days, which people of sentiment like to encourage in passing, to the extent of a bottle of beer and some bread and cheese or a chop perhaps. But for anything more durable the glamour of ancient history is not enough, and Shap struck me as somewhat doggedly conservative in this matter. Some traditions too are highly bad ones. When Prince Charles Edward passed through here on his way south for instance, I have read in a local handbook that he complained of the charges made and put a black mark against Shap in his household book to the effect that his landlady was " a sad imposing wife." It was no doubt a coincidence, but in taking a passing meal at a Shap inn a hundred and fifty-five years afterwards I had occasion for the first time I think in the Lake Country to observe that the accommodation, though respectable of its kind, was not quite in proportion to the price charged. A passing cyclist, who also thought himself injured, made more forcible observations than I did, and unlike myself derived no consolation whatever from the above mentioned highly interesting fact, of which I placed him in possession. For he remarked, and with much justice, that he was a member of the C.T.C., while the Prince was not. The latter however, poor fellow, had to walk on foot the whole twenty-seven miles from Penrith to Kendal, a point in which we had very much the better of him. But I should be sorry to take away Shap's character on grounds so slight. I am told that in August it is full to bursting, which is a good sign for its honesty. But a crowd that would strain the accommodation of Shap would after all not make much impress on the vast expanse of moor, fell and mountain which sweeps away so delightfully from its homely walls, and even in August solitude would not be far to seek. What Cerrig y druidion is to North Wales so is Shap to the Lake Country, save for the fact that it has a station at its door, which Cerrig y druidion is very far from having. Like the latter, it is

Shap Abbey.

sometimes registered as bleak in guide-books. But in summer time this often infers another and more attractive epithet. For myself I think it must be delightful. There is a sense of freshness and expansiveness about the outlook which has a great charm to my thinking. Formerly Lakeland visitors did not come on foot much east of the High Street range, and Haweswater was the limit of the carriage folk. But from Shap you may approach all this beautiful country just as readily and start as well as sleep, upon a fine elevation. It stands, as it were, upon a boundary, for the route of traffic from Penrith to

Kendal may fairly be said to divide the outer fringe of Lakeland from moorlands that belong in character, though not geographically, to Yorkshire and Northumberland.

There is a market in Shap and a quaint old market cross, now used as a parish room. There are several very old houses and a church too of the twelfth century in a commanding situation, and enfolded in summer time in a mantle of sycamore leaves. Altogether, as becomes a place that is a dozen miles from anywhere and so near the clouds, Shap has a character and originality all its own. Still more, it has the remains of a famous abbey, the only abbey in Westmorland; founded in the twelfth century by a son of that Gospatrick whom Rufus discovered lording it over Cumbria and kicked out so unceremoniously when he made it English ground. It was occupied by white canons of the Augustin order, was well endowed by Viponts, Cliffords, Lowthers, Curwens and others, and waxed wealthier as time went on. It must have had a great humanising influence over this wild and stormy country. A large block of the abbey church still stands amid the wreckage of what time and predatory builders and wall-makers have left of the main fabric. A mile from the village, poised in solitude upon a slope above the infant Lowther, it yet remains a noble relic of forgotten days, and gathers additional distinction from the loneliness of its site.

Away down in the low country at the back of Shap, eastward that is to say towards Appleby and the Eden, there is a region rich in the relics of old times—in manor houses built long since by Armigers, but now the abodes of farmers, and in churches raised before the days of Bruce. Crosby-Ravensworth, Strickland, the two Meaburns, Morland, Bolton, Kirkbythore, and many another spot lies down here that antiquaries at any rate hold in high regard, while the bright streams of the Lyvenant, which water all this region, give a further charm to many an unnoticed and old-world nook as they hurry by.

But it is to the wild and high country on the west that Shap chiefly sets its face, to Kidsty Pike and the High Street, and the eastern ridges of the great deer forest that rolls away to Ullswater and Patterdale. Swindale and Naddel, Mardale and Haweswater are all within an easy walk; the last named lake, though comparatively little known, being among the most beautiful of northern waters. Some three miles long and a bare half mile broad, it lies in the trough of hills that rise in height as they near the lake-head, where is a picture scarce less imposing, if on a narrower scale, than that of Ullswater.

Haweswater.

This is the best trouting lake too in the whole country, if one is not over critical as to size; and so it should be, seeing that it is strictly preserved by Lord Lonsdale. But the trout here are really free risers, an admirable quality which the strictest preservation cannot always ensure. Memories of a soft and breezy June day spent upon Haweswater, and of its sporting little trout, will remain with me for a long time. Indeed they kept me so busy that if this had been my only visit to the lake I should have but a confused recollection of dark wavelets rolling ceaselessly towards a wall of blowing woodland, and a vague vision on the other side of lofty fells and the white gleam of a cataract breaking down them.

Mardale too, in the deep glen at the head of Haweswater, is a hamlet unforgetable for the charm of its romantic beauty and seclusion from the world. Here is a snug inn—the Dun Bull—and an ancient church set among yew trees and of a size suitable to a valley that can scarcely contain a hundred souls in all. But there were kings in Mardale, as there were kings in Patterdale for all that, till some fifteen years agone, when the last representative of the reigning family, Mr. Hugh Holme, died, and with him the dynasty. The first Hugh Holme came to Mardale in 1209, and his descendants held the estate he then acquired in direct succession till the other day. And their kingship has been long undisputed. This is not quite so long as the Lloyds of Cwmbychan, near Harlech, dwelt in their savage mountain fastness, and the Welsh family, though Armigers, had no subjects to rule over; but otherwise there is something of a parallel. Near the foot of the lake too there is Thornethwaite Hall, which recalls a novel that was very famous when I was a boy, in which Anthony Trollope set the whole novel-reading world asking each other whether they could forgive a certain young lady or whether her folly was unpardonable. Few novelists, I confess, appeal very strongly to my topographical sentiment. Perhaps it is my fancy goes out so strongly for the things that have been there, there is no room left in the landscape for those that are creations of the midnight oil, though, as Trollope wrote before breakfast chiefly, the phrase is not a happy one. But as a staunch admirer of Trollope's I yield myself wholly to him in a Wiltshire water meadow or on the slope of a Wiltshire down, which on the part of a more than half native, is a strong mark of confidence. He has steeped his people in its atmosphere so thoroughly and yet with so little effort, so little vernacular, so little landscape painting, much less with the clumsy encumbrances of glossaries and maps. But the creator of Mrs. Proudie, and Archdeacon Grantly and Dr. Thorne would not take me a yard out of my way in Cumberland. Trollope's Vavasours were a Cumbrian family, it is true, but they might have lived in Wiltshire, at Bullhampton, for any local character that envelops them. Trollope's glimpse of Shap, however, forty years ago is not without interest, as the glory of the coaching period had recently given way to what for Shap

Near Bampton.

was the depressing influence of the railroad. The coach passengers, he remarks, stopped just long enough there " to thank Heaven they had not been born Shappites," and he pictures the place in his time as looking back with fond regret to what it conceived to be the lustre of its past. Tourist possibilities had not then dawned on Shap, and if all travellers shared Trollope's tastes they would still be in embryo.

After leaving Shap on our southward journey there are many miles of undulating but gradually ascending road before we

A WILD OUTLOOK

top the watershed. Fine fresh moorland sweeps all about us, and herds of small Highland cattle of every shade of colour known to the bovine race roaming restlessly about, not yet perhaps acclimatised to their change of scene, give a further touch of character to the landscape. The broken uplands of Shap Fell fill in the outlook to the right. Away beyond the hollow on our left, where the railroad is struggling over the apex of its long steep climb, the smooth crest of Crosby Fell rolls away by Orton Scaur towards the valley of the upper

Looking West from Shap Abbey.

Eden, to Kirkby Stephen and the wild sheep-walks that look out over Durham and Yorkshire. Down yonder too, near the railroad, though nearly as high above sea-level as Shap village, is Shap Wells, a solid, roomy mansion set amid an oasis of fir woods by the banks of the infant Lune. This is a really comfortable hotel, and you need not, of course, drink the waters which provide the motive for its existence unless you like. If a powerful taste is any test of efficacy in such cases, Shap Wells should be a spot blessed among health-seekers, for the flavour of rotten egg is as well imitated by the natural spring which bubbles up here in the wood as in any more famous resort. But the moorland air here must be at least as potent a restorative as the most nauseous water, and there is certainly a charm and a repose about the place that must be welcome to those whose health or fancy inclines them to take life quietly. The moorland breezes murmur soothingly in the pines. The fountains of the infant Lune sparkle beneath their shade and prattle their childish songs upon the rocks. The patient seeks his morning draught by bowery ways that wind cunningly through sylvan glens, while all beyond the peace and silence of the moorland reigns supreme. Life cannot be wildly exciting at Shap Wells, though three score people in one hotel are beyond a doubt capable of making it very hot indeed. But such are not the type, I fancy, who haunt this substantial, respectable and comfortable looking hostelry, which was originally, I believe, a nobleman's shooting-box. I have read somewhere, in a local publication probably, that once a visitor has tried Shap Wells he remains faithful to it unto death. I have come across this trite remark before of course, and sometimes applied by local patriots to places of most forbidding character. But Shap Wells, I think, merits much of the praise its *habitués* bestow upon it, if only for the fact that so far as I know Cumberland and Westmorland it is the only first-class hotel in the two counties set in a bracing air and on a high elevation. Personally I would sooner take the rougher accommodation, which is all that at present Shap village four miles away has to offer: for not only has it a railway station, but it is handier to the districts over which a sound man would by preference wander.

But to return to the Kendal road, from which Shap Wells is removed by a long half-mile of byway. The greater portion of what lies before us, main artery as it once was between north and south, though now but little trodden, traverses as wild a country as you could wish for. And something more too, for after losing sight of Shap Wells the solitude takes grand and striking shapes. Lofty fells fill the foreground upon either hand, bold in outline and clad from base to summit with that crisp verdure which Britain alone of all the countries of the earth can lay in such ample folds against the blue of heaven. One feels instinctively that if the upstanding hills, but little over two thousand feet any of them, showed their steep sides to you, washed gray and barren by rains and parched by fierce suns, and partly clad perhaps with hungry pine-woods, the spell in which they now hold you would have gone. You would hurry on your way and carry with you no impression worth mentioning to be a comfort in the smoky town or by the winter fireside. But these vast steeps of turf, fresh with the moisture of countless springs, of constant mists and nightly dews, and illumined with the suns of June, how beautiful are they—how sensitive to every swell and curve of the rock beneath, how quick to catch every passing movement of the sky! One might sometimes fancy the cloud shadows actually pressed the turf as they passed over it, so instinct with life and movement does it seem. With what admirable harmony too do the grey out-cropping rocks blend with the varied greens! How richly coloured are the sprouting brackens on the lower slopes, how black the water-channels that cleave the hollows, how white the water that leaps down them! But the Shap fells soon drop behind us. Wastdale and Yarlside, Lordseat and Barnsdale, rise and fall upon the West, while Rounthwaite and Whinfell, High Carlin and Greyriggs close in the east in long procession.

Whinfell, by the way, was one of the half-dozen official beacons of Westmorland in the old border days; the next one being Orton Scaur just across the Lune beyond Shap Wells. Among the chief items of border service by which the statesmen of the two counties held their lands was that of lighting the beacon fires when the alarm was sounded. It was no " red glare on Skiddaw " as in Macaulay's famous lines that " roused the burghers of Carlisle" when the Spanish Armada was on the sea. There would be too much cloud around the summit of these higher mountains for reliable signal beacons, and moreover the nimble horsemen from beyond the Solway would have covered too much ground while the most agile mountaineers were climbing 3,000 feet, nor yet again was Skiddaw in the main route of either soldier or moss-trooper.

The road is steep as well as solitary. Two or three farmhouses at long intervals are the only signs of man. The sound of falling water and the occasional bleat of a sheep alone break the eternal silence of the hills. One wonders what some of the cockney or Midland county passengers on the coach-top thought of this country as they passed through it for the first time. One knows the dread in which it was held in winter at any rate. To our friends bound for Gretna Green it must have been a sad trial at all seasons, for the road, though better probably then than now, was not less steep. There was plenty of movement along here too in the 'forty-five, and in the first chapter of this book we saw the Prince's army hurrying north again by this route with the Duke's close upon their heels.

As we break out of the high fell country into civilisation again, and begin the gradual descent into the rich basin in which Kendal lies, the outlook towards Windermere and the Lancashire fells comes as a sharp contrast after so long burrowing in the troughs of hills. Kendal is, I think, the pleasantest of all northern towns, even to look down upon from a height, a process trying to the complexion of any place where several thousand human beings, Anglo-Saxons at any rate, are busy making a livelihood. There is no disturbing factor of any consequence to break the harmony of the pleasant light grey tone which pervades the place as a whole, and the smoke from its thousand roof-trees steals up in peaceful and delicate clouds, as if nothing of greater distraction than the cooking of the family dinner, the dressing of May flies and March browns, or the tying of casting lines, with which industry Kendal seems to be inseparably associated, was filling the minds of the townsfolk. No belching chimneys, no garish factories, nor any other industrial monstrosity thrusts itself upon the artistic continuity of Kendal's subdued tones. And I think you like it as much on a closer acquaintance as from a bird's-eye view. It is an easy-going, well-to-do looking, self-respecting county town, freshened up and kept cheerful by a good outside income earned by the entertainment of strangers and foreigners. Even the early history of Kendal was comparatively uneventful, though Appleby was raided again and again, and in the fourteenth century, that wretched period for the border country, was so ruthlessly gutted that it never really recovered. But the seat of its sister barony was rarely attacked. The people round, however, were always liable to border service and might be called at any moment to aid in the defence of Cumberland. They had some fame too as archers, and at Flodden did notable service under Dacre of Gillsland.

> The left-hand wing with all his route
> The lusty Lord Dacres did lead;
> With him the bows of Kendal stout
> With milke-white coats and crosses read;
> There are the bows of Kendal bold
> Who fierce will fight and never flee.

Even in the Civil War Kendal escaped, while Appleby sustained a long siege for the King. All the gentry, tenants and statesmen of Westmorland went out willingly or unwillingly in the Royal cause, and the list of fines for the redemption of estates levied by Cromwell on the barony of Kendal alone reached a goodly sum.

In the arts of peace too Kendal was energetic, being famous in the Middle Ages for its woollen cloth, and doing a large trade in printed cottons during the seventeenth and early eighteenth century; long strings of packhorses carrying the bales south for shipment at Liverpool to the West Indies and North

American Colonies. It is worth noting that, on the plantations of Maryland and Virginia particularly the negroes hoed their corn and tobacco arrayed to a large extent in Kendal cottons. The revolt of the Colonies and the rise of Yorkshire together killed this industry, and then we are told that, just as Kendal had built up a very large business in the supply of knitted stockings to army contractors, the British soldier was put into trousers and short socks to the complete discomfiture of the Westmorland knitters. This is not the place however to write up the commercial history of Kendal or enumerate the many minor trades which even now make with other things for its contented appearance. Let us notice rather the ruined castle so proudly perched above the town, though to reach it we must cross the Kent, whose clear and rapid streams wash the outskirts of the ancient borough. One might weave much romance about Kendal Castle. Its ramparts and scanty ruins of grey silurian rock entirely cover the crown of the lofty, isolated hill from which it dominates the town and overlooks the vale below with rare significance—" a stern castle mouldering on the brow of a green hill " Wordsworth calls it.

But as a matter of fact no particular tales of blood and battle cling to Kendal Castle. Its history is but that of the baronial families and English monarchs who have in turn possessed it.

Founded or more probably rebuilt in some rude fashion when Rufus annexed this country, the two towers and encircling walls which yet remain are supposed to be the work of Henry III.

To go through a list of the Norman houses of Taillboys, Veteriponts, Rooses, and Lancasters, who by marriage, inheritance, or royal grant held the Barony of Kendal in whole or part would be an outrage here. It will be enough to say that in the early fifteenth century it fell to the Parrs, and after five descents the admirable Katherine was born here, who was fortunate, not of a truth in captivating the fancy of Henry

VIII., but in being the last lady to do so, and thereby acquiring immortality, without at the same time losing her head. She had been twice widowed it may be remembered, and at the age of thirty was just about to make a love match with Seymour, whom she ultimately took for her fourth husband, when the King pounced on her. She had spent much time too with her Strickland relatives at Sizergh, where their descendants still live, and was most intimately associated with Kendal. Specimens of her fancy work, says Miss Agnes Strickland, are still treasured there, and show that she was as gifted with her needle as in her head and heart. Her lofty character, her cheerfulness, her erudition and quick wit we know succeeded in keeping the ailing and irritable King in good humour, though enthusiasm for the new religion led her into arguments with his Majesty which very nearly cost even Katherine her head. For a breath of opposition on his pet subject was what this pious monarch even in his most genial moments could not tolerate. She married her old lover, Admiral Lord Seymour, two months after Henry's death, and in a little over a year afterwards died at the birth of her first and only child at the age of thirty-six. Surely as strange a career as noble lady ever had ! But her vicissitudes were not over, and continued after she had been centuries in the grave, beneath the chapel at Sudeley in Gloucestershire, her husband's property. Some of my readers will perhaps remember the gruesome story of the disinterment of her remains at the close of the eighteenth century, and though not quite in order, I cannot resist touching briefly on it here.

In the year 1782 a party of ladies were visiting at Sudeley, and while exploring the ruined chapel were moved by certain indications to excavate under the north wall. Their curiosity was rewarded by finding a leaden coffin within a foot of the surface bearing an inscription to the effect that it contained the remains of Katherine Parr. They caused the coffin to be cut open in two places, and found within a body wrapped in cerecloth. Lifting that part which covered the face, it disclosed the features of the Queen in the most perfect state of preservation, even to the eyes, and this after the lapse of two centuries and a half! The unexpected sight however seems to have unnerved the ladies, and omitting to replace either the cloth or the lead covering, they hastily ordered the earth to be thrown back. Soon afterwards, one, Mr. Lucas, the tenant of the ground on which the ruined chapel stood, reopened the grave and exposed the coffin. He moreover cut open the lid and discovered the entire body wrapped in six or seven cerecloths and quite uncorrupted. The flesh where he exposed it was quite white and moist. Two years afterwards some unauthorised bucolics took the body out of the coffin and laid it on a heap of rubbish for all to see. An eye-witness assured Miss Strickland's friend, Miss Jane Porter, that the features remained even then for some time perfect, showing distinct traces of beauty—that a costly dress, not a shroud, was on the body, which was of beautiful proportions, and shoes on the feet, which were extremely small. The vicar somewhat tardily, and not before decay had set in, caused the corpse to be restored to its grave and coffin. Even then curiosity does not seem to have been exhausted, for two years later another examination was made though this time under scientific auspices, and a report published in the *Archæologia* for 1787. The face had by now gone, but the body, even to the hands and nails, was in good preservation. The Queen must have been of low stature, since the lead coffin was but five feet four inches long. After that the poor lady was left in peace and has, I believe, been secured this many a long year from further intrusion by the owners of the property. Pity she had not lain in Westmorland among her kin in Kendal Church and in the soil of which in life she had owned so much and so greatly honoured by her virtue and her talents. There, alongside (to speak broadly) of Cicely Neville and Anne Countess of Pembroke, she would have completed the trio of historic Westmorland dames, and would have been saved at least from the neglect and indignities her remains suffered in her husband's country.

Kendal Church, which stands at the fringe of the town near the bank of the river, would catch at once the attention of the merest layman in such matters as something out of the common, and the layman would be right. There is nothing, I believe, quite like it in England, its prototype being generally looked for in the Church of St. John Lateran at Rome. Its great breadth, having no less than five aisles, together with the height of the square tower which springs from its west end, gives it a certain squat look which is not perhaps in strict keeping with the rules of art. But one may well waive such technicalities in a building so ancient, so spacious—for it is among the largest parish churches in England—and so rich in all that concerns the story of Westmorland.

The nave and two adjoining aisles seem to have been raised about the year 1200 on the ruins of a much older church, which had braved the centuries when Westmorland was a shuttlecock of contending nations and a cockpit for warring races. The remainder was added chiefly in the fifteenth century and early Tudor period, and contains no less than three private chapels—those of the Parrs, the Bellinghams, once of Levens, and the Stricklands of Sizergh. Restoration became urgent some fifty years ago, but the fine old building seems to have come out of the trying ordeal unscathed and to have successfully resisted all innovating tendencies. It was happily, too, re-pewed before the craze for seating a church like the top of an omnibus, or in other flimsy fashions, came into vogue. I am not surprised that the citizens of Kendal take infinite pride in their church. It is not many country towns that possess a building at once so wholly striking and with so many claims upon the affection of its people. There is, moreover, in the tower a chime of ten bells which are celebrated throughout the north for their sweetness, and owing, it is said, to the position of the church tower and the contour of the surrounding country, their melody is echoed among the hills by varying winds in remarkable fashion.

Beneath the private chapels and all about us lies the dust of famous folks beyond count, famous at any rate in the north country. All the earlier baronial stocks from the Castle contributed their quota, no doubt, though swept away and forgotten, while Parrs, Stricklands, Bellinghams, Rooses, Howards and Thornburghs crowd thick in brass or marble upon floor and wall.

Levens Hall.

The Bellinghams of Levens ran their course long since, and Bagots now live in the beautiful old Tudor house, whose topiary garden rivals that of Hampton Court, and is I believe the only other survival of this curious taste. Levens lies some six miles westward of the town upon the fine road which runs to Milnthorpe and the sea coast, and passes on its way the old turreted manor house to which the Stricklands have given peculiar distinction by an unbroken occupation that has hardly its like in England. They acquired the property in the thirteenth century by marriage with the Deincourts, and have lived there uninterruptedly ever since, always playing a leading part in the affairs of Westmorland, and often figuring on a more conspicuous stage. They are moreover among those old families of England that have retained the Roman faith. The house, which displays a peel tower of imposing size, is almost severe in its dignified simplicity and plain weather-beaten grey walls. It stands in a park above the Milnthorpe road and looks its part most admirably. The interior of such a house with such unbroken traditions, as may be well supposed, is rich in memories and in the things which awake them. To the world in general its connection with Katherine Parr will probably be the most interesting of these associations, the room she occupied and which still bears her name being in the main tower.

Some two miles beyond Sizergh, the road dipping suddenly to the Kent crosses the river on an old stone bridge that no one with his eyes about him would fail to pause on. The clear stream has by now gathered bulk and breadth and rushes under the arches in all the dignity of a salmon river. Stately timber and green park lands fringe its bank, and the last time I stood here a herd of fallow deer were drinking in the shallows within a stone's throw of the bridge. For this is Levens, and here touching the road are the famous gardens with the pointed gables of the ancient Tudor manor house rising behind them. Levens is as notable as Sizergh, except for the fact that its ownership has been more broken. The present proprietor, with most praiseworthy liberality it seems to me, seeing the nature of the treasure, throws the garden open to the public one afternoon in every week, and the opportunity should not be missed. This topiary garden, the pride of Levens, was laid out after the fall of the Bellinghams by Colonel Grahame, who owned the hall early in the eighteenth century. Beaumont, the gardener at Hampton Court, was employed in the cunning task, and all the quaint conceits in box and yew, such as were common once but are now no longer to be seen except as isolated specimens, have been sedulously maintained. There, says Lord Stanhope in his *History of England*, "at the fine old seat of Levens, along a wide extent of terraced walks and walls, eagles of holly and peacocks of yew still find with each returning summer their wings clipped and their talons pared. There a stately monument of the old promenoirs—such as the Frenchmen taught our fathers, rather I should say to build than to plant,

Milnthorpe

along which in days of old stalked the gentlemen with periwigs and swords, the ladies in hoops and furbelows—may still to this day be seen."

But it is not only this quaint company of cardinals' hats and lions, peacocks and umbrellas, pheasants, forensic wigs and what not, that make the garden of Levens worth seeing; but the possession of so great a treasure seems to have inspired its owners to unusual efforts to keep the rest of the garden and the spaces between in harmony with the main features, while above it all rises the grey peel tower and the flanking gables of the manor house.

A time-honoured custom still brings the mayor and corporation of Kendal to Levens every 12th of May, the primary excuse being the proclamation of Milnthorpe Fair. Rural sports are held in the park, and the civic dignitaries, with a host besides no doubt, are regaled with radishes and bread and butter. Till recent times audit ale of great potency was a feature of the entertainment. An old retainer of the House has frequently described to me the ceremonies in connection with this celebrated liquor that were punctiliously enacted in days long gone by the jovial burghers of Kendal. The uninitiated who aspired to the full honours of comradeship were required to drink a flagon of the potent brew to the toast of "Luck to Levens while the Kent flows" while standing upon one foot, and a shilling fine was exacted each time the other one touched the ground. But the peculiarity of this special tap, and my authority is unimpeachable, was, that it went to the legs instead of to the head. In short, that the mayor of Kendal himself, should he celebrate the occasion too enthusiastically, might have to call in assistance to help him to his carriage—might even be borne thither—but yet as regards his faculties remain as sober as the judge he aspired to be. But this part of the programme at any rate is ancient history now.

One may well feel tempted to wander further upon this admirable road, to follow it along the widening valley to where the river spreads into its estuary and opens to the sea by Milnthorpe to Grange and Morecambe Bay. For myself I would fain have accompanied my reader as far as Furness Abbey, whose beautifully situated ruins recall one of the most splendid monastic houses in Britain, and by very far the greatest in this north west corner of England. Indeed, I may as well say at once that I had fully intended to tax, if it were permissible, the limits of this little book, to return in Autumn and say something of this Duddon and Furness country, and so

Y

complete the circle of the outer fringe of Lakeland. But fate, in the shape of an untimely accident, nipped all such good intentions in the bud. Mr. Pennell happily was more fortunate, and the famous ruins are perhaps even a fitter subject for the artist than for the author. So here upon the old bridge by Levens Hall, unless indeed he will bear me company back again to Kendal, I must take my leave of the long-suffering reader. For I have dragged him over steep and rough places and by tortuous routes which I could not avoid,

Furness Abbey.

and at other times have gratuitously led him further afield and through regions that the orthodox Lake visitor takes no account of.

In conclusion, it may seem futile to suggest that a world which, from highest to lowest, sets out upon its travels at the close of summer, should bestir itself at its more beauteous dawn. But yet there are great numbers, beyond a doubt, who are hampered in their movements neither by fashion nor by business. And to such as are thus untramelled and would see the best bit of England in its brightest garb and above all in its kindest humour I would say be there when the cuckoo's note fills the dales; when the Mayfly is fluttering over lake and stream; when fell and woodland still wear that incomparable freshness which surely fades as June suns wax hotter and the short summer night begins once more to encroach upon the hours of day.

Leven Bridge.

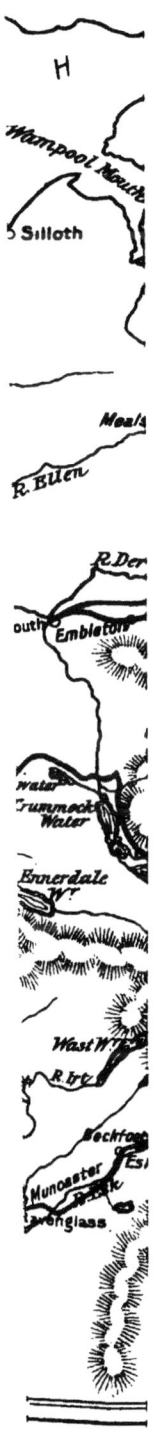

INDEX

INDEX

INDEX

A

AGLIONBYS, the, 161
Agricola, 268
Aira force, 57.
Allan Bank, 236
Ambleside, 83, 207, 209, 216, 217, 218, 228, 231
Angletarn, 60, 64, 67
Annandale, 291
Appleby, 20, 22, 305, 313
Applethwaite, 108
Armathwaite Hall, 104, 299
Armboth, 131, 232, 243, 245, 246, 247
Armstrong, the, 9, 283
Arnold, Dr., 218
Aske's rebellion, 93
Askham, 30
Athelstane King, 70

B

BANNERDALE, 59
Barf Mountain, 96
Barrow Bay, 118
Balliol, 19
Barnsdale, 311
Barton Kirk, 31, 32
Bassenthwaite, 82, 84, 96, 97, 98, 99, 101, 103, 247
Beauchamps, 69
Beaumont, 79
Bees, St. 145, 159, 164, 165, 166, 168
Bellingham, 317, 318
Bellisle, 204, 205
Binsey Fell, 250, 251
Birkfell, 56
Birthwaite, 209
Blacksail Pass, 136, 142, 146 147
Blamire, Miss, 200

Blea Tarn, 194
Blencathra, 18, 41, 72, 73, 74, 75, 78, 81
Blencoes, the, 70, 71, 105
Bolton, 305
Boot, 184
Borrowdale, 59, 80, 82, 122, 126, 128, 129, 130, 139, 233, 243
Bothel, 264
Bowfell, 195
Bowness, 203, 205
Braithwaite, 95
Brathay 193, 194
Brampton, 287, 288
Brayton, 264
Briggs, Colonel, 215
Briscoe, 161, 266
Brotherswater, 52, 65, 66
Brougham Castle, 16 to 23
Brownriggs, 104, 105
Bruce, 272
Budworth, 243
Burgh-on-Sands, 272
Burnmoor, 185
Buttermere, 122, 134, 135, 136, 147, 151, 152, 154, 156
Buttermere Hawse, 95, 132

CALDBECK, 153, 249, 251-260
Calderbridge, 172, 173
Calder, river, 145
Caldew, river, 254, 258, 259, 266, 268
Calgarth, 210, 212, 215, 246
Camden, 14
Canning, 207
Carling Knolt, 157
Carlisle, 23, 24, 263-291
Carlisle Cathedral, 272, 286
Castle Inn, 103, 104, 240

INDEX

Catchedicam, 42
Catterlan, 70
Caudale Moor, 65
Causey, 82
Charles Edward, Prince, 23, 287, 288, 303
Chester, 175
Chestnut Hill, 83
Cliburn, 30
Clifford, Roger, 18
Clifford, the Black, 15, 30, 76
Cliffords, the, 69
Clifton, 23-28
Cocker, the, 99, 137, 157
Cockermouth, 78, 92, 98, 99, 100, 145, 157
Coleridge, S. T., 52, 89, 150, 151, 153, 207, 218, 236, 237
Coleridge, Hartley, 223
Coniston, 82, 202, 216
Copeland, 185
Creighton, Bishop, 268, 272
Crinkle Crags, 195
Crofton Hall, 266
Cromwell, 286
Crosby Fell, 309
Crosby Ravensworth, 30, 305
Crossfell, 6, 227, 229, 300
Crossthwaite, 90, 92
Crossthwaite, Fisher, 119
Crozier, 77
Cumberland, Duke of, 25, 26, 288
Cumberland, Richard, 37
Cunedda, 9
Crummock Lake, 132, 154, 155, 156, 157

D

Dacre Castle, 68
Dacre Church, 70
Dacres, the, 69, 93, 285, 313
Dale Head, 131, 136, 245
Dalemain, 41
Dalston, 266
David, King of Scotland, 271
Dawes, the, 31
Debatable land, 274, 275, 278, 291, 296
Deincourts, the, 319
De Quincey, 90, 150, 151, 152, 207, 208, 212, 221, 222, 223, 224, 235, 236, 237
Derwent, river, 94, 99, 100, 101, 103, 157, 251, 264
Derwentwater, 82, 84, 109, 110, 111, 113, 122, 243, 247
Derwentwater, Countess of, 113
Derwentwater, Lord, 114
Dickinson, 142
Dockwray Hall, 8, 13
Dollywaggon, 241, 242
Dolphin, 270
Dove Cottage, 226, 234, 236, 237
Dove Crag, 218
Drigg, 177

Duddon, river, 185, 186, 192
Dunmail Raise, 207, 237, 238, 239
Dyvoke, 185

E

Eamont, river, 16, 33, 37, 41
Easdale, 237
Ecclefechan, 291
Eden Hall, 301
Eden, river, 5, 227, 263, 267, 269, 280, 291, 293, 299.
Edmund, King, 238
Edward I., 271, 272
Edward II., 69
Edward III., 272
Edward IV., 14
Egfrith, 270
Eglemore, Sir, 44
Egremont Castle, 164
Ehen, river, 145
Elfred, 270
Elizabeth, Queen, 100, 276, 280
Ellenborough, Lord, 301
Ellwood, 240
Embleton, 99
Ennerdale, 135, 136, 139, 140, 141, 142, 145, 146
Esk (northern), 271, 274, 280, 291, 293, 293, 294
Esk (southern), 178, 183, 184, 185
Eskat Woods, 146
Esthwaite, 203

F

Fairfield, 49, 80, 218, 238, 241, 242
Featherstonhaughs, 299, 300
Fell Foot, 192, 194
Ferguson, Chancellor, 18, 62, 181
Fish Inn, 132, 150
Fleetwith Pike, 136, 137
Flemings, the, 219
Fletchers, the, 71
Flodden Field, 313
Foxhow, 221
Franklin, B., 105
Friars Crag, 109, 110
Furness Abbey, 126, 142

G

Gatesgarth, 136, 137, 138
Giant's Grave, 15
Gibson Craig, 196, 197
Gibson's Knott, 238
Gilpin Miss, 200
Gilsland, 69
Gilstone, 114, 115
Glasgow, 271

INDEX

Glencoin, 45
Glenderamakin, 73, 75, 260
Glenridding, 49
Goldrill, 52, 55
Gosforth, 174, 180
Gough, 53, 54
Gowbarrow, 43 45, 57
Graham, Colonel, 319
Grahames, the, 279, 283
Grange, 124
Grassmere, 207, 226, 228, 229, 230, 231, 232, 234, 235, 237, 238, 243
Grassmoor, 82, 135, 156
Gray, 45, 109, 125
Gray Crag, 59, 67
Gray, Lady Jane, 71
Great Gable, 147, 148
Great Salkeld, 301
Greaves, Woodcock, 248, 255, 258, 259
Greenrigg, 253
Greenthwaite, 71
Greta Hall, 89, 108
Greta, river, 82, 83, 88, 89
Gretna Green, 291, 293, 294, 295, 312
Greyriggs, 311
Greystroke, 44, 69, 70, 71, 72
Grinsdale, 169
Grisedale, 49

H

HADRIAN'S WALL, 17, 268, 269
Hall, R., 109
Hallsteads, 43
Haltons, the, 71
Hardknott, 184, 185, 189, 237
Hartsop, 59
Hassells, the, 41, 161
Hassness, 135
Hatfield, 153
Hawkeshead, 195, 202, 203
Haweswater, 60, 304, 306, 307
Hayeswater, 60, 66
Haystacks, 135, 136, 155
Helm Crag, 237, 238
Helvellyn, 43, 46, 49, 54, 59, 74, 82, 131, 230, 239, 243, 245, 300
Hemans, Mrs., 218
Henry I., 271
Henry II., 271
Henry III., 271
Henry IV., 14, 273
Henry VI., 183
Henry VII., 19, 281
Henry VIII., 281, 314
Hesket, High, 263
Hesket Newmarket, 260
High Crag, 137
High Carlin, 311
High Stile, 134, 136, 156
High Street, 59, 67, 304, 306
Hindscarth, 137
Holme, Hugh, 307

Honeywood, Colonel, 25, 26
Honister, 131, 135, 155, 237
Horse Gill, 131
Howards, the, 69, 70, 71, 318, 285
Howtown, 41, 43, 59
Huddlestones, the, 41, 70, 162
Hutchinsons, the, 75
Huttons, the, 70

ICELAND, 239
Illbell, 193
Inglewood Forest, 15, 70, 300
Isell, 101

J

JACKSONS, THE, 245
James, I., 126, 127, 184
Johnby, 71
Johnstone, Chevalier, 23
Johnstones, the, 283
Jones, Wynn, 148

K

KENDAL, 5, 23, 24, 215, 298, 312, 313, 314, 315, 316, 317
Kent, river, 314, 319
Kentigerin, St., 72
Keswick, 68, 82, 83, 84, 85, 88, 90, 91, 104, 109, 118, 120, 146, 151, 156, 157, 232, 237, 238, 247, 249, 260, 262, 263
Kidsty Pike, 59, 67, 79, 306
Kinmount Willie, 276, 277, 279
Kinniside Fell, 145
Kirby Stephen, 309
Kirkbythore, 305
Kirkoswald, 69, 299
Kirkstone Pass, 47, 52, 59, 65, 237

L

LAMPLUGH, 158
Lancasters, the, 30
Langholme, 291
Langwathby Moor, 160, 161
Latting, 82
Lawson, Sir W., 101, 126, 129
Lawson, Miss, 101, 102
Lazonby, 301
Leathes, 245
Leslie, General, 286
Levens Hall, 318
Liddell, 274, 291
Lingmore, 194, 195
Lockerbie, 291
Lockhart, 207
Lodore, 112, 118, 122
Longstrath beck, 130

INDEX

Longtown, 291, 293, 294
Longwood, 291
Lonsdale, Lord, 99, 102, 306
Lord's island, 84
Lord's seat, 311
Lorton vale, 157
Lovell, Mrs., 89
Low Hartsop, 66
Loweswater, 142
Lowther Castle, 26
Lowther, Gerard, 13
Lowther, Robert, 31
Lowther, Miss, 102
Lowthers, the, 16
Lucy, de, 164
Lune, river, 309
Lyvenant, river, 305
Lyulph's Tower, 44, 57

M

MACAULAY, LORD, 106, 108
Magnusson, Eric, 240
Malcolm King, 238, 271
Manchester, 240
Mardale, 60, 306, 307
Marshalls, the, 50, 138
Martindale, 59
Martineau, Miss, 207, 218
Mary Queen of Scots, 13, 100, 283
Matterdale, 73, 74
Mayborough, 400
Meaburn Hall, 102, 305
Mellbreak, 156
Meschin, Le, 173
Millbeck, 104, 105, 106, 194
Mill Fell, 73
Milnthorpe, 318
Mite, river, 180, 184
Morecombe Bay, 4
Morland, 305
Mosedale, 147
Mounseys, the, 46, 63
Muncaster, 174, 176, 180, 183
Mungo, St., 73
Mungrisedale, 72, 75
Murgatroyd, 21
Murray, Earl of, 25
Musgraves, 161

N

NAB COTTAGE, 226
Naddle Fell, 82, 306
Naworth, 69
Needle Rock, 141
Neville, Cicely, 14, 15
Neville, Henry, 14
Nevilles, the, 7
Newby Bridge, 204
Newlands, vale of, 95, 132, 156, 237
Ninian, St., 72

Norfolk, Duke of, 40, 69
Northumberland, Duke of, 282

O

ORMATHWAITE, 105
Orris Head, 205
Orton Scaur, 311
Overwater, 250
Owen Cæsarius, 15

P

PARR, KATHERINE, 314, 315
Parrs, the, 314, 317, 318
Patrick, St., 72
Patterdale, 41, 46, 49, 52, 59, 64
Peel, John, 154, 251, 258
Peel, Willie, 255
Peel Wyke, 97
Pembroke, Anne, Countess of, 19-23
Pembroke, Earl of, 21
Pendragon, 20
Pennant, 294
Pennine Range, 5, 16, 300
Penningtons, the, 161, 180
Penrith, 5-16, 24, 54, 84, 262, 287, 288, 301
Penruddock, 72
Percies, the, 273
Petterell, the, 263, 268
Pheasant Inn, 97
Phillipsons, the, 215
Pike o' Blisco, 192, 195
Pikes, the, 65
Place Fell, 46, 59
Pillar Mountain, 140, 147, 148
Pillar Rock, 140, 141
Plumpton, 263
Ponsonby, Mr. 145
Pooley Bridge, 37, 41, 42, 68
Portinscale, 94
Powley, Miss, 199
Preston, 287

R

RADCLIFFES, the, 84, 93, 113, 114, 115, 129
Rannerdale Knotts, 156
Ratten Heath, 128
Ravenglass, 174, 175, 176, 177, 178, 180, 182, 184, 186, 272
Redbank, 229
Redgauntlett, 293
Red Pike, 134, 154, 156
Red Screes, 65, 218
Red Tarn, 53
Rest Dodd, 59
Richard II., 7, 14, 273
Richard III., 8, 14, 273
Rigg's Hotel, 205
Robinson, 82, 136
Robinson, Mary, 150, 151, 152, 153

INDEX

Rooses, the, 318
Rosamond Fair, 17
Rose Castle, 266
Rossthwaite, 130, 131
Rothay, the, 194, 217, 218, 226, 238
Rounthwaite, 251, 263
Rowan, Red, 279
Rufus, William, 239, 270, 314
Rumney, 266
Ruthwaite, 311
Rutland, Lord, 15
Rydal, 129, 217, 223, 226, 227, 228, 236
Rydal Hall, 219
Rydal Mount, 219

S

SALKELD OF CORBY, 277
Sandfords, the, 31
Sark, the, 294, 295
Savage, 25
Scafell, 147, 148, 216
Scale Hill, 157
Scardale, 218
Scarfgap, 136, 137, 138
Scott of Buccleugh, 277
Scott, Sir W., 207, 215, 280, 282
Scrope, Lord, 277
Seascale, 145
Seatoller, 129, 131
Seathwaite, 190
Seat Sandal, 238, 241
Sewell, the Rev., 192
Seymour, Lord, 315
Shap, 60, 302, 304, 305, 308, 309, 310, 311
Shap Fell, 23
Shelley, 83
Sherwin, Rev., 191
Simpson, 237
Sizergh, 319
Skiddaw, 74, 80, 92, 97, 104, 105, 121, 242, 247, 250, 251, 252, 260, 293, 300
Skipton Castle, 20
Sockbridge, 30
Solway, 251, 264, 268, 274
Solway Moss, 291, 293, 296
Soulby, 68
Sour Milk Gill, 133
Southey, 89, 90, 93, 108, 109, 124
Stagg, 200
Stake Pass, 130
Stanhope, Lord, 320
Stanley, John, 246
Stanwix, 291
Steel Fell, 238
Stephen King, 271
Strathclyde, 238, 239, 270
Stricklands, the, 305, 317, 318
Stricklands, Miss Agnes, 315, 316
Styborough, 55
Styhead, 130
Sudeley, 315

Swan Inn, 96
Swhirrel Edge, 53
Swindale, 306

T

TANKARDS, THE, 30
Taylor, Dr., 30
Taylor, the Water-Poet, 285
Thirlmere, 82, 83, 232, 243, 244, 246
Thirlspot, 246
Thornburghs, the, 318
Thornethwaite, 307
Thornthwaite, 96
Threlkeld, 74, 75, 77, 78, 82
Threlkeld, Sir L., 18
Thursby, 266
Thwaites, 161
Tillberthwaite, 195
Towneley, Colonel, 288
Trollope, A., 307
Troutbeck (Cumb.), 68, 73
Troutbeck (Westm.), 116
Tuftons, the, 23

U

ULLDALE, 251, 252
Ullswater, 41–67, 84, 238
Ulpho, 44
Underskiddaw, 104, 105

V

VIPONTS, the, 17

W

WADE, General, 287
Walker ("wonderful"), 189, 190
Walls Castle, 181
Warnscliffe, 137
Warwick, the Keymaker, 15
Wastdalehead, 82, 135, 136, 141, 147
Wastwater, 134, 136, 139, 142, 184, 185
Waterhead, 217
Watermillock, 43
Watson, Bishop, 210, 211, 215
Watson, George, 20
Weber, river, 265
Welcome Inn, 33
West, 36, 37, 126
Wheeler, Mrs., 200
Whinfell, 19, 311
Whinlatter, 80, 237
Whiteless Pike, 135, 156
Whitemoss, 231
Whittless Scaur, 264
Wigton, 265

BY THE SAME AUTHOR

SKETCHES FROM OLD VIRGINIA

Crown 8vo. 6s.

THE TIMES.—"A very charming series of sketches of Virginia as it was left after the war, still inhabited by a people who had been brought up under the institution of slavery, and who retained the ideas, traditions, the habits, the methods of thought of a system founded upon slavery. . . . Mr. Bradley has caught the sentiment of a region which is full of old world memories, and was still peopled at the time of which he writes by survivors of its old days of easy prosperity. The characters he describes are racy of the soil, and he paints their lives, occupations, and sports with a singularly sympathetic pen, with a gentle and subdued humour, which is finely attuned to the spirit of his theme, with the relish of a sportsman and a genuine appreciation of the more imaginative aspects of scenery."

DAILY TELEGRAPH.—" Mr. Bradley deserves the gratitude of every lover of open air life for this collection of his Virginian Studies which have appeared in Macmillan's and other magazines. His sense of style and humour lifts him far above the ordinary chronicler of woodlands and coverts. . . . The Old Dominion which he is so well qualified to sketch has vanished for ever, and the world is the poorer by the extinction of a picturesque and not ignoble society."

DAILY NEWS.—" Mr. Bradley's sketches of Old Virginia are delightful from first to last. They are the vivid, sympathetic, humorous picture of a social state which has passed away."

SPECTATOR.—" Nowhere have we met with more accurate accounts of the effect of the Great Civil War on the Old Southern States. Mr. Bradley, who clearly knows the 'Social Statics' of the South, paints for us the downfall and decadence of the Old Virginian landed gentry with a tender reminiscent hand. . . . Most agreeable matter for a delightful winter evening by the fireside."

SPEAKER.—" Mr. Bradley has found in the manor houses of the luckless Southron gentry the stuff for a charming book. He has lived and shot and fished among them. He has the descriptive touch, and he succeeds in enabling us to picture what Old Virginia really was like."

SATURDAY REVIEW.—" This is one of the pleasantest volumes that it has been our lot to handle for some time. Its people, its quaint aristocracy, the negroes before and after their emancipation, the 'poor whites,' the architecture, the aspect of the country—the trees, the birds of the air, and the fish of the rivers. All these after reading Mr. Bradley's book are as familiar to us as if we had lived in Virginia for half a life-time. The author has a sense of style and has personality. He is entirely possessed by the spirit of the country which he describes; he catches the lights and shadows that would escape the ordinary observer."

LITERATURE.—" Mr. Bradley has earned our gratitude by republishing in book form these charming studies of life in Old Virginia. . . . These (characters) are portrayed with excellent grace and quite delightful humour. Throughout the sketches breathes a spirit of loving kindness, of affection for the happier past, of sympathy with nature in all her forms. No lover of sport and scenery and old fashioned ways will read this book without peculiar pleasure."

FIELD.—" Throughout the book is pleasantly written; it contains many quaint stories, and gives an excellent idea of what things were in Virginia at the time of which the author writes. The descriptions of the scenery and the people possess considerable literary merit; and we can commend it to our readers as a most entertaining book."

ST. JAMES'S GAZETTE.—" The glory has departed from Old Virginia. And after reading Mr. Bradley's half-sad, half-humorous, wholly sympathetic 'sketches' we find ourselves more than a little inclined to sentimental regret that it should be so."

PALL MALL GAZETTE.—" A very agreeable book."

BIRMINGHAM POST.—" An entertaining volume. The sketches show a masterly hand and are full of humour and pathos."

BROAD ARROW.—" The reappearance of these sketches in their present form will be welcomed by many readers who appreciated the fidelity of description of southern men and manners, the shrewd and sensible views and the quaint and quiet humour displayed in them."

FISHING GAZETTE (R. B. Marston).—"One of the most charming little books imaginable. A series of sketches of scenes, sport and character all admirably done."

MACMILLAN AND CO., Ltd., LONDON

THE HIGHWAYS & BYWAYS SERIES

Extra crown 8vo. cloth elegant, gilt tops, 6s. each

Highways and Byways in the Lake District. By A. G. BRADLEY. With Illustrations by JOSEPH PENNELL.

Highways and Byways in East Anglia. By WILLIAM A. DUTT. With Illustrations by JOSEPH PENNELL.

WORLD.—"Of all the fascinating volumes in the 'Highways and Byways' Series, none is more pleasant to read. . . . Mr. Dutt, himself an East Anglian, writes most sympathetically and in picturesque style of the district."

MORNING POST.—"A most entertaining book. . . . Beautifully illustrated."

Highways and Byways in Normandy. By PERCY DEARMER, M.A. With Illustrations by JOSEPH PENNELL.

ST. JAMES'S GAZETTE.—"A charming book. . . . Mr. Dearmer is as arrestive in his way as Mr. Pennell. He has the true topographic eye. He handles legend and history in entertaining fashion. . . . Excellently does he second Mr. Pennell's beautiful drawings, and makes hackneyed places on the 'Highways' and in Mont-Saint-Michel, Rouen, Coutances, and Caen, to shine forth with fresh significance and 'new-spangled ore.'"

MORNING POST.—"A charming present for an intending or reminiscent traveller in the land."

Highways and Byways in North Wales. By A. G. BRADLEY. With Illustrations by HUGH THOMSON and JOSEPH PENNELL.

ST. JAMES'S GAZETTE.—"A worthy successor to Mr. A. H. Norway's *Highways and Byways in Devon and Cornwall*, and like that delightful book, has the inestimable advantage of illustration by Mr. Joseph Pennell and Mr. Hugh Thomson—an ideal partnership."

DAILY CHRONICLE.—"The illustrations are supplied by Mr. Joseph Pennell and Mr. Hugh Thomson, and it would be very difficult to see how Messrs. Macmillan could improve so strong a combination of artistic talent. . . . This book will be invaluable to many a wanderer through the plains and mountains of North Wales."

MACMILLAN AND CO., LTD., LONDON

Lightning Source UK Ltd.
Milton Keynes UK
UKHW052126221118
332624UK00026B/926/P